Flash™ MX
Complete Course

William B. Sanders

Wiley Publishing, Inc.

Flash™ MX Complete Course

Published by:

Wiley Publishing, Inc.
909 Third Avenue
New York, NY 10022
www.wiley.com/compbooks

Published simultaneously in Canada

For general information on our other products and services or to obtain technical support please contact our Customer Care Department within the U.S. at 800-762-2974, outside the U.S. at 317-572-3993 or fax 317-572-4002.

Library of Congress Control Number: 2002110245
ISBN: 0-7645-3685-0

Manufactured in the United States of America

10 9 8 7 6 5 4 3 2 1

» Credits

Publisher: Barry Pruett

Project Editor: Erik Dafforn

Acquisitions Editor: Michael Roney

Editorial Manager: Rev Mengle

Technical Editor: Kyle Bowen

Interior Designers: Edwin Kwo
                      Daniela Richardson

Cover Designer: Anthony Bunyan

Layout: Beth Brooks
        Sean Decker
        Melanie DesJardins
        Kristin McMullan
        Kristine Parial-Leonardo
        Heather Pope
        Erin Zeltner

Production: Kelly Emkow
            Gabriele McCann

Quality Control
Technicians: Laura L. Bowman
             Andy Hollandbeck
             Susan Moritz
             Angel Perez

Indexer: Lynnzee Elze

Special Help: Tim Borek
              Cricket Franklin
              Daniela Richardson
              Maureen Spears

» Dedication

This book is dedicated to my sister Dianne and my brother Stephen.

» Table of Contents

Confidence Builder

The Confidence Builder shows you that you can create a Flash movie using the major parts of Flash MX including tweening, drawing, and sound, and changing position and transparency. You will animate and coordinate different objects and throw in a sound for good measure. You've been provided with the sound and a couple of movie clips in the library, but that's just to save a little time in getting started. The rest is up to you.

TOOLS YOU'LL USE
Stage, Property inspector, Library, Color Swatches panel, Text tool, Oval tool

MATERIALS NEEDED
From the accompanying CD-ROM, you'll need the confidence.fla file.

TIME REQUIRED
15 minutes

Test Tutorial
» Opening Flash MX with a Flash File

You can get started in Flash MX by opening a Flash MX file from your CD-ROM.

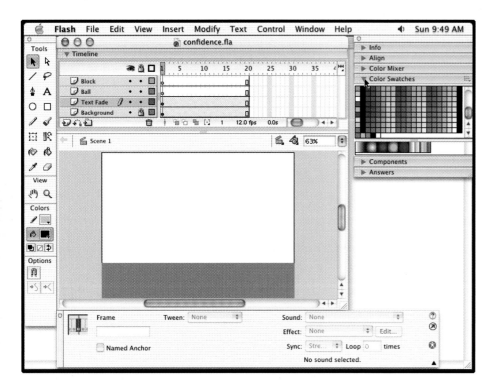

1. **Find the file confidence.fla on your CD-ROM.**

2. **Drag confidence.fla from the CD-ROM to your desktop.**

3. **Double-click the file to open it in Flash MX.**
   You will see the Flash stage with an olive gray block with a white outline at the bottom.

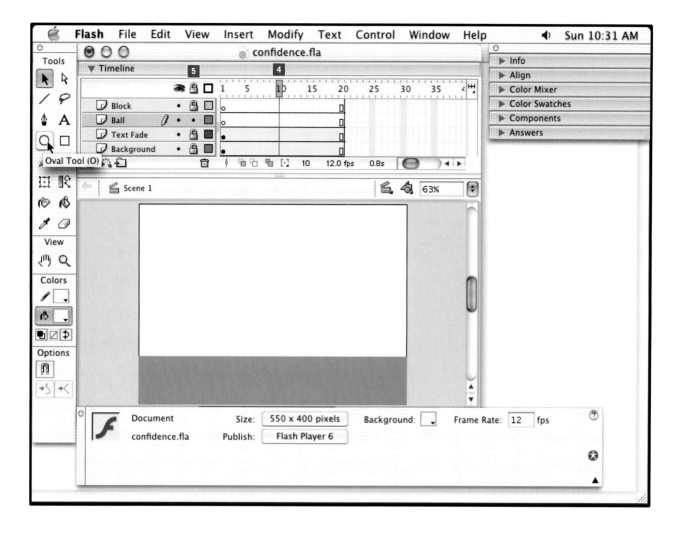

4. Click the playhead and move it from left to right.

The playhead automatically moves over the timeline when you play a movie.

5. Click several times on the lock icon next to the eye icon on the left side of the timeline.

The locks on the different layers will appear and disappear as you click the top lock. If you click the lock next to a layer, the individual layer's lock will appear and disappear. A lock on a layer means you cannot change it. As you are learning Flash MX, the locks help keep you from making mistakes.

Test Tutorial
» Drawing an Oval with a Radial Gradient

The first step is to draw an image on the screen that will become animated. A radial gradient gives the image a three-dimensional look.

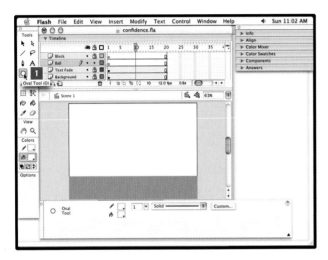

1. **Select the Oval tool in the Tools panel on the left of the stage.**
   After you select the Oval tool, the Property inspector beneath the stage changes to the Oval Tool inspector.

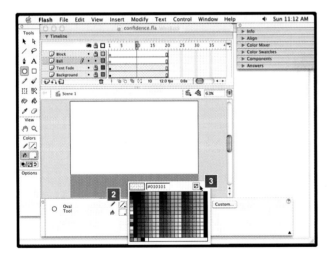

2. **Click the stroke (top) color well in the Property inspector.**
   A Swatch palette opens when you click the well.

3. **Click the square with the red slash in it.**
   The square with the red slash (sort of looks like a diver's flag) indicates that the drawing will have no stroke. Because you will be drawing a ball with a radial fill, you won't need a stroke around the ball. The *stroke* line in Flash is the line surrounding a drawing — something like an outline. Inside the stroke line is the *fill*. You can create a drawing with either fill or stroke turned off by selecting the white swatch with a red diagonal through it.

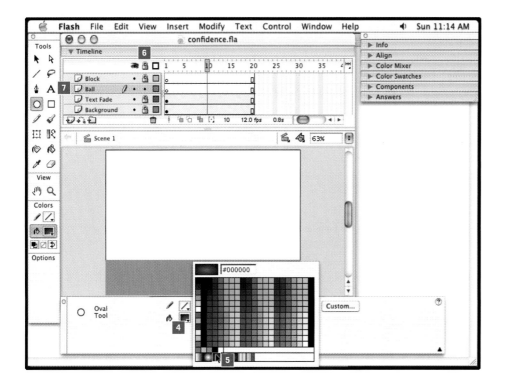

4. **Click the fill (bottom) color well in the Property inspector.**
   A slightly different Swatch palette opens, replacing the stroke color palette. At the bottom of this palette you will see several 3-D, ball-shaped images. These are the radial fills.

5. **Choose the red radial fill color at the bottom of the Swatch panel.**

6. **Click the lock column for all of the layers except the Ball layer.**

7. **Click the Ball layer.**

8. **Hold down the Shift key and drag the mouse across part of the stage just above the olive-colored rectangle.**
   You should now have a red ball on the stage.

Test Tutorial
» Positioning and Sizing a Shape on the Stage

Once you have a shape on the stage, you can easily get it exactly the size you want and place it precisely where you want it to go.

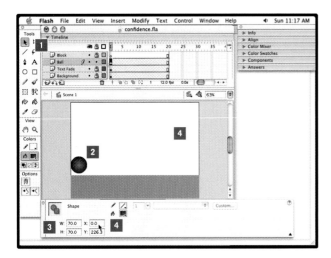

1. **Click the pointer tool.**

2. **Drag the pointer tool around the ball to select it.**
   The ball gets "dotty" (pixilated) when selected. All drawings that are not symbols take on that "dotty" look when selected. You will also notice that the Property inspector has changed again, indicating it is the Shape inspector.

3. **Type 70 in both the W and H text windows in the Property (Shape) inspector.**
   The ball becomes a 70 x 70 pixel sphere.

4. **Type 0 in the X text window.**
   The ball moves against the left side of the screen.

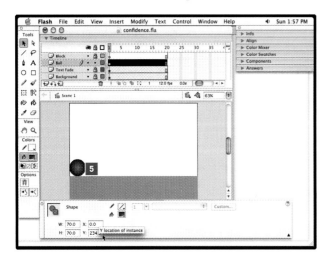

5. **Press the down arrow key until the ball sits directly on top of the stage.**
   The current position is the starting position for the object used in the next part of the tutorial.

Test Tutorial
» Animating a Drawing

After precisely positioning and sizing a shape on the stage, it's ready to be animated.

1. **Click Frame 20 on the timeline in the Ball layer.**

   The playhead moves to the frame when the frame is clicked.

2. **Select Insert→Keyframe from the menu bar.**

   A black dot appears in the frame after the keyframe has been inserted. Be sure that the playhead stays in Frame 20 for now.

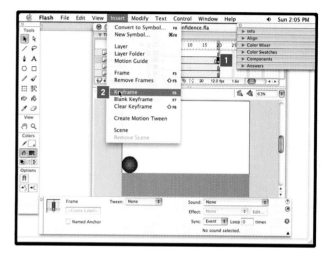

3. **Click the pointer tool and select the ball.**

4. **Hold down the Shift key and press the right arrow key until the ball is against the right side of the screen.**

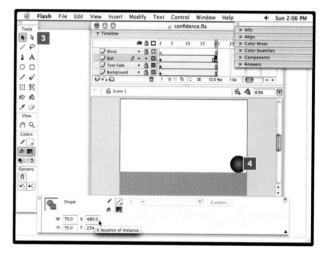

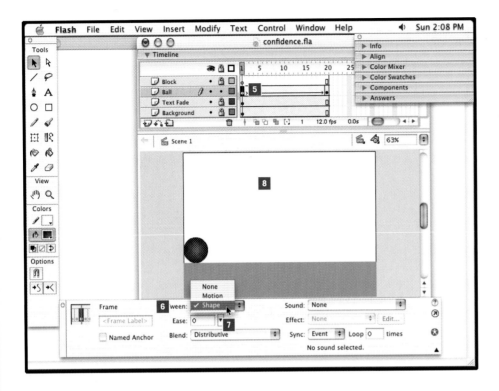

5. **Click the first frame of the Ball layer.**

6. **Click the Tween popup menu in the Property inspector (Frame inspector).**

7. **Select Shape from the popup menu.**
   A black arrow on a light green background appears in the Ball layer. That means you have successfully created a "tween" that will animate the ball.

8. **Click the stage and press the Enter (Windows) / Return (Macintosh) key to test your movie so far.**
   The ball should move across the stage to the opposite side.

Test Tutorial
» Adding More Components to the Movie

Animating shapes is only part of what Flash MX can do. By adding instances of symbols, you can do more things. This tutorial shows how to add different types of symbols and sound. Some ready-made elements have been placed in the Library and you will see how to use them to add to the movie.

1. **Select Window→Library from the menu bar.**
   The Library panel opens. You will see three items in the library.

2. **Click the Box Clip item.**
   The Box Clip is a movie clip and appears in the upper pane of the Library panel. As you will see, Flash MX has distinct icons for different symbols in the library.

3. **Click the lock icon next to the block layer to unlock it and click the lock column to lock all the other layers if they are not already locked.**

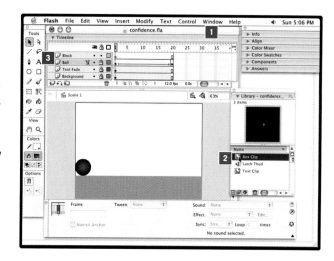

4. **Click the Block layer to select it.**

5. **Drag the Box Clip movie clip to the stage and place it on top of the olive-colored rectangle in the middle of the stage.**

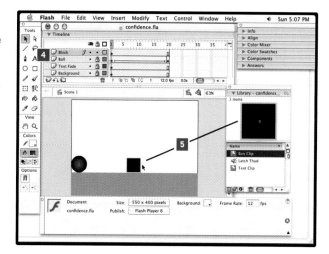

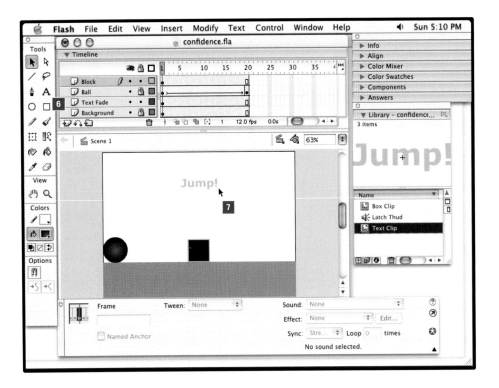

6. **Unlock the Text Fade layer.**

7. **Drag the Text Clip from the Library panel to the center of the stage above the Box Clip.**

Test Tutorial
» Adding Keyframes and Motion Tweens

After all of the movie components are on the stage, you need to add more keyframes and tweens. However, because the objects on the stage include movie clips in addition to a drawing, you must add a different type of tween.

1. **Drag the playhead to Frame 20.**
   Frame 20 is the last frame in this movie. Movies can have far more frames, but for purposes of getting started, this one is short.

2. **Hold down the Ctrl (Windows) or Cmd (Macintosh) key and click the Block and Text Fade layers.**
   By holding down the Ctrl/Cmd key, you can select multiple frames.

3. **Select Insert→Keyframe from the menu bar.**
   Keyframes are added to both of the selected frames. Two for the price of one.

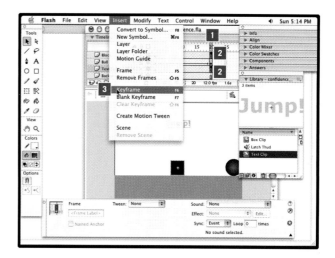

4. **Drag the playhead to Frame 1.**

5. **Hold down the Ctrl (Windows) or Cmd (Macintosh) key and click the Block and Text Fade layers.**

6. **Select Motion from the Tween popup menu in the Property (Frame) inspector.**
   The Property inspector turns into the Frame inspector. Only when a keyframe is selected can the Tween popup menu be used. This helps you from making the mistake of attempting to tween a non-keyframe or other object.

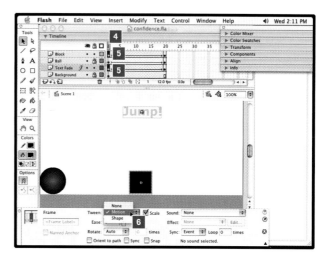

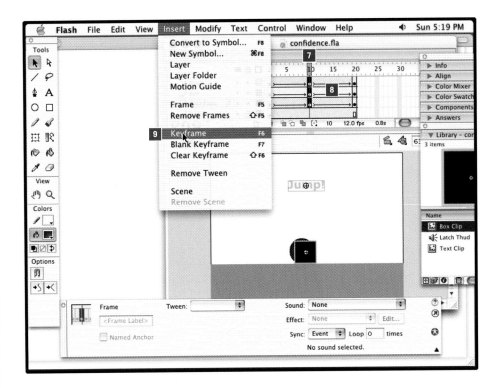

7. **Drag the playhead to Frame 10.**
   When you drag the playhead to Frame 10, the ball and box overlap.

8. **Hold down the Ctrl (Windows) or Cmd (Macintosh) key and click the Ball, Block, and Text Fade layers.**
   Be sure to have all three layers selected.

9. **Select Insert→Keyframe from the menu bar.**
   Keyframes are added to all three layers in the middle of tweens for all three layers.

Test Tutorial
» Coordinating the Parts and Adding Sound

With all of the parts in place and the tweens added, the elements will have to be coordinated so that they don't run into one another. The box must jump up when the ball comes rolling by and the Jump! sign should appear just at the right time. To make it more interesting, sound will be added when the box jumps out of the way of the ball.

1. **Click Frame 10 in the Block layer.**
   You will see the Box Clip selection indicated by a white circle and crosshair in the middle.

2. **Press the Shift key and press the up arrow key until the box is directly under the word Jump!**

3. **Click the last frame (Frame 20) of the Block layer and move the box back to its original position on the stage on top of the olive-colored rectangle.**

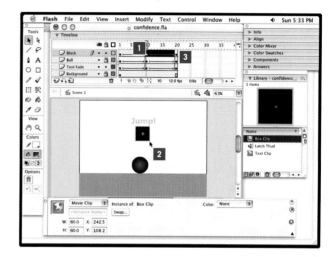

4. **Click the first frame of the Text Fade layer.**

5. **Select the Text Clip in the middle of the screen.**

6. **Click the Color popup menu in the Property inspector and select Alpha.**

7. **Move the slider next to the Color popup menu to 0%.**
   The word Jump! disappears because the movie clip is now fully transparent.

8. **Click Frame 20 and repeat steps 5 through 7.**

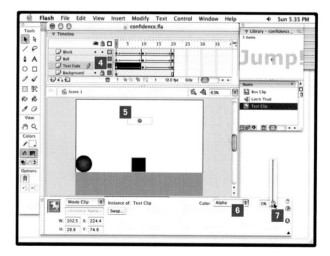

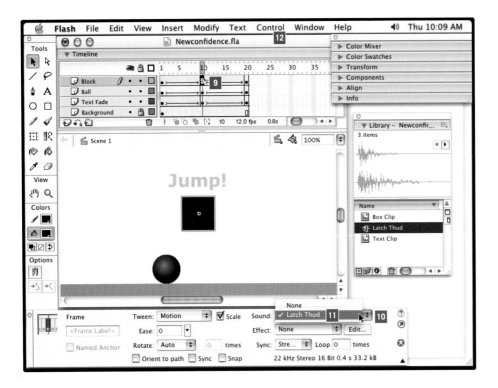

9. **Click Frame 10 in the Block layer.**

10. **Open the Sound popup menu in the Property inspector.**

11. **Select Latch Thud.**

    That is all there is to building your movie.

12. **Select Control→Test Movie from the menu bar.**

    You should now see the ball rolling across the top of the olive green "earth," the box jumping up out of the way with a "thud" sound, and the Jump! clip fading in and fading out.

That's all there is to it. It's a good idea to save your movie with a different name, such as NewConfidence.fla, so that you can start over and do it again if you want to use the original confidence.fla file. To save your movie with a different name, select Save As from the File menu on the menu bar, and give it the new name in the Save As dialog box.

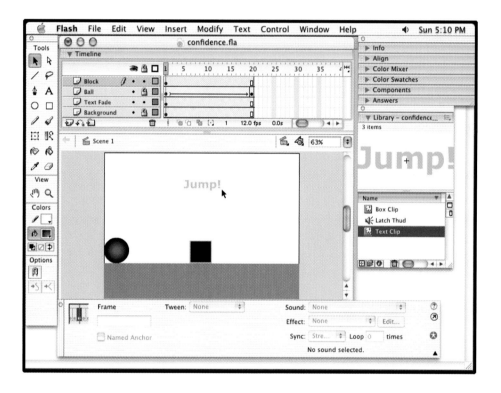

Part I:
Course Setup

Flash MX Basics

Flash is recognized as the most effective and efficient tool for creating sound and animations for the World Wide Web, and a Flash movie can be run on your desktop or on a CD-ROM using a Flash player. However, the important feature of Flash is that it gives you the ability to put together objects that normally have high bandwidth requirements and crunch them down into media that can quickly be transferred over the Web inside a Web page. That means that you can send out movies over the Internet and viewers won't have to wait an eternity for the movies to load and play.

With Flash MX come many improvements and enhancements, and so what started as an outstanding tool continues to develop in many different ways. Flash is easier to use and at the same time more powerful than ever. You can mix a rich combination of media by taking graphics and sound and putting them together in such a way as to present a full-fledged movie to a worldwide audience. Flash MX does Web animation with sound, including music, in a more compact fashion than any other software tool available. For example, after stuffing a Flash movie with a 10MB music file, several graphics files, little jumping graphics, lots of symbols, and ActionScript, it compressed to

141KB. I know 141KB is getting a bit weighty for the Web, so I revised the music down to an 884KB loop, and the Flash file compressed to 16KB. That'll do the job.

Think of Flash as a part of a larger toolbox, and while Flash can do many things, it is not the best tool for everything. Flash MX is becoming a better drawing tool than previous versions were, and it has some range of text manipulation. However, if your primary goal is to draw, you're better off with Macromedia FreeHand or Adobe Illustrator. If you want to create text for the Web, you can probably make better use of Microsoft Word or Adobe InDesign. For animation solely for CD-ROMs, I recommend Macromedia Director or Adobe Premier. For developing Web sites, use Macromedia Dreamweaver or Adobe GoLive. But when you want to focus on animating rich media on the Web, Flash MX does that better than any other tool available.

Flash specializes in using vector graphics instead of bitmapped graphics, so instead of needing a piece of code for every single pixel on the screen, vector points suffice to provide the information necessary for getting an image where you want it. For example, a bitmapped graphic of a line between point A and point B needs data for each bit between points A and B. Flash just needs the points. What's more, no matter the distance between A and B, vector graphics only need the two points. Therefore, a long line and a short line take the same amount of bandwidth (information sent over the Internet) and the line looks the same.

A related advantage to using vector graphics in Flash is how the graphics look in different sizes. An enlarged bitmapped graphic looks "blocky" because the size of the bitmap is set to a certain number of pixels on the screen. If the pixels used for a one-square-inch image are enlarged to fit in a two-square-inch image, the same bitmap is spread over double the space, giving it the blocky appearance. Conversely, when a large bitmap is made smaller, the image can blur with too much information. It's like trying to move all the furniture from a five-bedroom house into a one-bedroom apartment. You've got a mess on your hands as five bedrooms' worth of furniture is crammed into a single bedroom.

Vectors, on the other hand, retain their appearance because the drawings are created by vector points and not bitmaps. That means a big vector is going to look the same as small one and vice versa. That in and of itself is important, but for animation, it is vital. In animation, as in all drawings, a larger object appears to be closer and a smaller object appears to be farther away. An object must be made progressively larger when it's animated moving from a distant point to a closer point. With bitmapped graphics, a lot of bitmapped images would need to be streamed into the movie sequentially or you would risk having blurry and blocky images. If you use vectors, though, the animation can move seamlessly from one size to another with a single set of graphic information sent over the Internet.

Instead of using the built-in HTML or JavaScript interpreter in the major browsers, Netscape Communicator and Microsoft Internet Explorer, Flash has its own plug-in that interprets the code in SWF (Small Web Files) files. At last count (or estimate), about 350 million users have the Flash plug-in. Early on, many developers and their clients worried about using a nonstandard plug-in on the Web. However, the movies developed with Flash were so compelling that users wanted the plug-in. After version 4 of both major browsers was released, Netscape and Microsoft decided to make the Flash plug-in a standard part of their browsers.

The plug-in is also compatible with older Flash movies (ones made with Flash 2, 3, 4, or 5). However, a Flash 5 plug-in cannot read a Flash MX movie unless the movie has been saved in Flash 5 format. When you publish a movie for the Web, Flash MX places the necessary code in the HTML file so that if the wrong plug-in is present in the browser, a link to the Macromedia Web page appears; the Web page includes a link to the updated plug-in, which can be downloaded for free.

What You Can Do with Flash

With Flash MX, you can make anything from compelling animated banners to a full-fledged game that can be played over the Internet. You can make an eBusiness Web site, as was done for the main project that you will be following in this course. You can make your own cartoon show and present it over the Web if you want, or you can make an interactive classroom where students can learn anything from chemistry to psychology. In short, you can create a virtual reality for a Web environment.

The Internet has become a superhighway of communication between people, and the Web is its biggest attraction. Flash has become the tool of choice for creating lively and interactive media for the Web. Flash is an application that brings together active elements that extend well beyond HTML, and it's far less complex and time-consuming to use than Java and related programming environments.

On a basic level, Flash MX is a simple animation, drawing, and sound application. By gradually using more and more of Flash's powerful tools, you will be able to put your ideas into a format that more closely approximates the virtual reality you intend. A seamless graduation from Flash 5 makes adding the new and more powerful Flash MX elements intuitively simple.

New Tool for Experienced Web Designers

If you have experience creating Web pages and your clients want something more offered by Flash, you will find many cross-over elements between HTML and Flash. Both Adobe GoLive and Macromedia Dreamweaver include components that allow you to easily add Flash to your Web site. However, you will also find that if you simply publish a movie in Flash, you automatically get an HTML page with the code to embed a Flash SWF file. In addition, the code in the HTML file looks to see the kind of plug-in the viewer has and if it's not the right one, the viewer is automatically guided to the Macromedia site where it can download the plug-in.

Moreover, experienced designers are going to find out that making a good looking Flash movie follows the same design rules that are applied to any other design. Scale, proportion, color, shading, and every other artistic canon applied to Flash has the same effect on quality as it does a Web page or a brochure.

However, Flash is an animation tool and so you need to understand concepts that apply to cartooning and other motion graphics. Importing vector graphics from Adobe Illustrator or Macromedia FreeHand will go a long way making a good-looking movie, but pay close attention to how movies are animated in frames, keyframes, layers, and on the Flash stage.

Join a Flash Discussion Group or Users Group

It's 9 pm, and your Flash movie is just about done, but you run into a problem you just can't solve. You don't know who to call, and the project is due tomorrow morning. Here's where an online Flash discussion group comes in handy. I don't know how many times I've been stumped, at 9 pm (or 3 am) and have sent an e-mail to a Flash online discussion group and have received a reply in time to save my bacon. You will find online discussion and support groups at www.flashkit.com and Yahoo! (Flash Newbies).

If there is a Flash users group in your area, join it. You'll save yourself a lot of time and get more tips than you'll find anywhere else. Members are generous with their knowledge and time. It's like having your own private team of consultants, but without the expense. Check out www.macromedia.com/support/ programs/usergroups/ to find the users group nearest you. Often they're called MMUGs, for Macromedia Users Groups. A great example and one of the largest Users Groups is the Los Angeles Flash and Shockwave Users Group at www.flashcore.com.

Thinking Flash

Flash is a moviemaking software application. The files created in Flash are animated movies, and appropriately, they're called movies. Your basic mindset should be "I'm making a movie." Now, imagine a roll of movie film. It is made up of a series of little pictures called frames. As each frame passes in front of your visual field, you see the illusion of motion. You know it's an illusion because if you speed up the projector, the motion is faster, and if the projector is slowed, the motion slows.

In an animated movie, objects need to change. They can change in many ways. They can change position on a stage. They may change color, shape, sound, volume, transparency, visibility, and speed. Movement is one of the most fundamental changes that occurs in animation. An object moves from point A to point B. If you lay out a roll of movie film, you can see an object in Frame A at point A. However, movement to point B may not occur until 20 frames later. In animation, the frame where an action begins and the frame where it ends are called keyframes. The distance between keyframes may be great or small, depending on the nature of the change. Where dramatic change occurs in every frame in a moving collage, every frame might be considered a keyframe.

In-Betweening

Originally, when animators went to work, a master animator would create drawings at key points (keyframes), and other animators would draw the graphics in between the keyframes. The ones who drew the graphics in between the keyframes were called in-betweeners. Flash is an in-betweening tool because it automatically draws all the frames between two keyframes in a process known as tweening.

>> Keyframe A Drawing

    Frame→tween

    Frame→tween

    Frame→tween

    Frame→tween

    Frame→tween

    Frame→tween

>> Keyframe B Drawing

All of the drawings between the drawings Keyframe A and Keyframe B are tweens. In the Flash movie editor you can see that changes have been automatically inserted between tweened keyframes by moving the playhead back and forth.

Working with Digital Animation

In the early days of animated cartooning, animators were confounded by having to deal with a single plane. Either backgrounds remained stable and objects moved across the backgrounds, or the backgrounds changed to show animated objects moving in a certain direction while their arms and legs moved to indicate energy. A background automobile or character might move by, but the perceptual relationship between objects at different distances was extremely difficult to maintain. Among the early innovations that occurred in the Disney Studios was the use of glass layers. By placing cellophane cutouts (cells) on different pieces of glass stacked on top of one another, not only could animators create animated films that showed depth, they could make their jobs considerably easier. Cameras placed above the stacks and shooting downwards enabled the animators to present the movie as a unified whole. The top layer of glass would have the main character's body animation, the next layer of glass would contain the animation of secondary figures, and the background would have still and animated background features. More complex movies required more layers, and Disney used numerous layers in his early full-length animations.

Flash works in a very similar fashion. As the movie progresses frame by frame, you can have as many different layers as you want. Unless an opaque object in a layer blocks your view, you can see through all the frames just as if you were looking through clear glass frames. You will find that working in layers makes constructing an interesting movie much easier because you can focus on one animation or static element at a time and yet still see where everything else is on the different layers.

Objects

To successfully work with Flash MX, it helps to think in terms of frames, tweens, layers, and objects. An object is whatever you put in the movie — typically a graphic image or sound. You work with images that you draw in Flash or that you import from another source. Special objects called symbols can be used over and over again. There may be hundreds of instances of a single symbol in a movie, but when the movie loads into a browser, only the single symbol has to be loaded, thus reducing loading time. Different types of objects have different behavior, and in Session 3 you will see how to create symbols and instances of symbols.

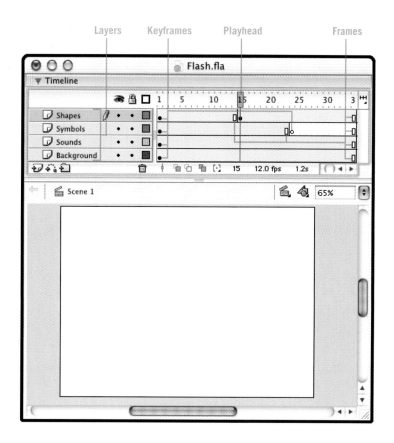

Flash Work Environment

The area called the stage is where most of the creative work is done in Flash MX. Above the stage are the key Flash development components — the timeline, layers, frames, and keyframes. The work area will be familiar to experienced Flash users, and although new tools and panels have been added, the workflow and process is very much the same as several earlier versions of Flash. The following figure shows the basic stage and the key elements around the stage.

The Stage

The stage is like a clean canvas or animation cell to which you add movie content. It's the area where you place the objects you'll be using in an animation. The appearance of the stage changes as the timeline moves, because with each frame, the objects can change appearance and position. As you move the playhead in the timeline, objects that have been changed at different frames or keyframes will change on the stage. If you place a drawing in one keyframe and a different drawing in another keyframe and then have Flash tween all of the frames between the two frames, as you move the playhead, not only will you see the differences in the two keyframes, you will see all of the additional drawings supplied in the tween by Flash.

Timelines

The timeline above the stage shows what frame number is currently being shown. As the playhead moves over the timeline from left to right, it shows each frame the playhead crosses in turn. All of the layers on the same timeline are shown together, allowing the effect of the stacks of glass with the individual cells used in early animation.

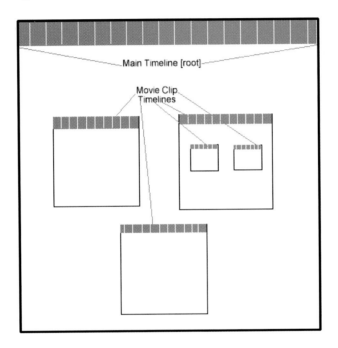

Something they could not do with the stacked glass and film cameras was to have multiple timelines. However, a central concept in Flash is the use of more than a single timeline. Imagine a movie, and in the movie is another movie — something like the picture-in-picture that some televisions have. The big movie can have other movies inside of it, each with it's own timeline, or position on the roll of film being shown. Multiple timelines in Flash are handled by movie clips. The main timeline is the root or base of a Flash movie, and all of the movie clips you want to put in your movie have their own timelines as well. This works well for animation. For example, suppose you have a character walking in your movie. The arms and legs have to be animated and coordinated. Likewise the character's position relative to the other characters on the stage and background need to be coordinated as well. By using a movie clip, you can put the walking motions into a separate object with its own timeline. The walking motions keep moving in the object no matter what the rest of the movie does. So now you can move the object on the main timeline while the movie clip's own timeline just keeps pumping those arms and legs. The figure below shows the general concept of multiple timelines.

Layers

The layers of glass from the dawn of the cartoon animation era have been replaced by digital counterparts. Layers help separate drawings and objects, and so if one object is going north and the other south, when they meet, they won't run into each other because they're on different layers. Further, layers help arrange foreground and background, and which objects will move behind or in front of other objects.

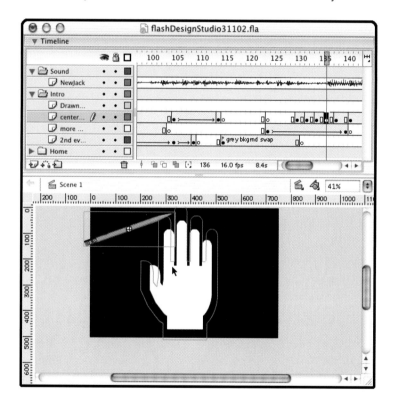

Layers can be locked so that while you're working on one layer, you don't accidentally change an object on another (locked) layer. Likewise, a layer's visibility can be turned on and off while you're working on a movie. This lets you see whether everything is where it belongs. Sometimes objects will begin a movie behind another object, and to help you see where the objects are, you can turn off the visibility of those objects blocking the view of other objects. Also, when you're working on a complex movie, turning off some layers helps reduce clutter so that you can see what you're doing. The following figure shows part of the introduction to the project movie. On the stage, you can see three different objects on different layers — the pencil, the hand drawing, and the outline of the hand.

Layers can be organized into folders so that when the number of layers is so large you cannot see the stage, you can put them into a folder and close the folder. Then by only opening the folder when you need to work on one of the layers in the folder, you can see what you're doing. The following figure shows three folders labeled Sound, Intro, and Home. The Home folder is closed, but you can see the layers in the other two folders. This new Flash MX feature significantly eases the task of creating movies with multiple layers.

Symbols

Besides using vector graphics where possible, Flash symbols reduce the amount of bandwidth required. Graphic images take up far more computer memory than text does, thus they take more time to download over the Web. Because animated graphics consist of a series of graphic images, they can take up the most memory. When you create or import graphics in Flash, you can turn the graphics into a symbol. Then you can use instances of the same symbol as many times as you want using the same graphic. For example, the time-series shown here, taken from the course project, shows a pencil spinning in a hand. In the old days, to make that simple pencil spin, you would need a total of six different drawings. Even with computer graphics, you would need six different graphic files because the pencil is displayed at different angles. However, in Flash MX the pencil has been converted into a graphic symbol. Instances of the same symbol are displayed at different rotation angles using only a single graphic. Thus, instead of requiring six images to be transported across the Web, in this case Flash only needs one.

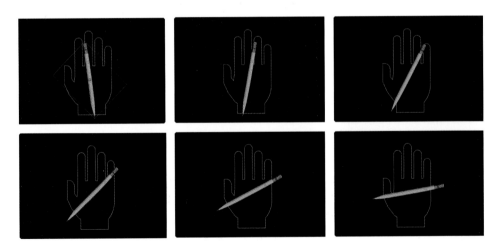

You can animate, rotate, expand, reduce, and color the instances of the symbol. The pencil could be enlarged, reduced, have its transparency changed, or transformed into a different color. However, all you need is the single graphic converted into a symbol and not several additional objects.

Toolbox and Panels

Two new Flash MX features make Flash MX's user interface an improvement over Flash 5: the Properties panel and docking. The Properties panel is a context-sensitive tool that replaces many of the old panels. The docking feature of Flash MX lets you place the different panels in a special area of the stage where they are available but out of the way. The figure below shows a panel open and on the stage, another open and in the dock, and others closed in the dock.

You can rearrange the tools, select just the panels you want, and customize the rest of the Flash MX work area so that it fits your needs. The rest of this section looks at different tools you have at your disposal.

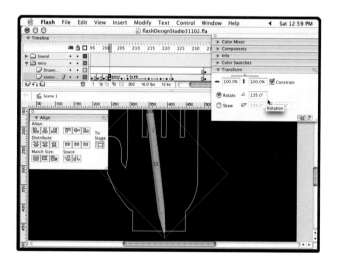

Toolbox

The primary collection of tools you need for creating different drawings and coloring are found on the Toolbox, typically set to the left of the stage.

The Toolbox has changed some since Flash 5, and the changes you will see are significant. Probably the most important new tools are the addition of the Free Transform and Fill Transform tools to the main set. The following figure shows the Toolbox and available tools in Flash MX, this book will teach you how to use them.

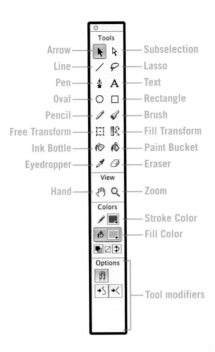

Arrow — Subselection
Line — Lasso
Pen — Text
Oval — Rectangle
Pencil — Brush
Free Transform — Fill Transform
Ink Bottle — Paint Bucket
Eyedropper — Eraser

View

Hand — Zoom

Colors

Stroke Color
Fill Color

Options

Tool modifiers

Drawing in Flash MX

Drawing with a mouse is not the most intuitive way for many to draw. You may find that it's easier to use the Flash MX drawing tools using a drawing tablet. Drawing tablets provide a stylus to use as a brush, pencil, or other drawing implement that provides better drawing control. Also, most drawing tablets come with a transparent cover so that you can place material under it to be traced. Prices range from under $100 to as high as you'd like to go. Having personally tested a Wacom tablet (cost: $99), I found that using the stylus made it easier to do line drawings and paintings — doing circles and squares is just as easy with the mouse, though.

When using the tools, you will be drawing on a specific layer and keyframe. Learning to use the tools depends on your familiarity with drawing tools in other applications such as Adobe Illustrator, Macromedia FreeHand, and similar applications capable of creating vector graphics. However, even if you have no experience using the tools in Flash MX, this book will teach you how to use them.

Properties panel

One of the best new features of Flash MX is the Properties panel. The Properties panel works as a "smart" or context sensitive panel. It provides the object information about any object you currently select on the stage or timeline. For example, if you select a keyframe, you will see all of the information you can change or add in a keyframe. However, when you select a movie clip (MC), the panel changes to show the properties of the selected MC. The Properties panel has replaced several panels from Flash 5. All of the Text panels have been replaced because as soon as you start working with text, the panel shows all of the options available for text. This panel has significantly reduced workplace clutter and you will find it easy to work with. The following figure shows several different configurations of the Properties panel.

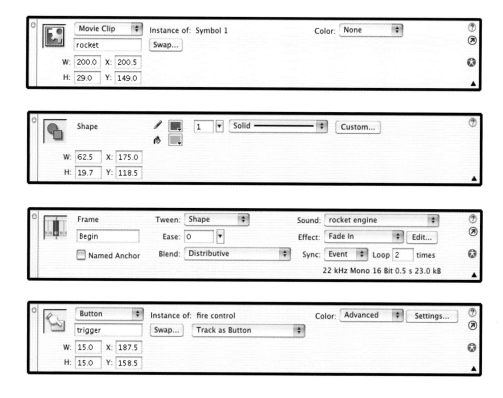

Other Panels

To work effectively with Flash MX, you will be working with a set of different panels, in addition to the Properties panel in all of its formats. Some of the panels are redundant with information found on the Toolbox and Properties panel. For example, if you begin using the Oval tool, you will find color wells on the Properties panel, Toolbox, and the Mixer panel. However, if you make a change on one panel, it will be reflected in the others. Sometimes you will have a lot of panels on the stage at the same time. You can minimize them and drag them into the dock area at the right of the screen or just press the Tab key and they'll disappear. Press it again and they'll return. In this next section, you will see a brief description of the major panels you will be using in developing your Web site.

Answers

This handy little panel helps you learn Flash MX. Whenever you need an answer to a Flash question use this panel.

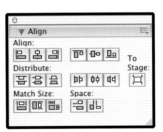

Align

Once you get used to using this panel, you'll find it indispensable. With it you align, arrange, resize, and generally set objects on the stage relative to other objects on the stage.

Color Mixer

Using the Color Mixer, you can create just about any color you want using decimal RGB, standard HSB percentages, hexadecimal, or just pointing to a color you like in the mixing table. You can select solid, gradient, or radial colors as well as add swatches to the Color Swatches Panel.

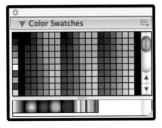

Color Swatches

After mixing colors in the Color Mixer Panel, you can put your palette into the Color Swatches Panel for use in coloring your movie elements.

Info

The Info panel contains the information about the position of an object on the stage as well as its height and width, its color, and the position of the cursor. The registration box in the panel lets you set the center as the upper left corner or the center of the object. The default zero point (X=0, Y=0) is the upper-left corner of the stage, but you can select the middle of the registration box for the zero point. All graphic drawings and symbols can be positioned and resized using this panel. (This panel is not as critical as it was in Flash 5 because the Properties panel usually has the same information when needed.)

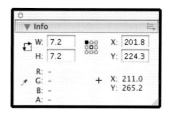

Scene

Use the Scene panel when you have to deal with more than a single scene and for renaming, switching to, and deleting scenes.

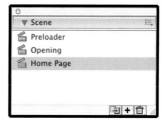

Transform

The Transform panel is used for changing the size of objects (in percentages), rotation, and skewing them to different shapes.

Actions

The Actions panel, available in both the Normal and Expert modes, is used to enter action scripts. It is a context-sensitive panel that displays frame or object scripts. All of the ActionScript actions are available from different menus in a list along the left side of the panel, and the scripts themselves are in the ActionScript pane on the right side.

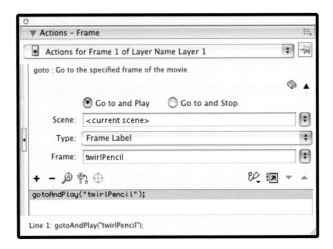

Movie Explorer

The Movie Explorer shows all of the objects that make up the movie in a hierarchical arrangement. All scripts associated with buttons, movie clips, and frames, the text fields and associated variables, and any static text on the screen are shown as well.

Components

Components are new to Flash MX. These ready-made graphic interfaces can be employed in your movies. They require ActionScript to correctly interface with your movie.

Library

The Library window shows the symbols and sounds currently being used in your movie.

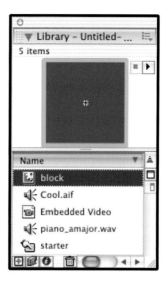

Common Libraries

The common libraries are made up of a button, learning interactions, and sound library. These ready-made symbols and sounds can be used as they are, or they can be changed to fit into your design.

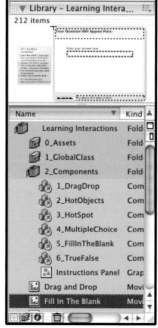

Specialized and Support Panels

The remaining panels are either specialized or used in support with the Actions panel. The Accessibility panel can be used to enhance accessibility for vision impaired users (Windows only). For example, a button could be made to work with a vocal response rather than a button click.

The Actions panel has three important support panels. The Reference panel is a quick look-up panel for the meaning and use of ActionScript terms. The Debugger panel is used in conjunction with the Actions panel to find errors in ActionScript code, and the Output panel is used for both reporting errors and showing output for developing scripts.

Menus

A number of pull-down menus on the menu bar along the top of the window provide other tools to use with Flash MX. Many of the tasks represented by the menu options can be also be accomplished via keyboard shortcuts or the panels. Finding your own preferences is simply a matter of using the program until you discover what feels best for your style.

File

- » New — Open a new movie
- » New from Template — A new movie begins with template elements in place
- » Open — Open an existing movie
- » Open as Library — Open a movie's components only
- » Close — Close currently selected movie
- » Save — Save currently selected movie as FLA file
- » Save As... — Save currently selected movie under another filename
- » Revert — Use a previously saved version of selected movie
- » Import — Import objects from other files (for example, sound, graphics)
- » Import to Library — Object is sent directly to library rather than the stage
- » Export Movie — Save currently selected FLA file as SWF file
- » Export Image — Save currently selected image as graphic file
- » Publish Settings — Set the parameters for publishing movies

» Publish Preview — View movie in Web page or Flash player (Other options for selected items)

> Default — (HTML)

> Flash

> HTML

> GIF

> JPEG

> PNG

> Projector

> QuickTime

» Publish — Export files as SWF file and generate Web page to embed SWF file

» Page Setup — Establish printer parameters

» Print Preview — Show what will be sent to the printer and printed out

» Print — Send page to printer for printing

» (Recent File) — A list of recently saved movies appear here for quick retrieval when working on a project

» Exit — Quit Flash MX and close all open movies

Edit

» Undo — Take away all changes last made. This can be done backwards over 100 steps

» Redo — Take away last Undo

» Cut — Delete selected items from movie and place them into copy buffer

» Copy — Place selected items into copy buffer

» Paste — Place items in copy buffer onto the stage

» Paste in Place — Place items in copy buffer in exactly the position they are copied or cut from

» Clear — Delete selected items but not place them into copy buffer

» Duplicate — Place a copy of selected items on stage but not place items into copy buffer

» Select All — All unlocked objects on all layers are selected

» Deselect All — All selected items are unselected

» Cut Frames — Selected frames and all objects on the selected frames are removed

» Copy Frames — Place selected frame information into copy buffer

» Paste Frames — Insert keyframe with copied frame information in selected insertion point

» Clear Frames — Delete all information on selected frames

» Select All Frames — Select all frames in current scene only

» Edit Symbols — Selected symbols are placed into Symbols editor window or in place

» Edit Selected — Edit group or objects in a group

» Edit in Place — Edit instance in its current position on the stage

» Edit All — Return to the stage after editing a group and restore objects to a group

» Preferences — General, editing, and clipboard settings desired by user

» Keyboard Shortcuts — User-set key combinations to be used instead of pull-down menus as shortcuts. Both user-set and existing shortcuts are available to be set and/or changed.

» Font Mapping

View

» Goto — Go to a specified scene to work on

First — Go to first scene

Previous — Go to previous scene

Next — Go to next scene

Last — Go to final scene

Scene # — Go to specified scene

» Zoom In — Increase page magnification

» Zoom Out — Reduce page magnification

» Magnification — Set specific page magnification relative to 100 percent

» Outlines — Set view to outlines

» Fast — Set view to normal without antialias

» Antialias — Smooth bitmapped edges and corners

» Antialias Text — Smooth jagged text

» Timeline — Toggle showing timeline

» Work Area — Toggle showing entire work area in current window size

» Rulers — Toggle showing pixel delineated rulers along left side and top of work area

» Grid — A superimposed grid on work area to help in placement and alignment

  Show Grid — Toggle showing grid on work area

  Snap to Grid — Objects will align with grid marks

  Edit Grid — Change or set grid parameters

» Guides — Guide layer paths drawings

  Show Guides — Toggle showing guides

  Lock Guides — Prevent guides from being changed

  Snap to Guides — Magnet to beginning and end position of guide

  Edit Guides — Change or set guide parameters

» Snap to Pixels

» Snap to Objects — Nearby objects act as magnets

» Show Shape Hints — Used in tweening to guide the tween process to change along guide points so to make the changes without distorting certain features of the shaped object

» Hide Edges — A toggle to show and hide edge points in drawings

» Hide Panels — Toggle to show and hide all panels

Insert

» Convert to Symbol — Convert selected drawing or text to a symbol

» New symbol... — Create a new symbol with no selected objects

» Layer — Add a layer

» Layer Folder — Add a folder to the layer column

» Motion Guide — Add a new guide layer

» Frame — Add a new frame at the selected frame on the timeline

» Remove Frames — Remove selected frames from timeline

» Keyframe — Add a keyframe in the selected frame

» Blank Keyframe — Place a blank keyframe in selected frame

» Clear Keyframe — Remove a keyframe but leave the frame

» Create Motion Tween — Create a motion tween from the selected keyframe to the next keyframe

» Scene — Add a new scene

» Remove Scene — Delete an indicated scene

Modify (Some selections vary depending on selected object)

» Layer... — Make changes to a layer's name, visibility, lock status, type, outline color, view as outline, and layer height as a percentage

» Scene... — Open scene selection panel

» Document... — Change movie's frame rate, dimensions, match with printer dimensions, background color, and ruler units of measure. Changes may be set to default

» Smooth — Smooth curves in lines

» Straighten — Straighten curved lines

» Optimize — Reduce the number of curves in a line on a sliding scale

» Shape — Use fill to adjust images

Convert Lines to Fills — Selected line is converted to fill

Expand Fill... — Specify a value for fill

Soften Fill Edges... — Smooth edges in fill

Add Shape Hint — Add points where shape will have more natural morph

Remove All Hints — Remove all shape hints

» Swap Symbol — Exchange selected instance for another symbol instance

» Duplicate Symbol — Duplicate instance as new symbol in Library panel

» Convert to Symbol — Change selected drawing into symbol

» Swap Bitmap — Exchange for bitmapped graphic in library

» Trace Bitmap — Convert selected bitmapped graphic to vector graphics

» Transform — Make changes in the selected object

Free Transform

Distort

Envelop

Scale — A box of eight handles (square) appear around the selected object so that its size can be reformed dragging the pull tabs

Rotate and Skew — A box of eight handles (round) appear around the selected object so that its rotation can be dragged 360° or skewed by dragging a single skew point

Scale and Rotate — A percentage value is assigned to scale and a degree value assigned to rotation

Rotate 90° CW — Selected object is rotated 90° from its current rotation angle in a clockwise direction

Rotate 90° CCW — Selected object is rotated 90° from its current rotation angle in a counter clockwise direction

Flip Vertical — Selected object is reversed on vertical axis

Flip Horizontal — Selected object is reversed on horizontal axis

Remove Transform — While transform handles are on object, it removes any changed. It is inactive after transform handles are no longer on the object.

» Arrange — Change symbols' depth relative to other objects on the stage

Bring to Front — Selected object placed on top level relative to depth

Bring Forward — Reduce depth by one

Send Backward — Increase depth by one

Send to Back — Selected object placed at lowest depth

Lock — Selected object cannot be moved or changed, but it can be part of a motion tween

Unlock All — All currently locked objects are unlocked

» Frames — Selected frames are modified

Reverse — Reverse the direction of motion tweened objects

Synchronize Symbols — Coordinate selected symbols and frames

Convert to Key Frames — Transform selected keys to keyframes

Convert to Blank Key Frames — Change any frame to a blank keyframe

» Group — Group selected objects into single or grouped objects

» Ungroup — Selected grouped object is returned to pre-grouping arrangement

» Break Apart — Text, bitmaps, and symbols are broken into shapes

» Distribute to Layers — Multiple selected objects are automatically sent to their own layer

Text

» Font — Fonts available in current system

» Size — Point size of font

» Style — Choice of plain, bold, italic, superscript, or subscript

» Align — Left, right, center, or justified alignment

» Tracking — Increase, decrease, or rest tracking space between characters

» Scrollable — Add horizontal or vertical scroll bars to text fields

Control

» Play — Run movie in work area

» Rewind — Move playhead to first frame

» Go To End — Move playhead to the end of the current scene

» Step Forward — Move the playhead one frame forward (to the right)

» Step Backward — Move the playhead one frame back (to the left)

» Test Movie — Create SWF file and play it

» Debug Movie — Show Output window and Debugger panel when movie runs

» Test Scene — Run current scene as SWF file

» Loop playback — Continuously replay the movie in work area

» Play All Scenes — When movie is tested in work area, all scenes will be displayed

» Enable Simple Frame Actions — Simple script is enabled in frames when played in work area

» Enable Simple Buttons — Simple button scripts and effects are enabled when played in work area

» Mute Sounds — Turn sounds off when movie is tested

» Enable Live Preview — Allow preview of components as they will appear in published movie

Window

» New Window — Duplicate current window on screen

» Toolbars

   Main — Toolbar with commonly used file and editing tools

   Status — Status bar along the bottom of the screen

   Controller — Panel with control icons used for testing movie

» Tools — Open the toolbar panel

» Timeline — Show or hide timeline

» Properties — Open context-sensitive Properties panel

» Answers — Open Answers panel for quick look-up for questions

» Align — Open Align panel for arranging stage elements

» Color Mixer — Open Color Mixer panel

» Color Swatches — Open Color swatches panel

» Info — Open Info panel (much of this panel's functionality has been duplicated in Properties panel)

» Scene — Open Scene panel to show all scenes in current movie

» Transform — Open Transform panel for re-sizing, rotating, and angling objects

» Actions — Open the Actions panel

» Debugger — Open debugger when movie is tested

» Movie Explorer — Open the Movie Explorer

» Reference — Open Reference Panel for looking up ActionScript terms

» Output — When a movie is tested, the output window opens

» Accessibility — Open Accessibility panel

» Components — Pre-assembled user interface elements

» Component Parameters — Use for naming and associating component with functions

» Library — Open library for current movie

» Common Libraries — Open library for specified library:

    Buttons

    Learning Interactions

    Sounds

» [NetConnect Debugger] — Debugger for application server

» Sitespring — Link to workgroup server

» [Server Console] — Console for working with Macromedia server

» Panel Sets — Select from default or saved panel layout

» Save Panel Layout — Save current layout of panels as a set to be opened in current configuration

» Close All Panels — All currently opened panels are closed

» Cascade — Organize desktop so that the different windows are at least partially visible for selection and use

» Tile — Organize a mosaic of open Windows so that all of the windows reduced in size are seen simultaneously on the screen

Help

Help menus will vary with the computer and operating system you are using. When you open the Help menu, you will see those help menus associated with your computer's system in addition to the following Flash MX Help menu items.

» Welcome — This page has some information to get you started

» What's New — Links to Web page with information about new features in Flash MX

» Lessons — A set of instructions for using Flash

» Tutorials — Step-by-step procedures for different Flash techniques

» Using Flash — Online Flash references and guides

» ActionScript Dictionary — Online guide to writing ActionScript in Flash MX movies

» Samples — Here you will find lots and lots of samples. The best part is that the FLA files are already on your system because they were installed when you installed Flash.

» Flash Support Center — A clearing house for various technical notes about Flash, workarounds, bugs, and tips for using Flash

Context Menus

In addition to the menus arranged along the top of the screen, Flash MX has several context menus that show different selections depending on what you happen to be working on. Context menus are shortcuts to menu items accessed by pressing the right mouse button or using Control+click on Macintosh computers. The following shows a collage of typical selections from different objects:

» Cut

» Copy

» Paste

» Select All

» Deselect All

» Free Transform

» Scale

» Rotate and Skew

» Distribute to Layers

» Edit

» Edit In Place

» Edit In New Window

» Actions

» Panels

   Info

   Transform

   Align

   Component Parameters

» Swap Symbol

» Duplicate Symbol

» Convert to Symbol

» Properties

Many users find context menus very convenient, whereas others prefer the main menu, the panels, or shortcut keys.

Shortcut Keys

Throughout this book, you will see a number of shortcut keystrokes used to issue commands. The shortcut keys are a combination of the Control (Command), Alt (Option), and Shift and other keys; they are used to complete a command that would require drilling down through the menus for the same behavior. Other commands have an F-key shortcut. The more you use Flash, the more you will find your own best combination of shortcuts using the keys, context menu, and panels. Common ones include the F6 key for inserting a keyframe, F8 to turn a drawing into a symbol, and Ctrl+F3 (Windows)/Cmd+F3 (Macintosh) to open the Properties panel. You can also create your own keyboard shortcuts. This option allows you to customize the keys to your specifications by using the Keyboard Shortcuts editor accessed through the Edit menu.

Project Overview

The project for this course is based on what a typical Flash-based Web site would involve. It opens with an engaging and interesting movie suggesting the nature of the site — a Flash Web design studio.

So as not to bore the viewer, the site begins with a preloader that lets the viewer see the progress in loading the movie. As soon as the movie loads, a strong musical track drives an abstract opening where a drawn hand fades into the abstract motion graphics, which leads to an artist's hand dynamically drawing three squares. These squares roll into three-dimensional wire cubes that rotate off the stage leaving three empty windows.

One of the three windows begins enlarging to fill the screen with a white fill, and then recedes into a black void. The black screen then becomes the background for an animated show that leads to a home page. The home page shows six portals the viewer may enter:

- » About Us
- » Animation Studio
- » Contact

» Fonts and Forms

» Portfolio

» The Basement

Each of these links provide the viewer (and you the reader) with information about the Web design company. First, viewers learn that all of the design work is done in a coast-to-coast collaboration using Flash in the About Us page. In the Animation Studio, viewers find out about different aspects of animation, including everything from simple tweens to animated text. The Animation Studio shows off the different types of animation techniques the company provides clients. The Contact link goes to a Flash-based form and optional e-mail link. The contact form asks for information about the client's needs and collects all of the information and sends it to a server-side script that handles the details. (A simple PHP script does all the work that you can actually use for your own site.)

Another link goes into a media-rich area that shows off what the designers can do with different aspects of text to enrich a site, as well as shows more about text forms and how they are used to take in information from a user and send back a response. Scrolling text explains how a site can be updated regularly by simply changing the contents of a text file.

At the Portfolio section, a different set of materials shows what the Flash design studio has done, including banners, animated logos, sound, and samples of Flash-based material that covers the wide range of Flash's domain.

Finally, in the Basement, the viewer finds an area of ActionScript code. Here, the viewer sees how different enhancements are added to Flash movies by using Flash's scripting language. In addition, the viewer sees a panel of different user interfaces newly available to Flash MX that require ActionScript coding.

Understanding the Process

In order to support the learning process and not to make an over-sized site that would take a long time to load, the different parts of the site are separate modules that load separately and can be created separately. Creating the site necessarily follows a learning process beginning with the simple features of Flash and gradually working into the more complex. In this way, you will not be overwhelmed by complex material at the outset, and as you gradually develop skills and understanding of Flash you will be able to see how a professionally designed and developed site is created.

Required Materials

» Windows Users: An Intel Pentium 200 MHz or equivalent processor running Windows 98 SE, Windows ME, Windows NT 4.0, Windows 2000, or Windows XP; 64MB of RAM (256MB recommended); 85MB of available disk space; a 16-bit color monitor capable of 1024 x 768 resolution; and a CD-ROM drive.

» Macintosh Users: A Power Macintosh running Mac OS 9.1 (or later) or Mac OS X version 10.1 (or later); 64MB RAM free application memory (256MB recommended), plus 85MB of available disk space; a color monitor capable of displaying 16-bit (thousands of colors) at 1024 x 768 resolution; and a CD-ROM drive.

Browser requirements

» Netscape plug-in that works with Netscape 4 (or later) in Windows, or works with Netscape 4.5 (or later) or Internet Explorer 5.0 (or later) on the Mac OS

» To run ActiveX controls, Microsoft Internet Explorer 4 or later (Windows 95, Windows 98, Windows Me, Windows NT 4.0, Windows 2000, Windows XP, or later)

» AOL 7 on Windows, AOL 5 on the Mac OS

» Opera 6 on Windows, Opera 5 on the Mac OS

Optional equipment and software

Several different tools can enhance your ability to create the kind of site you want. If you are not artistically inclined, get a good collection of digital art done with vector graphics, available on CD-ROM or from vendors on the Web. A flatbed scanner is another helpful tool. Even an inexpensive flatbed scanner can do wonders to your ability to create interesting materials to be used in your Flash site. Likewise, a digital camera is another source of graphic images you can import into Flash. As noted in the chapter, you may find that a drawing tablet that plugs into your computer can save you a lot of time creating the graphics you want. Many professional Flash developers prefer extra-wide screens or even dual monitors so that they can spread out a project over a wide area.

Stepping Through the Project Stages

Unlike some projects that you can begin with the beginning, the very first element in the Flash project that a viewer will see is a preloader that requires more advanced Flash materials you will see in the later sessions of the course, including the scripting language ActionScript. Therefore, the sessions begin guiding you through the basics first where you can use Flash to build different elements that make up the movie. As you develop skills, you will add more and more to the overall project. In this way you will have a better understanding both of Flash and what it takes to create the project.

However, some readers may want to skip around to the different sessions and yet see tangible results from their efforts. To accommodate those with a non-linear approach to learning, the sessions deal with different modules that will work on their own yet are linked to one another. Also, some readers may have had some previous experience with Flash and want to try out different aspects of Flash MX and so will cover the materials out of sequence. That is perfectly fine, and if you run into new materials you don't understand, just go back to one of the earlier sessions where the unknown technique is explained.

Choosing Project Options

Some of the modules may be considered project options. For example, the movie will load and run perfectly fine without a preloader, so if you don't want to spend time finding out how to build your own preloader, skip it. Likewise, any module or session that is either redundant to your own knowledge base of Flash or just something you'd rather not bother with can be skipped.

You are also welcome to make any changes that you want. In fact, I would encourage you to experiment with making changes so that you can add exactly what you may need for your own site. You can add, change, or enhance anything you see. If you accidentally destroy some part of the project beyond repair, you can always pull a mint copy of the project off the CD-ROM and start over. So, don't worry about marching through the sessions in a lock-step manner. Instead, use the sessions and tutorials to get the most of what you need out of them.

One suggestion is to set up dual projects. Take the project supplied with the course and replicate it by going through the different sessions and tutorials. At the same time, have another project of your own that changes the original project but requires the same or similar techniques. So as you develop your skills and see how the sample project has been created, you will also be creating a mirror project that reflects exactly what you need for your own site.

General Work Tips and Computer Instructions

Here are a few tips that are probably reminders for you rather than anything new and startling. I assume that you know your way around a computer, but it never hurts to have a few reminders that will help you get the most out of this course.

Organizing files

The first thing you should do is to copy all of the files from your CD-ROM to a folder on your desktop. First, create a folder on your desktop and name it "Flash Course" or some other name that clearly helps you remember what's in the folder. In Windows, the easiest way to copy the files to your hard drive is by installing them from the interface. The interface installs the files to a directory under Program Files named Flash MXCC. After the files are installed they can be accessed from the Start menu by selecting Flash MX Complete Course. On the Macintosh, simply select the Tutorial Files folder on the CD and drag it onto the desktop. Remove the CD-ROM from your disk drive and put it somewhere safe and out of the way. If you accidentally lose a file, you can just pull out the CD-ROM and drag a new copy to your computer.

Saving and backing up files

Create a set of folders for each of the sessions and another folder that contains the entire project. By watching your progress in developing the Web site, you will be able to see your skill set grow. For each session, you will have to have folders for both the work that you do as well as the original project segment. This will allow you to make all the mistakes you want — or introduce all the creativity you want and still have a complete set of session files you won't have to pull off the CD-ROM in case you lose a file.

Once you have completed a session or tutorial, save a backup copy. I generally save my files to a high capacity removable disk — a Zip disk. You can also save backups to floppy disks or even to your server. However, one of the few absolute truths about computer files I've learned over the years is that the only files that get destroyed permanently are those you neglect to back up. For some reason, you never lose original files that are backed-up. Once you're finished with a big project, take all of the materials from your backup drive and dump it all on a CD-ROM if you have a CD burner on your system.

Part II:
Getting Started

The Flash MX Environment

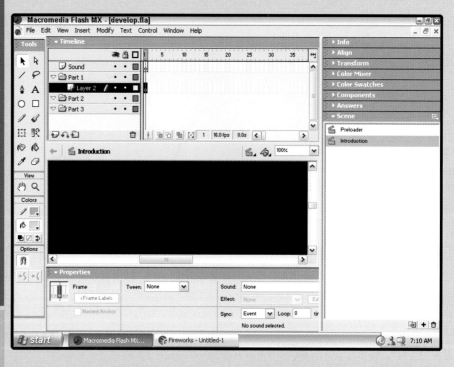

Introduction to Session

In this session you will jump right in with the different tools provided by Flash MX. We'll start with the menus and use them with different parts of the project and then go on to look at the rest of the environment. Throughout this examination, your course project is used to show both how to work in the Flash MX environment and how to create Flash applications.

TOOLS YOU'LL USE
Many different basic and advanced tools

MATERIALS NEEDED
Project from CD-ROM including IntroFinal3.fla

TIME REQUIRED
90 minutes

SESSION OUTCOME
Getting to know the tools and workplace

PROJECT PORTION
Different parts illustrating layers, scenes, and objects on the stage

Tutorial
» Changing the Default Panel Set

When you first open Flash, you see your stage, timeline, Toolbox, and default setup panels. The first thing you want to do is to select the panels with which you want to work. To do that you need to use the Window menu.

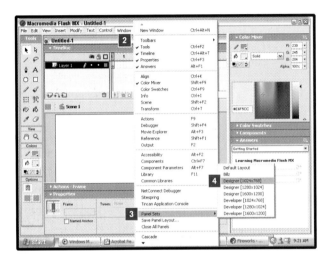

1. **Open Flash MX by double-clicking its icon.**
   The page appears with the default set of panels in the dock on the right side of the screen.
2. **Click the Window menu in the menu bar at the top of the screen.**
   On smaller monitors, or if you have your monitor set to use a lower resolution, the Panel Sets may be hidden below the bottom of the screen. Just click the arrow at the bottom of the menu to access the Panel Sets menu option.

3. **Select Panel Sets.**
   A submenu appears as soon as you select Panel Sets.

4. **Select Designer (1024x768).**
   You can select any one you want, but for purposes of illustration, select this one.

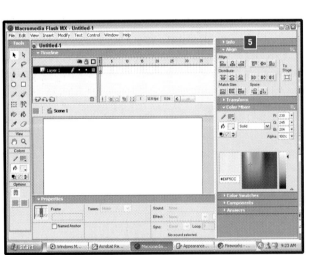

5. **The original panel set has been replaced by a new one in the dock.**
   The new panel set offers more, but you may want to add still other panels as you need them for your movie.

Tutorial
» Customizing the Panel Set

When viewing the panels in the dock, you might decide you want to add one or more other panels. With Flash MX, you'll find that as easy as loading the panel set initially. Because this project involves more than one scene, you may want the Scene panel handy.

1. **Select Window→Scene on the menu bar.**
   You see the Scene panel in the second grouping in the Window menu. You can select any of the panels you want and add them later.

2. **Click the arrow next to the word "Scene" to close the panel.**
   The Scene panel closes to a panel bar.

3. **Click the Scene panel bar in the "dot" area and drag it to the dock.**

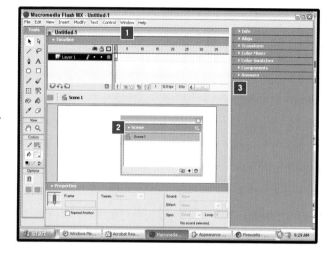

4. **When you see a bold outline around the dock, release the mouse button.**
   The Scene panel is now tucked into the dock.

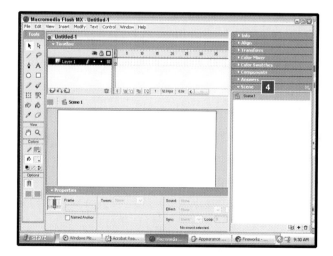

Tutorial
» Saving Your Customized Panel Set

Now that you have a customized panel set, you need to save it so that the next time you begin working with Flash, you can call up your own panel set. Make sure you have the panels in your set you want, and then follow these instructions:

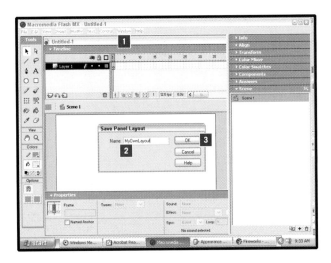

1. **Select Window→Save Panel Layout on the menu bar.**
   If you have a low resolution or smaller screen, you may have to click on the arrow at the bottom of the menu to see the Save Panel Layout selection.

2. **Type a name for your panel set in the Save Panel Layout dialog box.**

3. **Click OK.**
   Your panel set is now saved.

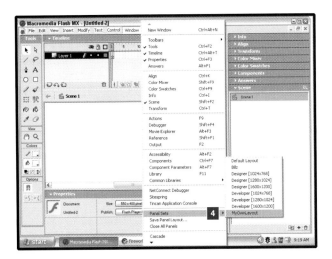

4. **Reopen the Panel Sets submenu to see that your panel set is indeed saved.**
   You may notice another "personalized" set named "Billz" in the Panel Sets portion of the illustration. That's the author's personalized set!

Tutorial
» Adding and Renaming Scenes

The course project has three main scenes. The first scene is a preloader that gives the viewer something to look at while the movie loads. As soon as the preloader detects the loaded movie, it jumps to the next scene, which is the introduction. Finally, the third scene is the home page. When you first load a new movie, it has only a single scene, named Scene 1. In this next set of tutorials, you see how to add scenes, rename them, and then move from one scene to another.

1. **Click the arrow next to Scene in the dock to open the Scene panel.**

2. **Select Insert→Scene.**
   As soon as you release the mouse button you will see a new scene in the Scene panel.

3. **Click the Add (+) button at the bottom of the scene panel.**
   This is another, simpler way to add a scene if you have the Scene panel in the dock or on stage.

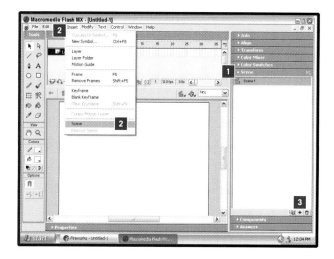

4. **Double-click the first scene in the Scene panel (Scene 1).**
   A black rectangle appears around Scene 1.

5. **Type the name** Preloader.
   The name changes from Scene 1 to Preloader in the Scene panel.

6. **Repeat Steps 4 and 5 for Scene 2 and rename the scene** Introduction.

7. **Click the Edit Scene button to navigate from one scene to another.**
   At this stage, all the scenes look alike. As you develop the project, each scene will be completely different from the other two.

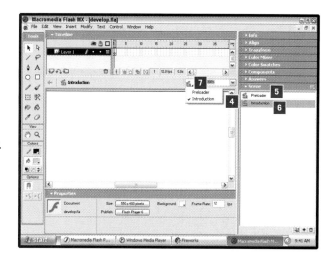

Tutorial
» Setting Background Color, Dimensions, and Frames Per Second

Three settings in your movie affect all the scenes and movie clips loaded into the movie. These are called *global settings*. First, because the background color remains the same for all scenes, you need to select a color for the background. You can place a large rectangle of a different color to simulate a different background color in your movie, but the background color itself remains the same. Second, your movie's dimensions stay constant for all scenes. Third, the frame rate (Frames Per Second—fps) remains constant throughout a movie. Streaming sound may affect the frame rate, but otherwise, once selected, the frame rate stays the same for all movies. The default fps is 12, and the site is set up to use a higher frame rate. The higher the frame rate, the better the animation, but higher fps generate more images, which require more bandwidth. Lower fps can save bandwidth but produce poorer animation. The setting 16 fps provides better animation but does not have a major impact on the animation.

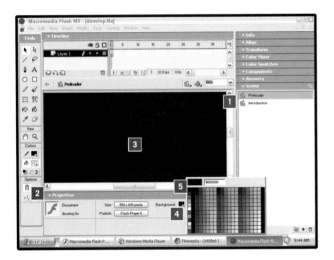

1. **Select the Preloader scene.**

2. **Open the Properties panel if it's not already open.**

3. **Click the stage area to select the Document properties.**

4. **Click the Background color well popup menu arrow to open the color swatches.**

5. **Click the color black.**
   You can make sure that you have selected black and not a dark blue or dark green by the value in the hexadecimal value window. It should be #000000. That's it, your entire movie's background color for all scenes is now set.

6. **Click the Size button in the Properties panel.**
   The Document Properties dialog box opens.

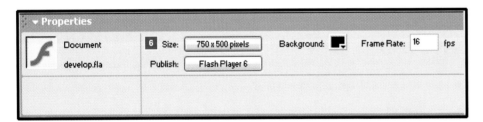

7. **Type** 750 px **for the width and** 500 px **for the height in the Document Properties dialog box.**

These dimensions define your work area. The default size is 550 by 400 pixels, so you have more room to work in with the larger dimensions. Macromedia recommends a monitor capable of 1024 by 768 pixels, but even with those set at a lower resolution of 800 by 600, you have ample room to see the entire movie. However, if your target audience uniformly has older monitors with maximum resolutions of 640 by 480, they may miss part of the movie on their screens.

8. **Click the Frame Rate option in the Document Properties dialog box.**

9. **Type** 16 **(if it's not already set to 16).**

10. **Click the Ruler Units popup menu and select Pixels if it's not already set to pixels.**

Pixel measurement units better reflect screen resolution.

11. **Click OK to save your settings.**

12. **Select File→Save from the menu bar.**

13. **Type** project **for the movie name, or any other you would prefer, and click Save.**

Having set up the scenes and global settings, you need to save your work. Each time you complete a segment of the project, remember to save it.

Tutorial
» Adding Layers and Folders

The next step is to organize your movie into layers and folders. The layers let you place objects at different levels in the movie. Those layers on higher levels overshadow those on lower levels. For example, if you animate a woman on Layer 1 and a man on Layer 2, and Layer 1 is higher in the stack than Layer 2, when you animate the woman, she appears to move in front of the man. If you switch the layers, the woman appears to move behind the man. Folders help you organize the different layers. In movies with lots of layers, the collapsible folders give you more room to see what you're working with on the stage.

1. **Click the Insert Layer Folder button.**
   A new folder appears above Layer 1.

2. **Drag Layer 1 so that it is positioned above Folder 1.**

3. **Double-click Layer 1 to see a white background behind the layer name.**

4. **Type the name** Sound**.**
   The top layer is now labeled Sound.

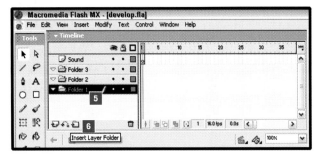

5. **Click Folder 1 to select it.**

6. **Click the Insert Layer Folder button twice.**
   Two more folders appear above Folder 1.

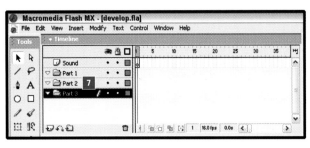

7. **Rename the folders so they are labeled Part 1, Part 2, and Part 3.**
   These labels are not too descriptive, but they do provide an idea of the developmental sequence of the introduction. They reflect sequence rather than object groups.

Tutorial
» Organizing Layers and Folders

Now that you have a start on your layers and folders, you can organize them so that you can work with them more easily. The better organized your layers and folders at the outset, the fewer problems you encounter later.

1. **Click the Part 2 folder to select it.**

2. **Click the Insert New Layer button.**
   A new layer appears above the Part 2 folder. The layer is not "inside" the Part 1 folder and that is where you want to place it.

3. **Drag Layer 2 so that it is on top of the Part 1 folder icon.**
   As soon as you release Layer 2, it appears beneath the Part 1 folder but is now indented. Layer indentation beneath a folder indicates the layer is inside the folder above the layer. You can place as many layers inside a folder as you want. You can also place folders within folders.

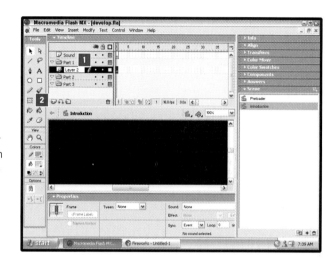

4. **Select Layer 2 and click the Insert New Layer button 11 times.**
   Twelve layers now appear in the Part 1 folder. They are all indented because when you initially select a layer within a folder and insert a new layer, that new layer appears inside the same layer that was selected when you clicked the Insert New Layer button.

5. **Drag four layers into the Part 2 folder and one layer into the Part 3 folder.**
   All of the layers you need for the Introduction scene are now in place. The last step is to rename them to more meaningful terms.

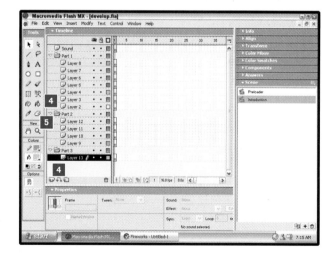

Tutorial
» Optimizing Layers and Folders

Finally, you want to rename the remaining layers so that you know their function. When not in use, you should close the folders to open up more room in the stage area where you can work. Remember to use names that help you remember the contents of the layer. Keeping layers straight is essential to successful Flash movies, and the clearer the layer names, the better.

1. **Rename the layers inside the folders, from top to bottom:**

Part 1

> Skip Intro
> White lines
> Animated rectangles
> Background moving
> Vertical rectangles
> Vertical center
> Background fades

Part 2

> "To The" Clip
> Frame swap
> Sequential Multiple clips
> The Edge

Part 3

> Cubes

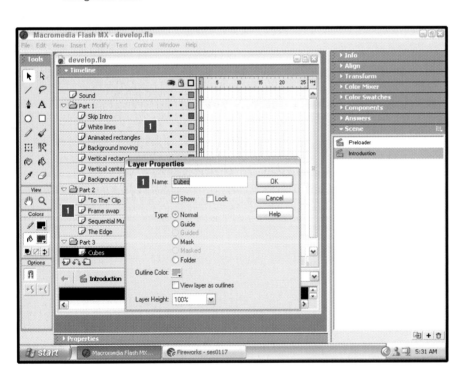

2. **Click the arrows next to the three folders.**

   All of the layers disappear.

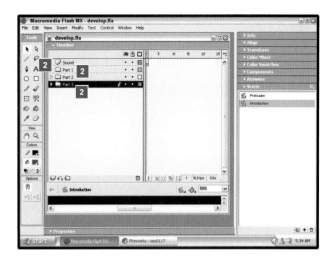

3. **Drag the bottom of the timeline upward to make room for more stage area.**

   With the layers tucked away, you can make more room to work on the stage. To remove the dock and panels, just press the Tab key. Press the Tab key again, and the dock and panels all reappear.

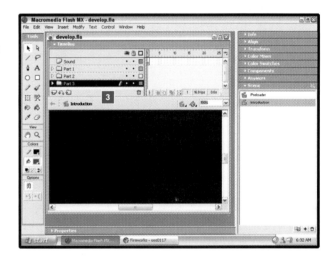

Changing Layer Properties

If you click directly on the icon next to the layer name, the Layer Properties dialog box appears. In this dialog box, you can rename the layer; lock it; change the outline color; convert the layer to a guide, guided, mask, or masked layer; or convert it back to a normal layer. You can also lock or hide the layer and make it two or three times (200–300 percent) as high. Further on in the course, you learn about other aspects of layers to make your movies more interesting, but here, you should know where to find the Layer Properties dialog box for future reference.

Tutorial
» Setting General Preferences

Before going further, you want to set your preferences. Flash has five sets of preferences to set: General, Editing, Clipboard, Warnings, and ActionScript. Each preference set has several options that you need to understand to maximize working with Flash.

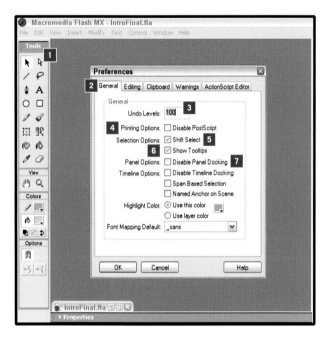

1. **Select Edit➔Preferences.**
   The Preferences dialog box appears.

2. **Click the General tab to bring it to the front if it's not already in front.**
   The General tab provides 11 different options. Each option depends on what you personally want.

3. **Type the number of levels you want Flash to undo mistakes in the Undo Levels text window.**
   The more undo levels, the more mistakes you can correct by selecting Edit➔Undo. The default of 100 is usually enough, but if you have lots of RAM and a large project, you may want to add more.

4. **Select Printing Options to disable PostScript Printing.**
   The default is deselected, and unless you have difficulties printing to a PostScript printer, it should be left deselected.

5. **Select Shift Select for controlling how multiple items are handled.**
   If you leave this option deselected, when you click an item on the stage it is selected, even if you have other items selected. Otherwise, to select multiple items, you have to hold the Shift key down. Because you often only want a single item selected, use the default and keep this option requiring a Shift key press for selecting multiple items.

6. **Select Show Tooltips to bring up the tool names when you move the mouse pointer over a control button.**
   For learning all of the different elements in Flash, keep this option selected. If the Tooltips become irritating, you can turn them off later.

7. **Select Disable Panel Docking to keep panels from arranging themselves in the dock area.**
   If you select this option, the panels are in a free-floating panel container or out on their own. If you have a small screen, select this option to give yourself more horizontal room on both the stage and timeline. However, you lose the convenience and organizing assistance you get with the dock feature.

8. **Select Span Based Selection to use a span-based selection method as used in Flash 5 instead of the frame-based selection native to Flash MX.**

   If you prefer the older, Flash 5, method of selecting frames, choose this option. If you're new to Flash, consider leaving this option deselected.

9. **Select Named Anchor on Scene to enable the viewer to use the forward and back buttons on browsers to jump to the next or previous scene.**

   In some applications, you may find this option very handy. If you choose this option, Flash automatically places an anchor at the first keyframe of each scene. If you arrange your scenes so that each has a distinct element of your site, you can let the viewer use the browser keys to move back and forth.

10. **Select either Use this color or Use layer color, a mutually exclusive choice.**

    When you place objects on different layers, you can highlight them with the layer color or a general color that you select here. For example, if you select a red layer color, and place a text field on the stage, when you select the text field, it appears with a red border around it. If you select a general color for all objects on the stage, whenever you select any one of them, regardless of layer, they appear in the same color.

11. **Choose a font from the popup menu to use as a "replacement" font when the font you use in a movie is not on the viewer's system.**

    Be sure to select a fairly generic font that you are likely to find on all of your viewers' computers, such as the default _sans. Some good choices are Times, Verdana, or Courier because they tend to be on most computers.

12. **Click OK to apply your settings.**

<TIP>

You should become familiar with the different Preferences as soon as possible because you need to know their various functions as you develop your skills in Flash MX. However, until you become more familiar, use the default settings. In that way, you can have a stable set of parameters while you learn all of Flash's nooks and crannies.

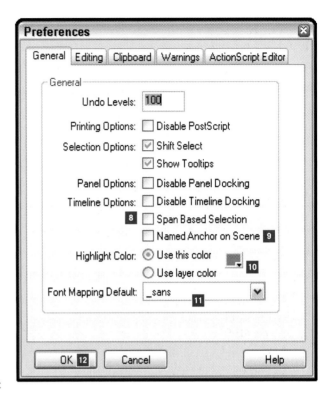

Tutorial

» Setting Editing Preferences

The Editing preferences contain a number of drawing and text options. Generally, the text options are left in their default state of unselected. However, you can experiment with some of the Pen and Drawing settings. As with all other Preferences, if you change your mind, you can always changes the Preferences.

1. **Select Edit→Preferences.**
   The Preferences dialog box appears.

2. **Click the Editing tab.**

3. **Select from three Pen Tool options.**
   The Pen tool is a Bezier pen and takes some getting used to. By selecting Show Pen Preview, you can get a better idea of what your drawing will look like. Choose Show Solid Points to better show the different pivot points in a drawing, and Show Precise Cursors to get a cross-hair type of cursor.

4. **Select from three Text options.**
   By and large, you can leave these three selections disabled. You may find some benefit if you select the Default Text Orientation option, when you work with some Asian language fonts. Select Right to Left Text Flow, when you work with languages that you write from right to left, such as Arabic. By selecting No Kerning, you can turn off font spacing that uses kerning.

5. **Click the Connect lines popup menu to choose options.**
   You may select from Must be close, Normal (default), or Can be distant.

6. **Click the Smooth curves popup menu to choose options.**
   You can select Off, Rough, Normal, or Smooth. The smoothness of a line can affect your drawings in a positive or negative fashion. When you want angles in some areas and smooth curves in others, it is best to minimize the number of smooth curves so that the angled drawings are not curved in a way you do not want.

7. **Click the Recognize lines popup menu to choose options.**
   If you want straight lines with the Pencil tool, such as when drawing triangles or other geometric shapes, select Strict, but if you do not want Flash to recognize the pencil's drawings as straight lines, select Off. If you desire something in between, select Normal or Tolerant. You may want to test different options before making a final selection with this tool, and you can always select a pencil line and straighten it using Modify→Straighten from the menu bar.

8. **Click the Recognize shapes popup menu to choose options.**
   You can select from Off, Strict, Normal, and Tolerant depending on how close you want your drawing to be recognized as a geometric shape such as an oval, circle, triangle or different angle.

9. **Click the Click Accuracy popup menu to choose options.**
   Click Accuracy refers to how close an item must be to the mouse pointer before Flash recognizes it as an object and selects it. The options are Strict, Normal, and Tolerant. Strict means you must have the pointer very close while Tolerant means that it can be in the general area.

10. **Click OK to apply your changes.**

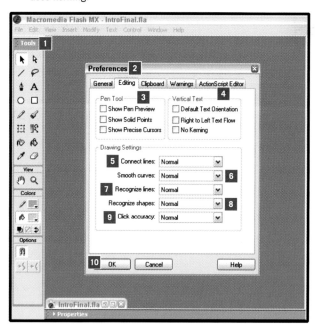

Tutorial
» Setting Clipboard Preferences

The Clipboard Preferences may seem like an odd name for selections that apply to bitmaps, gradients, and PICT files. However, the settings refer to how the different options are copied to the clipboard, and so it makes sense to call the options Clipboard Preferences. Bitmap and Gradient settings apply only to Windows operating systems and PICT settings are only for Macintosh OS.

1. **Select Edit→Preferences.**
   The Preferences dialog box appears.

2. **Click the Clipboard tab.**

3. **Select from the Bitmaps options (Windows only).**
   The Color Depth and Resolution refer to the number of bits the color will use (4–32 or match the screen) and the bit resolution (72, 150, or 300). Generally, you want to use Screen resolution unless you're certain of the resolution on the receiving computer monitor. You can increase the size limit to above or below 250Kb depending on the size of memory in the receiving computers. Generally, you do want the graphics to be smooth (anti-aliased) and so be sure to check the Smooth check box if it is not already selected.

4. **Click the Quality popup menu in the Gradients box (Windows only).**
   The gradients quality refers to the number of transition levels between two or more colors in a gradient. The higher the quality (Best), the more memory and bandwidth used. You may also select None, Normal, or Fast.

5. **Select PICT settings (Macintosh only).**
   To preserve data copied to the Clipboard as vector graphics, choose Objects. Otherwise select a bitmap format to convert the copied artwork to a bitmap. Type in a resolution value for the screen. To include PostScript data, choose Include Postscript. The gradients quality refers to the number of transition levels between two or more colors in a gradient. The higher the quality (Best), the more memory and bandwidth used. You may also select None, Normal, or Fast.

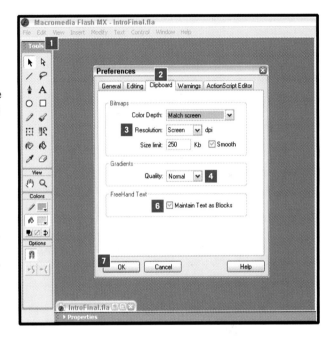

6. **Select FreeHand Text to Maintain Text as Blocks for editing in Macromedia FreeHand.**
   The gradient quality refers to the number of transition levels between two or more colors in a gradient. The higher the quality (Best), the more memory and bandwidth used. You may also select None, Normal, or Fast.

7. **Click OK to apply your settings.**

Tutorial
» Setting Warnings Preferences

The Warnings Preferences allow you to select the conditions under which you want a warning dialog box to appear. To get started, your best bet is to leave them all selected, and then later, if certain ones become annoying, you can deselect them.

1. **Select Edit→Preferences.**
   The Preferences dialog box appears.

2. **Click the Warnings tab.**

3. **Select/Deselect Warn on Save for Macromedia Flash 5 Compatibility.**
   If you use new features of Flash MX but you have your file type set to be saved as Flash 5, you will receive an error message in both the Output Window and a dialog box. This is a very good option to have selected!

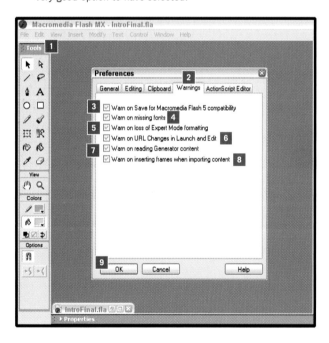

4. **Select/Deselect Warn on Missing Fonts.**
   If the file you are loading has fonts not in your system, it warns you and provides you with an option to use a default font or select one from your system.

5. **Select/Deselect Warn on Loss of Expert Mode Formatting.**
   You will find this option important to keep selected, especially if you use both Expert and Normal modes of entering ActionScript. Some ActionScript terms and formats entered in the Expert mode cannot be shown in the Normal mode, and if you lose any formatting or terms, you should definitely know about it.

6. **Select/Deselect Warn on URL Changes in Launch and Edit.**
   A warning appears if a Web address (URL) has been changed.

7. **Select/Deselect Warn on Reading Generator Content.**
   Flash MX does not support Generator objects, and if you load a pre-Flash MX file with Generator objects, this warning places a large red "X" over any such objects.

8. **Select/Deselect Warn on Inserting Frames when Importing Content.**
   Selecting this option alerts you when frames are inserted into your document for audio or video files that you import into your movie.

9. **Click OK to apply your changes.**

Tutorial
» Setting ActionScript Editor Preferences

Setting the preferences for the ActionScript Editor deals with formatting options. The ActionScript Editor tab is divided into three areas: Editing Options, Text, and Syntax Coloring. Although initially you won't deal with ActionScript, as your skills grow, you may find yourself doing a good deal of scripting with the Actions panel. You can use the default settings initially, but later you may want to customize them to your own tastes.

1. **Select Edit→Preferences.**
   The Preferences dialog box appears.

2. **Click the ActionScript Editor tab.**

3. **Choose selections from the Editing Options.**
   The Automatic Indentation formats ActionScript along standard scripting format conventions making it easier to read. Code Hints are a new and valuable feature of Flash MX. They show hints to correct formatting in ActionScript, making it easier to learn. The Delay gage shows the amount of delay before the code hints appear. The Tab Size requires a value for the number of spaces you want the indentations to be tabbed.

4. **Click the Text popup menus for font selection and size selection.**
   You may find it easier to write code with a mono-spaced font like Courier or Courier New rather than a font such as Times or Arial, which have kern values. Font size becomes crucial because you don't want font so large that you can only see a small portion of your code.

5. **Select Syntax Coloring from the color well popup menus.**
   Other than keeping the background color white or a very light color, the color selection is a matter of taste. However, you will find that selecting different colors for different types of actions and terms will help you learn ActionScript more easily and help you avoid mistakes.

6. **Click OK to apply your changes.**

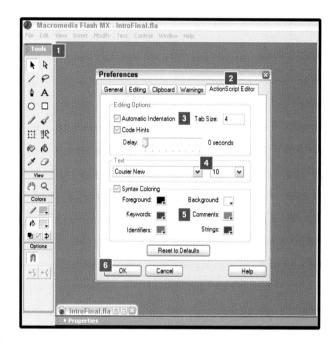

Tutorial
» Adding Frames

Once you establish your layers, you need to add frames, keyframes, and blank keyframes. Generally, you add frames for the length of the movie, and then depending on what objects you want in the movie, you add keyframes where the object first appears. You then add another keyframe where the object changes. Flash automatically fills in the intermediate steps between the first and second keyframes in a process called tweening. In the project movie, you first see the Preloader scene, which shows how much of the movie you have currently loaded. You then see the Introduction scene, which consists of several different objects. The objects in the Introduction begin at one point, go through a number of changes, and then are replaced by new objects. Depending on what level you want the object to appear, you place the objects on a specific layer. You must place the frames and keyframes on the level where you are working with an object. Before attempting this tutorial, you may find it useful to review the tutorials on adding and naming layers in this session.

1. **Click the Scene Edit button and select Preloader.**
   The Preloader Scene appears.

2. **Add three layers to the existing layer in the Preloader scene and name the four layers as follows:**
   Loading Message
   Chart Overlay
   Graphic Load Chart
   Percent Loaded

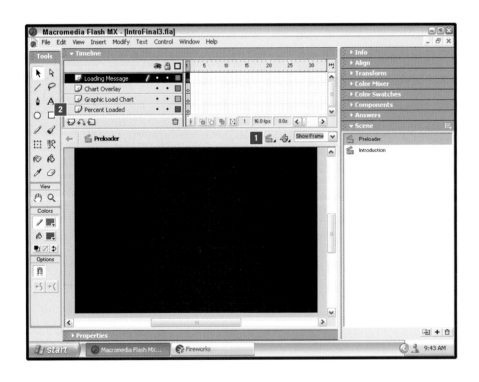

3. **On the Loading Message layer, click the second frame column on the timeline.**

    All movies begin with a keyframe in the first frame column, so when you begin adding frames, you begin in the second or high frame columns.

4. **Select Insert→Frame from the menu bar.**

    You see a little block in the second frame. The block indicates that the frame is the last frame in the layer after a keyframe and before any new keyframe in the layer.

5. **Select the second frame column on the Chart Overlay layer and press the F5 key.**

    Pressing the F5 key is a shortcut to insert a frame. Using certain shortcuts, rather than menus, saves you time. Because inserting frames is a common task in creating Flash movies, it's a good shortcut to learn.

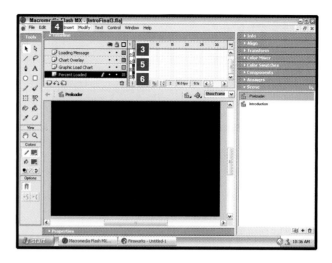

6. **Hold down the Shift key and drag the mouse downward from the second column in the Graphic Load Chart layer to the Percent Loaded layer.**

    Both of the bottom two second frame columns are selected.

7. **Press the F5 key.**

    Two new frames are added with a single action. All four frames could have been added at once using this technique.

8. **On the Percent Loaded layer, click the second frame on the timeline.**

9. **Select Insert→Keyframe from the menu bar.**

    The second frame now has a clear circle in it indicating it is a keyframe rather than a regular frame. Only the Percent Loaded layer requires a second keyframe. When you load an object onto the stage from a selected keyframe, the clear circle becomes solid. If you have an ActionScript script, you see a little 'a' above the keyframe.

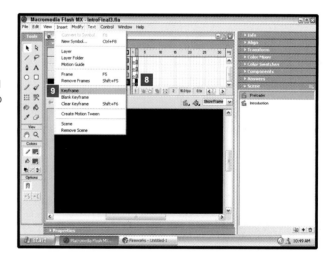

Tutorial
» Placing Objects on the Stage from the Library

Once you have frames and keyframes, you can place objects on the stage. You can either draw objects with the drawing tools or import objects into the library. Also, whenever you create a symbol object, Flash places it into the library. In addition to a regular library, you have special libraries called Common Libraries. The Common Libraries include pre-made Buttons, Learning Interactions, and Sounds. You can drag any of the objects in any of the libraries onto the stage. The following set of examples shows how the Preloader scene was built. To make it simple, first load the main program's library only. Then you can take objects from the library and place them on the stage.

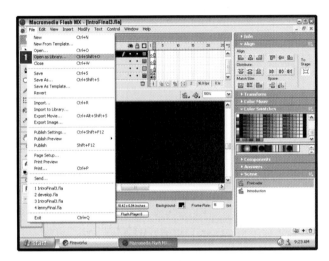

1. **While your current project is on the stage, select File→Open as Library.**

2. **When the Open as Library dialog box appears, select the IntroFinal3.fla file.**
   You current project stays put and a Library panel with several items already in it appears over the stage. This library contains all of the objects in the main introduction and preloader.

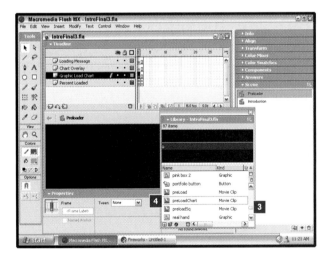

3. **Click the scroll arrow on the Library panel until you see preLoadChart.**
   With a total of 87 different items in the library, you have a bit of scrolling to do to find the item.

4. **Click the preLoadChart item in the Library panel.**
   You will see a purple bar in the top pane of the Library panel.

5. **Select the preLoadChart item in the lower panel and drag it to the stage.**

The purple rectangle is now on the stage.

6. **Drag the rectangle on the stage so that the Properties panel shows its position to be X=277, Y=379.**

If the Properties panel is not open, select Window→Properties to open it. The position values are in pixels.

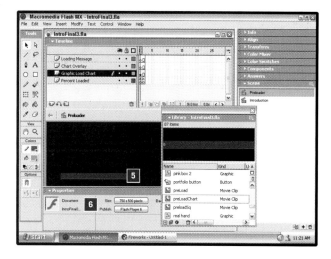

7. **Click the Loading Message layer to select it.**

As a reminder, you may want to lock the other layers so that you don't mistakenly place the item on the wrong layer.

8. **Select the preLoad item in the Library.**

The item is directly above the preLoadChart item. In the top pane of the Library pane you will see the movie clip and a little control panel. When you see a control panel in a Library item, it means that the item is a movie or sound that can be played by pressing the right arrow button in the control panel.

9. **Drag the preLoad item to the stage and position it directly above the purple rectangle.**

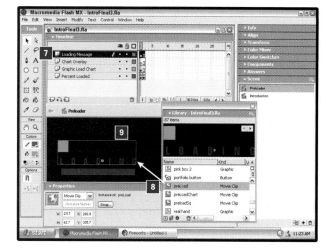

Tutorial
» Creating Objects on the Stage

To create an object on the stage, use one of the tools available in Flash MX. In Session Two, you learn how to use all of the tools in the Flash MX toolbox, but now you will see how to use two tools. You use the rectangle tool and line tool to make an overlay for the preloader chart.

1. **Lock all of the layers except the Chart Overlay layer.**
   When using drawing tools of any sort, you can avoid mistakes by locking all layers except the one on which you are working.

2. **Click the Chart Overlay layer to select it.**

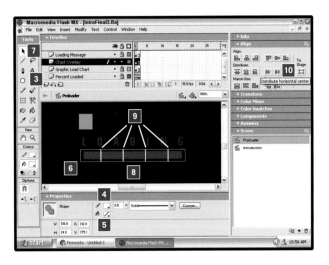

3. **Click the Rectangle tool in the Toolbox to select it.**
   The square icon on the Toolbox is the Rectangle tool. As soon as you select the Rectangle tool, you see the Properties panel become the Rectangle tool panel.

4. **Click the top color well on the Properties panel and select white as the color.**
   The top color well is the stroke color.

5. **Click the bottom color well and select the box with the red diagonal line through it.**
   The bottom color well is the fill color. The selection with the red diagonal line turns off the fill. If you select it in the top color well, Flash turns off the stroke color.

6. **Draw a white rectangle over the purple color bar.**

7. **Select the Line tool from the Toolbox.**

8. **Draw four vertical lines inside the rectangle distributing them as evenly as you can.**

9. **Hold down the Shift key and click on each of the four vertical lines.**

10. **Open the Align panel in the Dock, and select the Distribute Horizontal Center button.**
    The four bars will distribute themselves evenly within the rectangle.

11. **Lock the Chart Overlay layer.**

Tutorial

» Adding Text Fields to the Stage

The last topic this session covers is adding text fields to the stage. Like adding an item from the Library or drawing, the other main kind of object you will be adding is text. In the Preloader, you can add a dynamic text field that updates the viewer on the percent of the movie that's loaded. Further on in the course, you learn far more about text in Flash. This is just to get started.

1. **Lock all of the layers except Percent Loaded.**

2. **Click on the first frame of the Percent Loaded layer.**

3. **Click the "A" (Text tool) on the Toolbox.**
   The Properties panel becomes the Text properties panel. Next to the large letter "A" you will see a Text Type popup menu.

4. **Click the color well on the Properties panel and select green.**
   The green you select should match the green square above the LOADING movie clip.

5. **Click on the Text Type popup menu and select Dynamic Text.**

6. **With the Text tool still selected, click the stage to the left of the purple rectangle.**
   A text field looking like a white rectangle with a small square in the lower right-hand corner appears. This is the dynamic text field. Because two keyframes are in this layer, you will need to make a copy of the text field and paste it into the second keyframe in the layer.

7. **Select the Pointer tool (arrow) from the Toolbox and click the text field.**
   You will see a blue outline if you've successfully selected the text field.

8. **Select Edit→Copy from the menu bar.**

9. **Click the second frame in the Percent Loaded layer.**

10. **Select Edit→Paste in Place from the menu bar.**
    The text field is now in both frames in exactly the same place. Near the end of the course you will learn about the ActionScript that generated the text output and the bar graph that shows the viewer how much progress has been made.

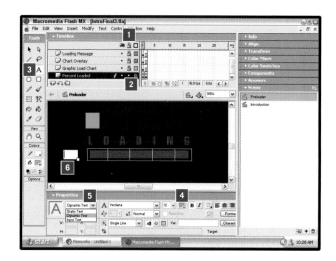

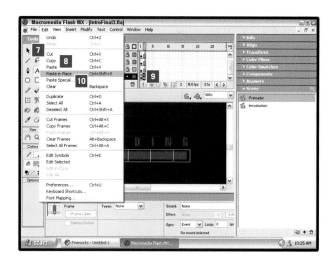

Tutorial
» Testing Your Movie

Creating Flash MX movies successfully rests in part on your ability to see what you've created. In this section, you learn three ways to test your movie. First, the simple technique of dragging the playhead over a section of the movie lets you see how a movie segment is working. This kind of testing is for fine-tuning your movie. A second testing method involves running the movie in the Flash editor. Here you can see the whole movie running at the correct frames-per-second (FPS) rate. Finally, using the Control menu, you can see the whole movie play in a special preview controller that shows what the movie looks like when you view it outside of the editor environment.

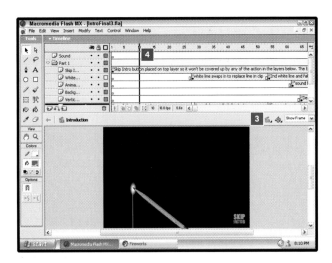

1. **Drag the main project movie file from the CD-ROM onto your desktop.**

2. **Double-click the main project movie icon to open the movie.**

3. **Select the Introduction from the Edit movie popup menu.**

4. **Click the playhead in the timeline and hold down the mouse button.**
   The playhead is a red, but when you press it, it turns into a solid vertical black line.

5. **Drag the playhead to the left and right.**
   As you drag the playhead you can see the movie change and animate.

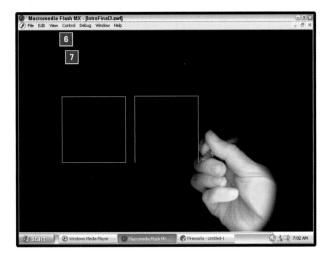

6. **Select Control→Play from the menu bar.**
   The movie automatically plays in the editor. You can elect to enable simple frame actions and buttons by choosing those options from the Control menu as well. You can also see what takes place off the stage area. The offstage area helps you understand some of the tricks for making Flash MX movies. (The shortcut for playing your movie is to press the Enter or Return key.)

7. **Select Control→Test Movie from the menu bar.**
   A special player window opens, and you can see what the movie looks like outside of the editor and how it appears in a browser or on a Web page. In the developing stage, you need to test your movies frequently. When you test your movie in this manner, Flash automatically creates an SWF file (the file that goes on the Web). So after testing your movie in the editor, test it in the Test Movie mode.

Tutorial
» Saving and Publishing Your Movie

Like any other computer-based project, you need to save your work often so that if you lose power or your computer crashes, you can reload your file and resume work without having to start all over again. When your movie is ready for the Web, you can access the SWF file directly on the Web, or, more commonly, make it part of a Web page. To automatically create a Web page for your SWF file and create an SWF file if you have not tested the movie to make one, you must *publish* your movie. Before publishing it, you can look at in a browser using Publish Preview.

1. **Select File→Save from the menubar.**

2. **Provide a filename with the FLA extension when requested in the Save As dialog box.**
   The first time you save your file, you will be in the Save As dialog box. Flash has no Save dialog box. In subsequent saves of the same file, all you will need to do is select Save from the File menu or use the Ctrl+S/Cmd+S keyboard shortcut.

3. **Select the folder or drive where you want your file saved.**

4. **Click Save in the dialog box.**
   Provide a filename with the FLA extension when requested in the Save As dialog box. Also find the folder where you want to save your file.

5. **Select File→Publish Preview from the menu bar.**
   A submenu opens, and you can choose the default (HTML unless changed), Flash, or HTML if it is not the default.

6. **Select Default (HTML) from the Publish Preview submenu.**
   You will see your movie in a browser as a viewer will see it once published on the Web.

7. **Select File→Publish from the menu bar.**
   Both an HTML file and SWF file are created. The HTML file has a link to the SWF file, and so when you put them on a Web host (a server), make sure they're in the same folder. The publish option has several different selections that are explained further on in the course. For now, though, you can save and publish your Flash pages.

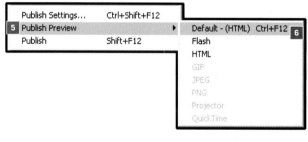

» Session Review

1. How do you change the panel set so that just the panels you want appear in the panel dock? (See "Tutorial: Saving Your Customized Panel Set.")

2. What settings in Flash are the same across all scenes? (See "Tutorial: Setting Background Color, Dimensions, and Frames Per Second.")

3. How can you reduce the number of layers that appear on the screen without deleting any? (See "Tutorial: Optimizing Layers and Folders.")

4. What are the different Preferences you can set? (See various "Preferences" tutorials.)

5. How do you add frames to a movie? (See "Tutorial: Adding Frames.")

6. What are some key ways items can be added to the stage? (See "Tutorial: Creating Objects on the Stage" and "Tutorial: Adding Text Fields to the Stage.")

7. What are different ways you can test a movie? (See "Tutorial: Testing Your Movie.")

» Additional Projects

» The most important project you can do in Flash is to try out different ideas. At this stage, you're just learning about the Flash work and creation environment, but still you can experiment with different ideas and play around with the different features discussed in this first session.

» A good exploration project in Flash MX involves using the Buttons library in the Common libraries. Begin by creating a new movie (File→New from the menu bar). Then open the Buttons library (Window→Common Libraries→Buttons). Enable the buttons by selecting Control→Enable Simple Buttons. Now drag the different buttons and button components to the stage. It's not important that you won't know what to do with them, but you should have some idea of the different ready-made items available to you. You will find 122 different button-related items in the library.

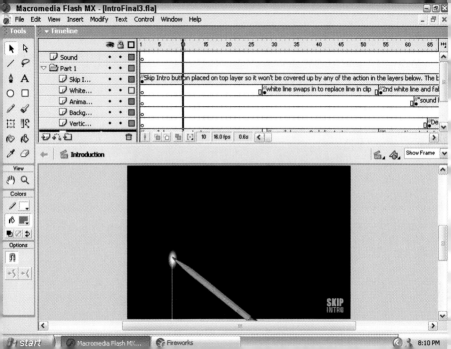

Session 2

Drawing in Flash

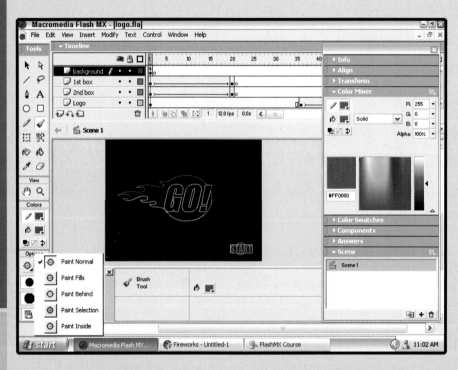

Session Introduction

In this session you will you will learn how to use the different tools in the Flash Toolbox for drawing, changing, coloring, and erasing vector graphics. Session 1 introduced you to rudimentary drawing using the rectangle and line tools, and in this session, you will see how to use the tools in conjunction with the ever-important Properties panel. As you select each tool, the Properties panel changes to accommodate using that tool. This new feature in Flash MX is important to understand because once you do, you'll see how easy it is to use the tools to create what you want on your Flash pages.

One of the movies in the Portfolio section of the project provides an animated tour of using the Paint Brush tool in its several variations. You will also be guided through a tutorial, however, so you can work on the project without having to run the movie continuously!

What you learn in this chapter can be applied to the entire project. Everything you draw can be created using the Flash MX drawing tools. You can use tools from Macromedia FreeHand or Adobe Illustrator to create vector graphics and then import them into Flash if you are more familiar using them than the Flash tools. The important feature of Flash MX drawing tools is that they create vector graphics instead of bitmapped graphics.

TOOLS YOU'LL USE
All of the tools in the Toolbox that create vector graphics and the following panels: Properties, Color Mixer, Color Swatches, Align, Transform, and Info

MATERIALS NEEDED
From the accompanying CD-ROM you'll need paintbrush.fla and logo.fla.

TIME REQUIRED
120 minutes

SESSION OUTCOME
Building and manipulating Graphics and Graphic Tools in Flash

PROJECT PORTION
The different drawings in the movie are shown here, illustrating different aspects of each using the various Flash MX tools.

Tutorial
» Toolbox Orientation

The Introduction to Part I introduced you to the different tools in the Flash MX Toolbox. In this tutorial, you will see how the Properties panel changes with the selection of different tools. In addition, you will see that different options appear depending on what tool you have selected. Many of the selections are duplicated in the panels.

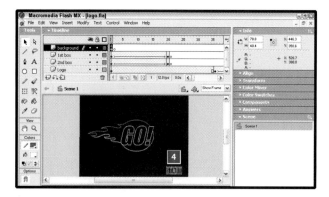

1. **Copy logo.fla from your CD-ROM to the desktop.**

2. **Double-click the logo.fla icon to open it and Flash MX.**

3. **Select the Arrow tool from the Toolbox by clicking it.**

4. **Click the START button in the lower-right corner of the screen to select it.**
   As soon as you click the button notice that the Properties panel shows the button's dimensions and position on the stage. The same information is in the Info panel. The redundant information can be handy if one of the panels is not on the stage. Keep in mind that when you select an object, every panel with information related to the object is available in one or more panels.

5. **Select the Pencil tool from the Toolbox.**
   Note that the Properties panel shows the Pencil tool as the selected object and note that a color well, a line stroke value (1.5), and line-format drop-down box appear.

6. **Click the Pencil Mode option at the bottom of the Toolbox.**
   A very important feature of Flash MX is the Options section of the Toolbox. Like the Properties panel, the options are context-sensitive and are available only for certain tools. For the Pencil tool, you can choose from Straighten, Smooth, and Ink. The Straighten option straightens lines with slight curing, while the Smooth option refines a curve by making it more of a curve shape. The Ink option does a little smoothing, but is primarily for free-hand drawing without straightening or smoothing.

7. **Click the Paint Brush icon on the Toolbox.**

8. **Open the Color Mixer panel.**
   With the Color Mixer panel open, you can see three different color wells, all the same color. The Fill color (illustrated by wells with the Paint Bucket next to them) is used to select the color for the Paint Brush tool. If you change the Fill color of any of the color wells, the other two will change as well.

9. **Click the Brush Mode option in the Toolbox.**
   A whole different set of options appears for the Paint Brush tool than for the Line tool. That fact should serve as a reminder that different tools evoke different options.

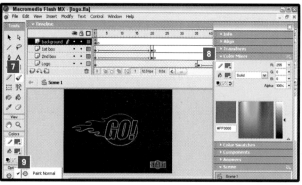

Tutorial
» Selecting with the Arrow Tool

While the Arrow tool is generally used to select items by clicking them, the Arrow tool in Flash MX has other uses as well. Many objects in Flash are multi-tiered. In other words, one object is likely to be inside another object, and the second object may contain further objects, and so on. To open the nested objects, you double-click each one with the Arrow tool. Likewise, you use the Arrow tool to drag the playhead back and forth on the timeline. So while the arrow tool doesn't actually create anything, you can fine-tune line drawings and open symbols to their root contents.

1. **If it is not already open, open the file logo.fla.**

2. **Click the Arrow tool to select it.**

3. **Click the top portion of the GO! in the outline fireball.**
   When you select the top portion, you will see that the Properties panel indicates it is a Graphic. A Graphic in Flash MX is a type of Symbol. If it were a drawing, it would indicate a Shape. Graphic symbols are treated as unit entities instead of several pixel points that make up the drawing. Another clue that the object is a symbol is the name "black top square." That is the symbol's name.

4. **Double-click the top portion of the GO! in the outline fireball.**
   By double-clicking a symbol, you automatically go into the Symbol Editing Mode. You can now make changes to the symbol. Note that above the stage in addition to Scene 1, you can also see "black top square" (the name of the Graphic object). Also note that you are on a different timeline. The main timeline has four layers, and this object has only a single layer. You can also edit selected symbols by choosing Edit→Edit Selected or by right-clicking (Control-clicking on the Macintosh) the mouse and choosing Edit or Edit In Place from the context menu.

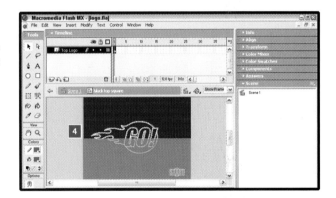

5. **Drag the playhead to Frame 36.**
   By dragging the playhead to another keyframe (in the Logo layer), you have uncovered another symbol. The Properties panel indicates it is an instance of the Go Logo color symbol. It too is a Graphic symbol.

6. **Select Window→Library from the menu bar.**

7. **Scroll down the bottom pane until you find Go Logo and then click it.**
   You can now see the Symbol used on the stage. All of the symbols you create are automatically placed into the Library panel.

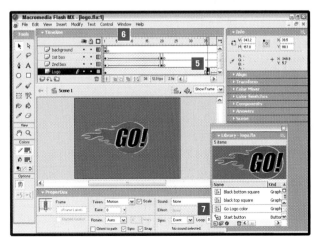

Tutorial

» Using the Subselection Tool

The Subselection tool reveals all of the anchor points in a drawing. Additionally, you can change a drawing using the Subselection tool. By dragging a vector point, you can alter the shape of a drawing to anything you want. So while the Subselection tool looks like a reverse Arrow tool, it is in fact much more.

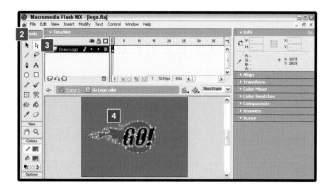

1. **Open the logo.fla and drag the playhead to Frame 36.**
   You will see an instance of the Go Logo color symbol.

2. **Select the Arrow tool from the Toolbox and double-click the symbol instance.**
   You are now in the Symbol Editing Mode.

3. **Select the Subselection Tool.**

4. **Click the edge of the fireball shape.**
   When you click the edge, you will see all of the anchor points on the shape.

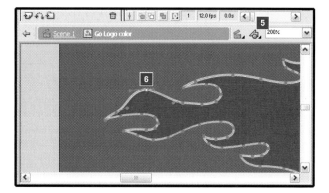

5. **Set the magnification to 200%.**

6. **Click one of the anchor points with the Subselection tool and pull or push the point.**
   When you pull or push an anchor point, the tangent handles appear. You can use these handles to change shapes to a desired angle.

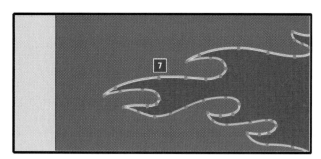

7. **Push and pull the anchor points and tangent handles until you have the shape the way you want it.**
   If your original shape created with the other drawing tools does not result in the shape you want, readjustments with the Subselection tool can give you exactly the shape you want.

Tutorial
» Drawing with the Line Tool

The Line tool is used for drawing straight lines. No options are available for the Line tool, but the Properties panel provides both a color well and Stroke style menu when the tool is selected. In addition, you can choose from Custom options, also on the Properties panel, that provide the additional option of Sharp corners and another selection for stroke size and line type.

1. **Open logo.fla, drag the playhead to Frame 36, and double-click the object on the stage to enter the Symbol Editing Mode.**

2. **Magnify the stage to 200% and move to a blank portion of the stage.**

3. **Select the Line tool.**

4. **Choose white for the color, and 1.5 for the size of the solid line.**

5. **Draw four parallel but staggered lines.**

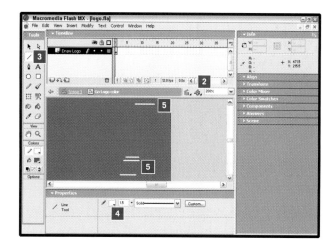

6. **Draw two parallel, nearly vertical lines to create a parallelogram on the bottom of the shape.**

7. **Draw another line from the horizontal line above the parallelogram to the top horizontal line.**

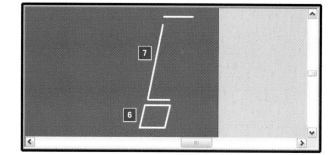

8. **Complete the drawing by adding a second vertical line to join the top horizontal line.**

   The exclamation mark at the end of GO! was completed using the Line tool! To make it complete, you will need different tools that you will see further on in this session.

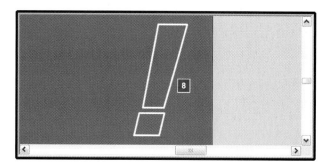

Tutorial
» Lasso Irregular Shapes

If you hold down the mouse button and drag the Arrow key around an object, it will define a rectangle and select the object or section of a shape. However, for irregular shapes, you need the Lasso tool to make the selection, and as you will see, there's more than one way to use the Lasso.

1. Open logo.fla, drag the playhead to Frame 36, and double-click the object on the stage to enter the Symbol Editing Mode.

2. Magnify the stage to 200%.

3. Move the horizontal and vertical stage scroll bars so that you can see the exclamation mark.

4. Select the Lasso tool and carefully draw a line around the parallelogram-shaped exclamation point.
   As soon as you release the mouse button, the Lasso tool draws a straight select line from the last point to the first point. If you release the button too soon, you'll see the shape you attempt to select dissected by a selection line.

5. Increase the magnification to 400%.

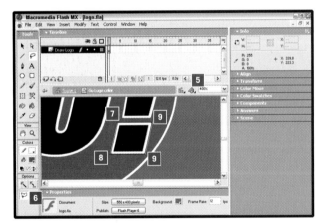

6. Click the Polygon Mode button in the Options section of the Toolbox.
   When you select the Lasso tool, one of the options is the Polygon Mode. When you draw in the Polygon Mode, you click the mouse at each point around the object you select.

7. Click the Lasso tool icon in the upper-left corner of the exclamation point.

8. Place the mouse pointer on the bottom-left corner of the exclamation point and click the mouse.
   A straight line appears between the first and second points.

9. Click the mouse at the two remaining corner points.

10. Click the starting point.
    The entire area is selected. Because the parallelogram is an irregular shape but still a polygon, using the Lasso tool in conjunction with the Polygon Mode selects the precise area you want.

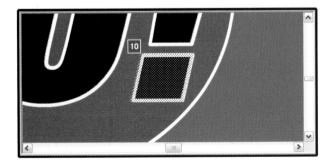

Tutorial
» Working with the Bezier Pen

The Pen tool works as a Bezier (bay-zee-air) pen. Named after the French mathematician Pierre Bézier, the pen creates a curve defined by a mathematical formula. Used for drawing curves, the Pen tool will take some practice to become accustomed to, but you will find it a great resource when you have curves to draw.

1. **Open logo.fla, and double-click the top portion of the logo to enter the Symbol Editing mode.**

2. **Click the Pen tool to select it.**
   To show how the Pen tool works, the last section of the "fireball" drawing is used to illustrate its use. You can draw the entire top section, or you can cut out the portion of the fireball and re-draw it following the illustrated case.

3. **Click the *ending* point for the drawing segment.**

4. **Click the starting point for the drawing segment and drag the tangent bar to describe the curve.**

5. **Pull the curve to the segment ending point.**

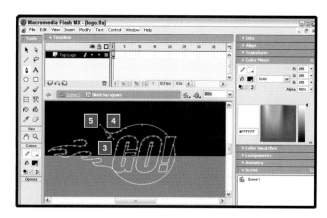

6. **Move the pen to begin the next segment and repeat steps 3–5 to complete the second segment.**
   Note the angle of the tangent bar and the curve of the line from the end of the second segment to the completion point. Getting the Pen tool to describe the right curve for your line takes patience and practice.

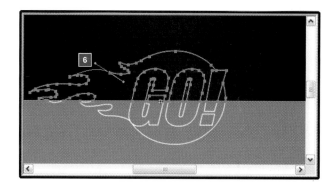

7. **Double-click the Pen tool to finish up.**
   When you use the Pen tool on a project, it is "active" until you double-click the ending point. The Pen tool has no options in the Toolbox, but you can change the line type and size as well as the color. Note that when the Pen tool is selected, the Properties panel displays two color wells. The stroke color is used for the drawing itself, and the Fill color is applied only when the Pen tool creates an enclosed area.

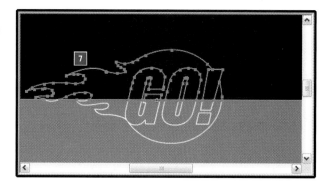

Tutorial

» Writing with the Text Tool

The Text tool is one of the most powerful tools in the Toolbox. In this tutorial, you will see how to work with the fundamental components of the tool, and in Session 5, you will learn to do far more with the Text tool and text fonts in animation and learn how to create forms using the Text tool. In this tutorial you will see how to place text on the stage and change its size and style. You will be taking the first step in creating the "*GO*" in logo.fla.

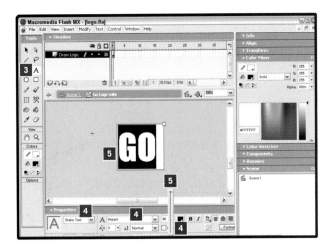

1. **Open logo.fla, move the playhead to Frame 36, and double-click the object to enter the Symbol Editing mode.**
   Note the large GO! in the fireball. The word GO is created using the Text tool and then converting the text into a graphic. Session 5 shows how to change the text into a graphic.

2. **Move the horizontal and vertical scroll bars until you find an empty space on the stage.**

3. **Select the Text tool.**
   In the Properties panel, you will see the Text tool icon (a large A).

4. **Select Impact from the Font menu, Static Text from the Text type menu, and black from the color well all on the Properties panel.**

5. **Type the word GO and set the size to 96 by moving the size slide to the very top.**
   Font size is not limited to 96, but that's as large as the size slider can handle.

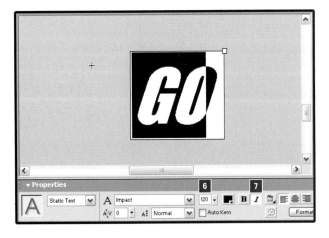

6. **Select the word GO by dragging the mouse over the word with the Arrow tool selected and type 120 next to the Font size slider.**

7. **Select the text and click the Toggle the Italic style button.**
   Compare the word "GO" with the text tool and the GO in the logo. It should be close, but as you will see in Session 5, when you change the text to a graphic, you can place a white (or any other color) outline around it.

Tutorial
» Drawing with the Oval Tool

The Oval tool is used for drawing circles and ovals. Certain familiar Flash images such as buttons are often initially created with the Oval tool. However, as you will see in this tutorial, other shapes that are only partially oval begin as oval shapes and then are made into different, more complex, shapes. Perfect circles are achieved with the Oval tool by holding down the Shift key while dragging the oval.

1. **Open logo.fla, drag the playhead to Frame 36, and double-click the object on the stage to enter the Symbol Editing Mode.**

2. **Move the horizontal and vertical sliders to find an unoccupied portion of the stage.**

3. **Select the Oval tool and red for both the Stroke and Fill colors.**
   You can use color wells for the Oval tool on the Properties panel or those on the Toolbox.

4. **Drag the pointer on the stage to create an egg-shaped oval.**

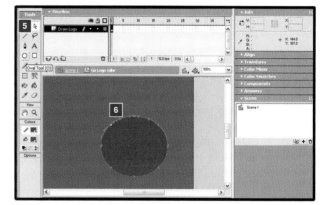

5. **Select the Subselection tool.**

6. **Click the pointer on the oval you just created.**
   All of the oval's anchor points appear on the oval.

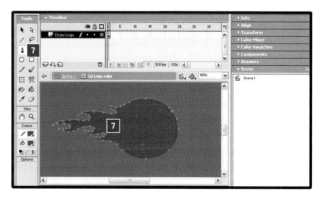

7. **Use the Pen tool to add the flames to the oval to create the fireball image.**
   You can compare the fireball you made with the one provided in logo.fla.

Tutorial
» Drawing with the Rectangle Tool

Using the Rectangle tool is a lot like using the Oval tool. It's used for creating a single shape. One option available for the Rectangle tool that is not available for the Oval tool is the Round Rectangle Radius. This Toolbox option lets you set the degree of roundness to be added to the rectangle's corners. In this tutorial, you will be using the default roundness of 0, but if you're interested in creating rectangles with rounded corners, all you need to do is to set the Round Rectangle Radius to greater than 0 with higher values for more roundness.

For this tutorial, you will be looking at a simple yet effective way to create different-sized rectangles for the abstract motion art in the Introduction scene. The rectangles are all part of a movie clip that adds a set of dancing rectangles to the movie.

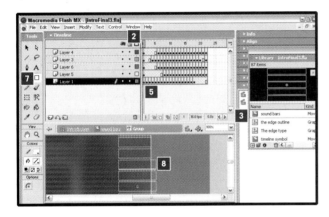

1. Open introFinal3.fla, drag the playhead to Frame 63, and double-click the group of rectangles in the upper-right portion of the stage to enter the Symbol Editing Mode.

2. Select Window→Library to open the Library panel.

3. Scroll down the library bottom pane to locate "sound bars."
   The selected object you are about to edit is a movie clip named "sound bars."

4. In the Symbol Editing Mode, double-click the rectangles again.
   Within the movie clip named "sound bars" you will find a group made up of rectangles.

5. Move the playhead to the first frame.

6. Remove one of the rectangles by selecting each of the four sides with the Arrow tool and pressing the Delete key.
   When you remove a rectangle, you will notice that each of the four sides is a separate piece even though the rectangle was created as a whole unit with the Rectangle tool.

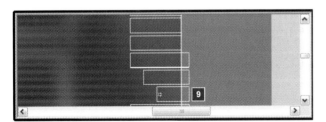

7. Select the Rectangle tool and set the stroke color to white and the Fill color to "none."

8. Drag the Rectangle tool in the space where you removed a rectangle to replace it.

9. Move the playhead to Frame 5 and repeat steps 6 through 8 choosing one of the smaller rectangles.
   When you replace the rectangle, use the Arrow tool to select each of the sides of the rectangle to see how it breaks down into four lines.

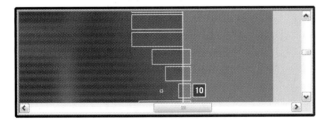

10. Move the playhead to Frame 8 and repeat step 9.
    You should be able to see how the different rectangles dance back and forth on the side of the larger movie clip now. The designer simply created different-sized rectangles in different frames, and when the movie runs, they bob in and out.

Tutorial
» Making Shapes with the Pencil Tool

The Pencil tool is several tools in one because of the different options available to the designer. When you select the Pencil tool, you can choose from three optional modes: Straighten, Smooth, and Ink. The Straighten mode is good for drawing objects made up of straight lines, like triangles. If your line is a little crooked, it is straightened automatically. The Smooth mode is best used when you have a number of curves and arcs in your drawing because the mode detects curves and smoothes them. Finally, the Ink mode is best for free-hand drawing that you don't want smoothed or straightened.

1. Open introFinal3.fla, drag the playhead to Frame 381, and double-click the hand object to enter the Symbol Editing Mode.

2. Drag the playhead in the Symbol Editing Mode to Frame 19 and double-click the blue hand outline.
   You will be able to draw the blue hand at this level. Directly above the stage you should see icons next to the labels, Introduction, hand and pencil, and bluehand outline.

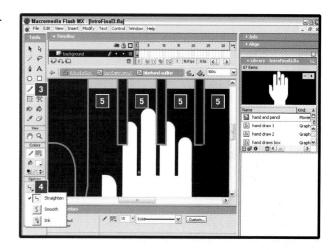

3. Select the Pencil tool from the Toolbox, and set the color to blue and the stroke to 1.5 in the Properties panel.

4. Choose the Straighten Pencil Mode option from the Toolbox Options section.

5. Draw the straight portions of the hand such as the finger sides.

6. Choose the Smooth Pencil Mode option from the Toolbox Options section.

7. Draw the curved portions of the hand such as the fingertips.

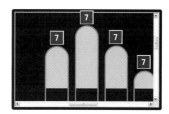

8. Choose the Ink Pencil Mode option from the Toolbox Options section.

9. Draw the mixed portion of the hand such as the area above the wrists where you have both curved and straight lines.

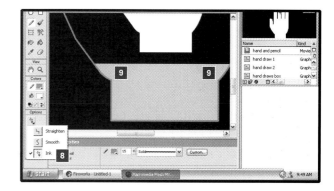

Tutorial
» Creating Masterpieces with the Paint Brush

The Paint Brush tool deserves its own movie where you can not only see how to use the Paint Brush tool but learn how to provide clear instructions with Flash. The Paint Brush has several options. First, you can choose from Brush Mode where you can select one of five different modes for painting. Second, you can choose a brush size, and third, a brush shape. In the Portfolio section of the project, you will find a little paintBrush.fla movie that animates the process of using the Paint Brush tool. Open it up and take a look at it and then look at the following screens.

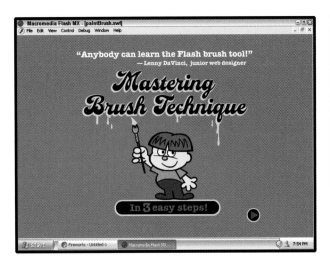

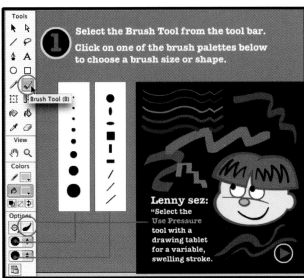

In the introduction, the viewer sees a "brushed up" scene with dripping paint.

The brush and shape choices for the Paint Brush tool provide options for many different types of brush strokes.

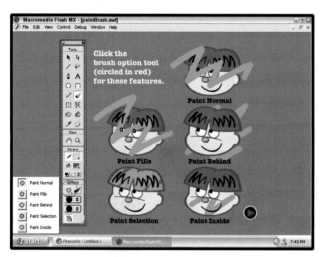

Depending on the task, you can set the Brush Mode to paint different parts of a shape.

The Paint Brush tool is a free-hand one used to create shapes and add color to the shapes.

Given the versatility of the Paint Brush tool, you can create just about anything!

Tutorial
» Changing Shapes with the Free Transform Tool

Using the different tools separately or in combination with one another, you will find yourself making changes to animate an effect. You can change horizontal and vertical size and rotation using the Free Transform tool. When you select the Free Transform tool, you will see push-pull points on objects when you select them. These points allow you to push or pull to resize the object. By selecting the area near the object's corners, you can rotate the objects.

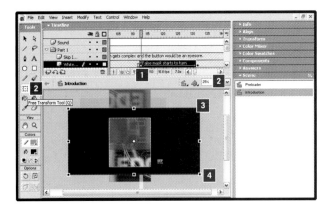

1. **Open introFinal3.fla and drag the playhead to Frame 113.**

2. **Set the stage magnification to 25% and select the Free Transform tool from the Toolbox.**
   The large black object is a "pseudo-mask" created by using a rectangle with a transparent hole in the middle. (It has its uses that are a bit different from the masks you will learn about in Session 6.)

3. **Click the large black "mask" object.**
   When you select an object with the Free Transform Tool, a rectangle appears around the object, no matter what the shape. Each side and each corner contains a push-pull point that you can drag to change the object's shape.

4. **Place the mouse pointer near one of the four corners.**

5. **When you see a looping arrow pointer, you can pull or push to rotate the object.**
   If you put the pointer directly on the corner, you will see an arrow pointer in a diagonal orientation. To activate the rotation pointer, you need to be off the corner just a little.

6. **Place the pointer at the top of the mask object.**

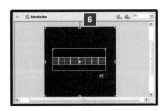

7. **Push the object downward until it is a long narrow rectangle.**
   In later sessions you will see how to animate the rotation and narrowing.

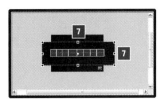

Tutorial

» Altering Fills with the Fill Transform Tool

The Fill Transform tool can be used to change gradient (including radials) or bitmap fills. Gradient fills have vertical orientations, and so when you use a gradient tool, it automatically shows gradients in vertical stripes. The Fill Transform tool can change the orientation of the fill only. Unlike the Free Transform tool, which changes the entire object, the Fill Transform tool is only supposed to change the fill, but if it is reduced severely, the object itself can be changed. Because the project had no gradient or bitmap fill, a simple ball with a radial fill is used.

1. **Use the Oval tool to draw a circle with a radial fill.**
   Once you select the Oval tool, you will see different colored radial fills at the bottom of the Swatches panel. You can use any color you want.

2. **Select the Fill Transform tool.**

3. **Click the radial fill area of the circle.**
   You will see the pull points and center point.

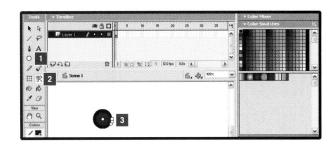

4. **Drag the center point to the upper-left portion of the circle.**
   As a general rule, dragging a radial center point to the upper left gives the object a convex appearance.

5. **Drag the square pull handle to change the width of the gradient fill.**

6. **Drag the circle pull handle at the bottom to rotate the radial fill.**

7. **Drag the circle pull between the circle and square pull handles to change the radius of the circular gradient fill.**

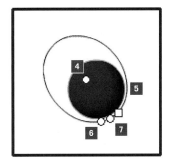

8. **Create two concentric circles, the inner about 60% the size of the outer, using the black and white radial fill and a 3-point stroke.**

9. **In the smaller circle, use the Fill Transform tool to drag the center to the upper-left quadrant of the circle.**

10. **Drag the center of the larger circle to the lower-right quadrant of the larger circle.**
    The effect is that of a stereo speaker. Add a box around the back of the two circles to create the appearance of a speaker box.

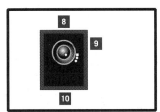

Tutorial
» Coloring Edges with the Ink Bottle

Often you will want the stroke color to be different from the Fill color of an object. The Ink Bottle tool takes care of coloring the stroke (outline) of an object. Likewise, you can change the color of line drawings using the Ink Bottle. To see how the Ink Bottle can be applied, use logo.fla from your CD-ROM.

1. **Open the logo.fla file from the CD-ROM and move the playhead to Frame 36.**
   If you have been following the course and drawing your own fireball, use it. Otherwise, move the playhead to Frame 36, and use the completed fireball with the GO! message.

2. **Double-click the fireball object with the Arrow to select it in the Symbol Edit Mode.**

3. **Click the Ink Bottle tool to select it.**

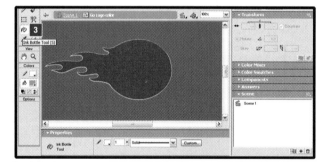

4. **In the Properties panel, select white from the color well.**
   If you're using the completed fireball, used another color than white. Try changing it to red and then back to white. With the Ink Bottle tool selected, any object's stroke will change to the color of the color well in the Properties panel.

5. **In the Properties panel, select yellow from the color well.**
   By testing different colors, you can determine which looks best with the fireball. You'll find no penalties for determining the color you like best.

Tutorial
» Filling Up with the Paint Bucket Tool

The Paint Bucket tool fills your drawings with a Fill color, including radials and gradients. Any drawing that encloses an area can be filled, including areas that may have gaps in the drawing that surrounds an area to be filled. If Flash detects an area that does not enclose an area or an area with very large gaps, it will not act as a fill. (Some fills spill the Fill color all over the stage if an enclosed area has a gap in it.) In this tutorial, the big exclamation point created using the Line tool will be filled. The point in the exclamation point has a gap to illustrate how gap-control is used by the Paint Bucket tool.

1. **Open the logo.fla file from the CD-ROM and move the playhead to Frame 36.**

2. **Find the large exclamation point after *GO!* that was drawn using the Line tool.**
   If you did not draw the exclamation point using the Line tool, do so now. Put a gap in the point of the exclamation point.

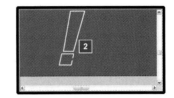

3. **Select the Paint Bucket tool.**

4. **Select black from the color well in the Properties panel or the bottom color well on the Toolbox.**
   Note the options that appear when you select the Paint Bucket tool.

5. **Place the Paint Bucket pointer over the top portion of the exclamation point and click the left mouse button.**
   The interior of the surrounded area turns black. You may want to consider magnifying the stage to 200% to better see where to position the Paint Bucket tool.

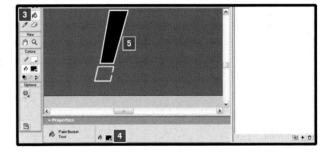

6. **Select Close Large Gaps from the Options section of the Toolbox.**

7. **Place the Paint Bucket over the bottom portion of the exclamation point and click the left mouse button.**
   The interior of the object, even with a gap, is filled with the selected color. The gaps stays put, but the Fill color remains within the surrounded area. To finish it up properly, you will want to use the Line tool to patch up the gap.

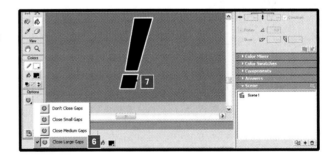

Tutorial

» Matching Colors with the Eyedropper Tool

The Eyedropper Tool has many uses, but its primary use is to match colors. Whenever you build a Flash MX movie, you want to use a consistent set of colors. As you probably know, the color "green" can be many different shades and tints, and you want to be sure to get exactly the right one. When a color is selected with the Eyedropper tool, all of the color wells generate a matching color, including an Alpha (transparency) level. Because the movie can be spread out over thousands of frames and all different levels, you have to have some way of creating a consistent set of colors.

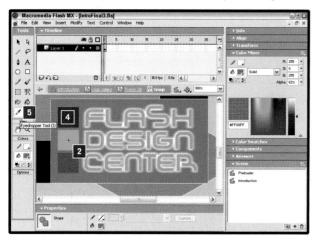

1. Open introFinal3.fla and select Control→Go To End from the menu bar.

2. Double-click the color bar next to Flash Design Center and then select Control→Go To End from the menu bar.
   You're not seeing double. In the first move, you sent the movie to the end of the main timeline, and in the second move, you sent the movie to the last frame in the movie clip.

3. Double-click twice on the grouped set of color boxes.
   Once again, you're not seeing double. You first opened the symbol, and then you opened the group. You will now be able to select the colors in each of the three boxes.

4. Select the Arrow tool and click the top of the three color boxes (pink one).
   The box should be "pixelated," indicating it has been selected.

5. Select the Eyedropper tool.

6. Click the green box.
   The selected pink box now turns green, and the open color wells indicate green and an alpha (transparency) level less than 100%. Whenever a color has less than 100% alpha, a grid shows through the color in the color well.

7. Move the playhead to Frame 523.
   Leave all of the color wells unaffected. You will want the color.

8. Double-click the hand to open the color boxes graphic symbol.

9. Move the playhead to Frame 150 in the color boxes timeline and select the keyframe in the more stuff layer.

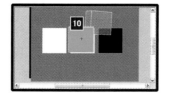

10. Double-click the green box.
    Look at the color in the Color Mixer. You will notice that the color value is #05FE05 (hexadecimal value of the color) and the Alpha is 54%. That is exactly the same color as used in the color blocks at the end of the movie. By using the Eyedropper, you are able to match any color simply by clicking the color with the eyedropper.

Tutorial
» Correcting Mistakes Using the Eraser

The Eraser tool, as its name implies, erases drawings and parts of drawings. However, unlike a normal eraser, the Eraser tool has several different options. To see how the Eraser tool works, this next tutorial takes the main drawing in logo.fla and shows how different eraser options remove different portions of the drawing. Also, you will see all of the different shapes and sizes available for the Eraser tool.

1. **Open the logo.fla file and move the playhead to Frame 36.**

2. **Double-click the object on the stage to open it in the Symbol Editing Mode.**
   Now you will be able to make changes to the drawing.

3. **Select the Eraser tool, and in the Toolbox Options open the Eraser Shape popup menu.**
   In the example, the third largest square shape is selected, but you can select any shape and size you want.

4. **Select Erase Normal from the Erase Mode menu in the Options section of the Toolbox.**

5. **Drag the eraser over the middle of the *GO!* fireball object.**
   All of the drawing where the Eraser passed is removed. On multiple layers, all drawings on all unlocked layers are affected!

6. **Select the Erase Fills Eraser Mode.**

7. **Drag the eraser across the center of the drawing.**
   All of the lines are left unaffected, but all of the fills where the eraser crossed are removed.

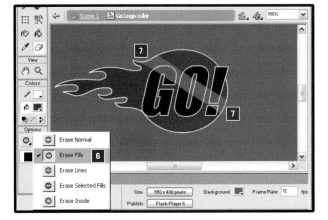

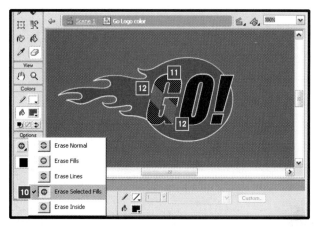

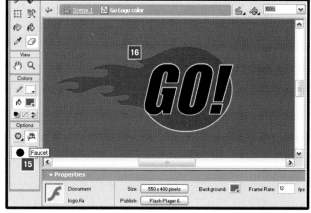

8. **Select the Erase Lines Eraser Mode.**

9. **Drag the eraser across the center of the drawing.**
   All of the fills are left unaffected, but all of the lines where the eraser crossed are removed.

10. **Select the Erase Selected Fills Eraser Mode.**

11. **Click the inside of the "G" to select the fill.**

12. **Drag the eraser across the entire drawing.**
    Only the selected fill area is erased and the unselected fills and line are left in tact.

13. **Select the Erase Inside Eraser Mode.**

14. **Drag the eraser across the flaming tail of the drawing.**
    Only the area inside the lines is erased. Each time you want to erase a different part of a fill, you have to release the mouse button and press it again to erase inside a different set of lines.

15. **Select the Faucet icon in the Options area of the Toolbox.**

16. **Place the faucet over the line around the top of the drawing and click the mouse.**
    The entire stroke line is erased to the point of an intersecting stroke line.

Tutorial
» Using the Hand and Zoom Tools

A couple of "little" tools that are very handy are the Hand and Zoom tools. Both tools are used to better see what you need to see on the stage. The Hand tool drags the stage area to a position where you can best see what you need to view. The Zoom tool acts likes a zoom lens, making the stage larger and smaller relative to the objects on the stage. When you use either tool, nothing on the stage is moved or changed other than the view, so you can use them without fear of putting an object out of its intended position.

1. **Open IntroFinal3.fla and move the playhead to Frame 523.**
   You will see a hand-and-pencil object.

2. **Double-click the object twice.**
   In the bar above the stage you should see Introduction I color boxes I hand draws box. In the timeline you will see lots of black dots indicating keyframes.

3. **Click the Hand tool in the Toolbox to select it.**

4. **Drag the stage area upwards and to the right.**
   The object on the stage is revealed to be part of an object within a rectangle object that extends beyond the visible stage. Because it is easier to see in context now, you will have a better idea of where to place it. (It's supposed to extend beyond the stage, but the viewer only sees what's on the stage.) Note that when you drag the stage with the Hand tool, the scroll bars on both the horizontal and vertical axes move.

5. **Select the Zoom tool.**
   When you select the Zoom tool, note the two zoom options. The icon with the plus mark (+) magnifies the object, and the icon with the minus mark (–) zooms out to give a wider view.

6. **Click the hand object to magnify it.**
   You want to magnify the hand to better see the exact position of the pencil because it is animated to draw a series of squares, and you want to be sure to place the hand directly over the area where the line is drawn.

7. **Click the zoom Reduce icon.**

8. **Click the stage area until you can see the entire stage and the object with the hand.**
   By zooming out or reducing, you can better see the stage and its objects in context. Some movies begin with several objects off the stage, and this "bird's eye view" lets you position everything in relationship to both the stage and other objects on and off the stage.

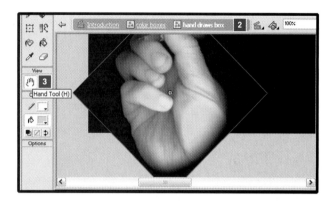

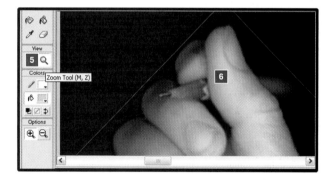

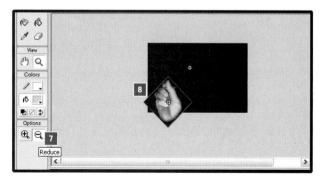

Tutorial
» Using the Toolbox Color Tools

Besides the color wells in the Toolbox, two little-noticed tools are on either side of the No Color box (the box icon with a diagonal through it). On the left is the Black and White tool. It will fill the color wells with a black stroke and white fill. Because that combination is so common, you will find it useful at different times when you want a shortcut to put black and white in the color wells.

On the right side of the No Color box is the Swap Colors tool. This tool swaps the Stroke and Fill colors. Any two colors, including black and white, are swapped as soon as this tool is clicked. All of the color wells swap and any object with a stroke and Fill color are swapped. A simple effect this creates can be seen when a button has its colors swapped in mouse-over states. One important exception to swapping colors is when you have a gradient or radial fill. Strokes cannot have any type of gradient, and so when you swap, the stroke takes on one of the colors of the gradient, and when you swap back, the stroke color is transferred to the non-gradient Fill color.

1. **Open the logo.fla file and move the playhead to Frame 36.**

2. **Double-click the object on the stage to open it in the Symbol Editing Mode.**

3. **Select the drawing.**

4. **Click the Black and White tool.**
   The colorful logo turns black and white. Note that the stroke is black and the fill is white on all aspects of the drawing.

5. **Select the entire drawing using the Arrow tool.**

6. **Click the Swap Colors tool.**
   Now the stroke is white and the fill is black.

» Session Review

1. What are the different uses for the Arrow tool? (See "Tutorial: Selecting with the Arrow Tool.")

2. After selecting a drawn object, what drawing ability does the Subselection tool have? (See "Tutorial: Using the Subselection Tool.")

3. What options are available with the Lasso tool? (See "Tutorial: Lasso Irregular Shapes.")

4. How can the Pen and Subselection tools be used together? (See "Tutorial: Using the Subselection Tool" and "Tutorial: Working with the Bezier Pen.")

5. When using the Oval and Rectangle tools, what role does the Properties panel play? What options are similar and different with these two tools? (See "Tutorial: Drawing with the Oval Tool" and "Tutorial: Drawing with the Rectangle Tool.")

6. What different shaping options are available with the Pencil tool and how do these options affect drawing? (See "Tutorial: Making Shapes with the Pencil Tool.")

7. When using the Paint Brush tool, what different brush and brush size shapes are available? What are the different Paint Brush modes and how do they affect a drawing? (See "Tutorial: Creating Masterpieces with the Paint Brush.")

8. What are the differences between the Free Transform and Fill Transform tools? How is each used with a drawing? (See "Tutorial: Changing Shapes with the Free Transform Tool.")

9. When are the Ink Bottle and Paint Bucket tool best used? How are stroke lines and fills affected by both? (See "Tutorial: Coloring Edges with the Ink Bottle.")

10. How is the Eyedropper tool used to match colors? What color wells are affected by the Eyedropper tool? (See "Tutorial: Matching Colors with the Eyedropper Tool.")

11. How is the Eraser similar to the Paint Brush in its various modes and sizes? (See "Tutorial: Correcting Mistakes Using the Eraser" and "Tutorial: Creating Masterpieces with the Paint Brush.")

12. How are the Hand and Zoom tools best used to change the view on the stage? (See "Tutorial: Using the Hand and Zoom Tools.")

13. What are the effects of the Black and White and Swap Colors tools? When are they most effectively applied? (See "Tutorial: Using the Toolbox Color Tools.")

» Additional Projects

» Using only the Rectangle, Oval, and Line tools along with the color panel and Properties panel, see what kind of objects you can create. Be sure to use the different options available with these tools. The purpose of this project is to practice creating complex shapes using simple shapes. Also, think about pivot points that you might use if you wanted to animate the different shapes.

» Using the Pen, Pencil, and Subselection tools, draw and adjust different shapes. Then, using the Ink Bottle and Paint Bucket tools, change the fill and stroke colors of the shapes you drew.

» Using the whole Toolbox, practice drawing different shapes found in the project from the CD-ROM. Use the Arrow tool to break the objects down to the point where they can be edited. Erase them and then see if you can reproduce different objects.

Session 3

Arranging and Changing Objects

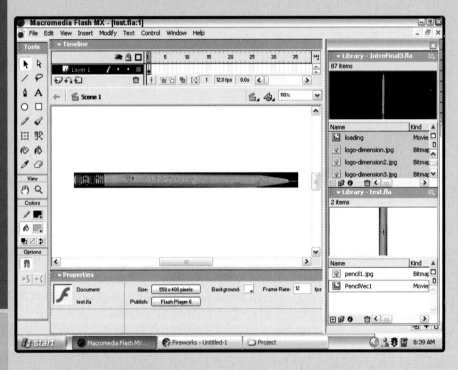

Session Introduction

This session shows you all of the ways that you can change objects. The essence of animation is a series of small changes over time. By understanding how to take an object, whether it is a drawing or symbol instance, and make changes in it, you can learn how to set up animations. Flash animation is simply an object in one state in one keyframe and in a different state in another keyframe. The Flash tweening process handles all of the little changes required to transform the first frame into the state in the second frame.

The first issue we discuss in this session is further examination of vector and bitmapped graphics. You see how to change bitmapped graphics into vector graphics. More important, though, you see how to determine when such a transformation is optimal for your site. Flash MX provides color wells for stroke and fill in several different panels and the Toolbox. In this session, you mix colors to get exactly the color you want and then create a color palette to use for your site. Another important Flash MX feature covered in this session is the different techniques for editing shapes and symbols. When you change an independent shape, all that changes is the single shape. However, with symbols, you apply some changes only to instances of a symbol, while you apply other changes to the entire symbol and all of the instances of the symbol. Lines and fills make up the last important portion of this session. In one of the tutorials, you learn how to change lines into fills so that you can use the Paint Bucket to add gradient colors to an object's "line."

TOOLS YOU'LL USE
Toolbox tools and Menu effect tools. Important panels include the Color
Mixer, Color Swatches, and Properties.

MATERIALS NEEDED
From the accompanying CD-ROM you'll need the files logo.fla,
IntroFinal3.fla, and PaintBrush.fla.

TIME REQUIRED
120 minutes

SESSION OUTCOME
Manipulating different aspects of graphic objects

PROJECT PORTION
All of the drawings in the movie are completed in this chapter. Rotations,
scales, and skews are taken from drawings in the different portals.

Tutorial

» Bitmapped and Vector Graphics

The example project makes extensive use of both bitmapped and vector graphics. As much as possible, the project was constructed using vector graphics because they tend to be far smaller in terms of bandwidth than are bitmapped graphics. Bitmap graphics store information for each pixel, while vector graphics store information in formulas using vector points. However, in some circumstances, you may find it difficult to avoid bitmapped graphics because of the nature of the drawing or digitized photograph. In this tutorial, you learn how to use bitmapped graphics in the project movie.

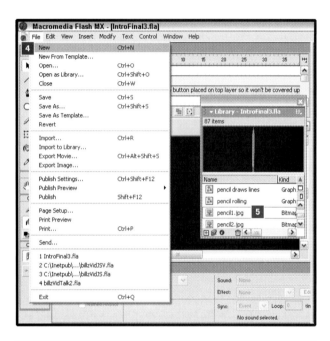

1. **Remove IntroFinal3.fla from your CD-ROM.**

2. **Double-click IntroFinal3.fla. to open it in Flash MX.**

3. **Select Window→Library from the menu bar.**

4. **Select File→New from the menu bar.**
   A new window opens, but you still have the library with all of the objects from IntroFinal3.fla.

5. **Scroll down the Library panel until you find the bitmapped graphic pencil1.jpg.**
   All bitmapped graphics have an icon with a little green tree. While looking for the pencil bitmapped graphic, note the others in the library. Most are digital photographic images.

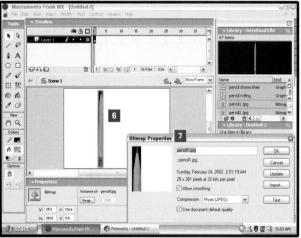

6. **Drag the pencil object to the stage.**
   Bitmapped graphics can be integrated into a Flash movie like any other object. However, as you will see further in this session, you will generally want to create a symbol from a bitmapped graphic.

7. **Select the pencil bitmapped graphic in the Library panel, and click the small info icon ("i") at the bottom.**
   The Bitmap Properties window appears. If you deselect the Use document default quality option, a Quality text window appears where you can adjust the quality from 1–100. Otherwise, you can choose either Allow smoothing or select the alternate compression.

Tutorial

» Converting Bitmapped to Vector Graphics

In this tutorial, you see how to convert a bitmapped graphic into a vector graphic. Depending on the bitmapped graphic and quality of the converted vector graphic, you can save or gain "weight" in your movie. (This tutorial is a continuation of the previous one, which explains why the numbering begins with 8. So if you're starting here, take a look at the preceding tutorial to see where the pencil bitmapped graphic came from.)

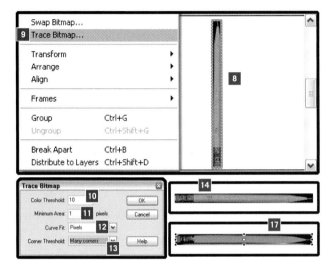

8. **Drag a copy of pencil1.jpg from the Library panel to the stage.**
   When you first drag a bitmapped graphic to the stage, note the dotted (zipper-like) border it has. This unique selection border helps identify it as a bitmapped graphic.

9. **With the pencil object selected, select Modify→Trace Bitmap.**

10. **In the Trace Bitmap dialog box, type** 10 **for the Color Threshold.**
    The Color Threshold text box accepts values from 1 to 500. The lower the number, the greater the number of colors. If the difference between the two RGB color values is less than the threshold, both pixels are considered the same color. For example, if one color is cc27ab and another is cc27ae, the difference is 3. If the threshold value is 10, the two colors are considered to be the same. If the threshold value is 1, each color will be treated as unique. However, the smaller the color threshold value, the more memory it takes to create a vector graphic, and that vector graphic takes more memory as well.

11. **Type** 1 **for Minimum Area.**
    Values range from 1 to 1,000 and determine the number of pixels to consider when assigning a color value. For more detail, select fewer pixels. The price is a greater memory use.

12. **Set the Curve Fit popup menu to Pixels.**
    Curve Fit values include Pixels, Very Tight, Tight, Normal, Smooth, or Very Smooth. The smoother the object, the fewer vector points there are and the less memory consumed. Set to Pixels for a more exact rendering of the image.

13. **Set the Corner Threshold popup menu to Many Corners.**
    The more corners you have, the more exact the rendering but the more memory it uses.

14. **Select the converted image.**

15. **Press the F8 key to open the Symbol Conversion dialog box.**

16. **Select Movie Clip as Behavior and type** PencilVec1 **for the name and press OK.**
    Now the vector graphic image is converted into a symbol and can be used again by using instances of the symbol. The converted image has the same high resolution as the original, but takes up 55KB of memory — far too much.

17. **Repeat steps 8–13, but use 200 for Color Threshold, 10 for Minimum Area, Normal for Curve Fit, and Normal for Corner Threshold.**
    This new image is far less crisp and much of the detail is lost. It only takes 3KB of memory, and so using it will allow your movie to load much faster. However, the original bitmapped graphic transformed into a symbol also took only 3KB of memory. When you do not have to change the size or scale of a bitmapped graphic, it can work quite well in a movie. However, when you do, bitmapped graphics are a visual disaster, and you should convert them into vector graphics.

Tutorial

» Understanding Drawings and Symbols

The most essential differentiation in Flash MX is that between drawings and symbols. When you convert a drawing to a symbol, any number of instances of the same symbol on the stage actually use only a single symbol. So rather than having to send several copies of a drawing over the Internet, a single symbol sent can use as many instances of that symbol as needed, but the bandwidth "cost" is only the single symbol. For example, in the preceding tutorial, you saw how you can change a bitmapped graphic into a vector graphic; however, if you convert the bitmapped graphic to a symbol, the bandwidth consequences are far more important. That's because the single bitmapped graphic used as a symbol can have as many different angles and instances on the stage at the same time, but you only need to import a single bitmapped image as a symbol. The movie then uses several instances of the symbol.

You can convert drawings into three types of symbols: movie clips, buttons, and graphics. The project movie uses a good deal of graphic symbols, so this next example shows how you create a graphic and how it becomes a symbol. In fact, the example shows that you can make graphics part of other graphics.

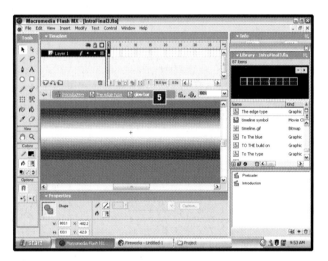

1. **Open the file IntroFinal3.fla and move the playhead to Frame 132 of the Introduction Scene.**

2. **Click the first frame on The Edge layer.**
   By clicking the first frame, you automatically select the symbol instance named "The edge type."

3. **Double-click the symbol instance to open its timeline.**

4. **In the new timeline, move the playhead to Frame 9 of the glow bar layer.**

5. **Double-click the symbol between "The" and "Edge" to open the glow bar symbol.**
   You are now in the Symbol Editing Mode for the glow bar symbol. This is where the drawing was originally created. The next step shows you how the glow bar symbol was created from this drawing.

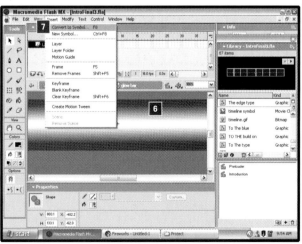

6. **Select the drawing made up of a rectangle with a gradient color scheme.**

7. **Select Insert→Convert to Symbol or press the F8 key.**

8. **When the Convert to Symbol dialog box opens, select Graphic as the behavior.**

Tutorial
» Coloring Objects in Flash

To color objects in Flash MX, you must be at the drawing level. *Drawing level* refers to a level where you can use the different tools to add color to an object. Symbols can have color changes and tint changes, but you must first enter the Symbol Editing Mode to color them. This next tutorial shows how to remove and change color in a graphic symbol. The same techniques apply to movie clip and button symbols as well.

1. **Open the file paintBrush.fla and both the Color Mixer and Color Swatches panels.**

2. **Click the character with the paint brush — Lenny.**

3. **Right-click (Windows) or Control-click (Macintosh) the mouse.**
   A context menu appears. Virtually every aspect of Flash MX has an associated context menu accessed by right-clicking/Control-clicking the mouse button.

4. **Select Edit in Place from the context menu.**
   Because the object is on the stage and not inside of another symbol or group, you can begin editing the colors immediately. You are in the Symbol Editing Mode.

5. **With the Arrow tool selected, click right between Lenny's eyes and press the Delete key.**
   The painted area first becomes "dotty" (selected) and then disappears with the area being replaced by the background color.

6. **Repeat step 5, but select Lenny's cheek to remove the rest of the white flesh tone from his face.**

7. **Select the Paint Bucket tool and the white fleshtone color from the Color Swatches panel.**
   The white fleshtone (a pinkish white color) is part of the color palette for the movie. Further on in this session, you will learn how to create a color palette for any movie.

8. **Click Lenny's cheek.**
   The area fills with the selected color. When you color a symbol in the Symbol Editing Mode, all instances of the symbol will change.

9. **Click right between Lenny's eyes.**
   You've restored Lenny to the original colors.

Tutorial
» Breaking Up and Coloring Text in Flash

You can color an entire text block by selecting a text block and adding color using the Properties panel's color well. However, if you break up text, you can color both the fill and the stroke of a text block. By breaking up the text, it is no longer text, but instead it's a shape. You can add all the colors and strokes to it you want. In this tutorial, you first see how to color the banner text, and then see how to begin with regular text and break it up for multiple colors.

1. **Open the file paintBrush.fla and both the Color Mixer and Color Swatches panels.**

2. **Select the banner "Mastering Brush Technique" object on the stage.**

3. **Select Modify→Break Apart from the menu bar.**

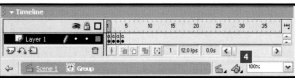

4. **Magnify the stage to 100%.**
   The broken apart text can be seen by the "dotty" black part of the text.

5. **Select each black fill area and press the Delete key.**
   You can now see the underlying stroke of the text. A very wide stroke has been used, leaving a thick background.

6. **Press Ctrl+Z (Windows) or Cmd+Z (Macintosh) to restore the material to its original.**

7. **Magnify the stage to between 600%–700% and use the Hand tool to drag the stage to a place where no images exist.**

8. **Select the Text tool and type a 24-point letter** A.
   In the example a Victorian letter A has been employed.

9. **Select Modify→Break Apart from the menu bar.**
   The text looks "dotty" indicating it is now a selected shape.

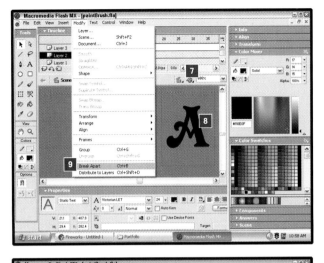

10. **Select the stroke color in the Color mixer and put in the values R=204, G=216, B=229.**
    The resulting color is a light blue-gray.

11. **Select the fill color in the Color mixer and put in the values R=119, G=209, B=68.**
    The resulting color is a light green.

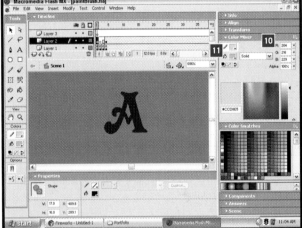

12. **Select the Paint Bucket tool and click the solid area of the A.**
    The letter turns green. Actually, just the fill turns green.

13. **Select the Ink Bottle tool and in the Properties panel change the stroke value to 0.5.**

14. **Click the stroke areas of the A.**
    Be sure to click the "inside" stroke area that is made up of the interior of the letter A as well as the outside area. Now you have a Victorian A in Victorian colors.

15. **Select the graphic text, and press F8 to open the Convert to Symbol dialog box and select Graphic for the Behavior.**
    You cannot change the graphic text back into a regular text block after you have colored it. However, you can change the text into a graphic symbol and use it multiple times as an instance of the symbol.

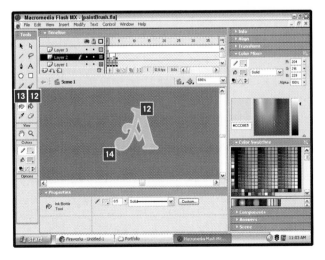

Tutorial
» Setting a Color Palette

Any colors you select should not be random; instead, they should complement one another and create a theme for your site. In the paintBrush.fla movie, you may have noticed a group of colors near the bottom of the Color Swatches panel. These colors represent the color palette. A good color scheme doesn't look planned. The colors go together naturally. In this tutorial, you learn how to create a color palette using the paintBrush.fla movie as an example.

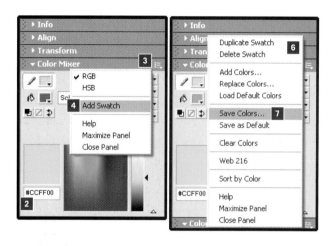

1. **Open the file paintBrush.fla and both the Color Mixer and Color Swatches panels.**

2. **In the Color Mixer, enter #CCFF00 in the hex color window.**
   You will see the yellow-green used as a stroke color in the movie.

3. **In the upper-right corner of the Color Mixer window, click the arrow there to open the popup menu.**

4. **Select Add Swatch from the menu.**
   You will see a yellow-green swatch added to the end of the Color Swatches panel.

5. **Repeat steps 2–4 until you have all the colors you want.**

6. **In the upper-right corner of the Color Swatches panel, click the arrow to open the popup menu.**

7. **Select Save Colors.**

8. **In the Export Color Swatch dialog box, type a filename with the CLR extension.**

9. **Click the Save button.**
   Your color scheme is now saved to disk.

10. **Select the popup menu from the corner of the Color Swatches panel and select Add Colors or Replace Colors to recall the saved color combination.**
    If you select Add Colors, the colors are added to the current set of swatches. Selecting Replace Colors removes the current set of swatches and replaces them with the one you saved.

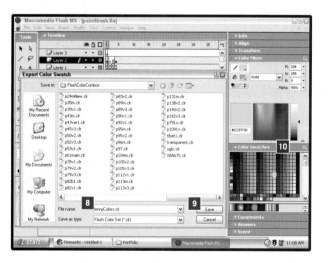

Tutorial

» Understanding the Differences between Windows and Macintosh Coloring

The Windows and Macintosh operating systems have different color mixers. You can access the native mixers of each operating system. The Windows mixer is very similar to the Flash MX Color Mixer, providing both RGB and HSL (Hue, Saturation, Luminance) mixing with a luminance slider. All values entered are decimal, and you rarely need to use it. The Macintosh OS provides a wider choice for mixing colors. Importantly, they include CMYK (cyan, magenta, yellow, and black) using percentages. Many books on color combinations use the CMYK formulas and so Macs have a bit of an advantage if all you've got are the CMYK values. (*The Designer's Guide to Color Combinations,* by Leslie Cabarga (North Lights Books), uses CMYK percent values.) The Macintosh also offers HSV (hue angle, saturation, and value), crayon named colors, Web-safe colors in hexadecimal, and RGB colors defined as percentages. You can find a collection of color combinations with both RGB and CMYK formulas in *The Designer's Guide to Global Color Combinations,* by Leslie Cabarga (HOW Design Books), that you can use with both your Windows PC and Macintosh. (Leslie did all of the artwork in this book.)

Windows Only

1. **Select the popup fill colors from the Fill color well on the Toolbox.**

2. **Click the color ball on the upper-right corner of the swatch menu that opens.**
   You will see a Color window open with different mixing schemes.

3. **Select a color for the Color|Solid window by changing the HSL or RGB values or by clicking a color from the Basic colors or Custom colors.**
   The color that you create or select for the Color|Solid window will be passed to the Flash MX color well.

Macintosh Only

1. **Select the popup fill colors from the Fill color well on the Toolbox.**

2. **Click the color ball on the upper-right corner of the swatch menu that opens.**

3. **Select a mixing selection from CMYK, Crayon, HSV, Name (actually Web safe), or RGB.**
   Mix your colors with whichever technique you require. If you use the RGB color, be advised that it uses percentages instead of either decimal values or hexadecimal ones. (The RGB values in the Flash MX RGB mixer uses decimal values between 0 and 255.)

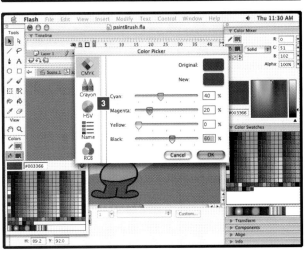

Tutorial
» Editing Symbols

When you edit symbols in the Symbol Editing Mode, you edit all of the instances of the symbol as well as the symbol in the Library panel. Because instances of a symbol are subject to the same drawings as all other instances, when you edit the instance, you actually edit the symbol, even though you have selected an instance of a symbol to edit.

1. Open the logo.fla movie and move the playhead to Frame 36.

2. Select Window→Library or press Ctrl+L/Cmd+L to open the Library panel.

3. Click the Logo layer, select the Go Logo color graphic symbol from the Library and drag a copy to the stage placing it beneath the identical object on the stage.

4. Set the magnification to 50% and drag the two logo objects so that one is on top of the other.

5. Double-click the top graphic to enter the Symbol Editing Mode.

6. Open a Fill Color well and select a green swatch.

7. Select the Paint Bucket tool and touch the area just to the left of the G in GO! to fill the fireball with green.

   The fireball in the edited symbol turns green, as it does in the other instances on the stage and in the Library panel.

8. To tidy up, use the Paint Bucket tool to fill the center of the O in GO!

   You may want to magnify the stage to better target the center of the O. When you're finished, reset the magnification to 50%.

9. Select the Oval tool.

10. In the Properties panel, select red for the stroke color and No Color for the fill.

11. Place an oval drawing around the top logo.

    The same oval appears around the other instance of the symbol and the symbol in the Library panel.

<TIP>

When you are finished with this tutorial, close the logo.fla file and when asked if you want to save the changes, indicate you do not. In that way, you'll have your original logo.fla file without having to get another one from the CD-ROM. Alternatively, you can use Save As and save the file under a different name, such as greenLogo.fla, so that you can use it again if you want a green fireball.

Tutorial
» Adjusting Alpha and Brightness in Symbols

A previous tutorial showed that if you change one instance of a symbol, all instances change. However, you can make some changes to symbol instances that affect only the instance itself and not the entire symbol. When you select a symbol instance, the Properties panel shows a popup menu labeled Color. This popup menu has the parameters you can change in a symbol instance without affecting other instances. The parameters include Brightness, Tint, Alpha, and Advanced options.

1. **Open paintBrush.fla.**

2. **Select Window→Library or press Ctrl+L/Cmd+L to open the Library panel.**

3. **Select File→New from the menu bar to open a new movie.**

4. **Click the Insert Layer button to add a layer to the existing layer.**

5. **Rename the bottom layer Background and the top layer Foreground.**

6. **Draw two lime green vertical rectangles on the Background layer and lock the layer.**

7. **Drag two instances of the symbol Lenny head on the Foreground layer.**
   Each instance of the symbol should be centered over the two rectangles.

8. **Select the Lenny object on the left.**

9. **Open the Properties panel and select Alpha from the Color Styles popup menu on the Properties panel.**
   The Color Styles popup menu is labeled Color and it defaults to None. So look for the Color label and None in the menu selection.

10. **In the text window to the right of the Color Styles popup menu, type** 50%.
    You can see that the object on the left is now partially transparent, but neither the object on the right nor the symbol in the Library panel has been changed.

11. **Repeat steps 8–10, but select Brightness from the Color Styles popup menu instead of Alpha.**
    Now you can see that the object on the left looks almost identical to the one where the alpha was changed. However, you can no longer see the rectangle behind the object. It is wholly covered by the symbol instance.

<TIP>
You should be judicious in using alpha. Generally, alpha is changed to fade in or fade out an object, but changing alpha significantly adds to the size of your movie. If you plan to create a fade-in/fade-out sequence more than once in a movie, create a movie clip symbol, and in that way, you only "pay" once for the bandwidth cost.

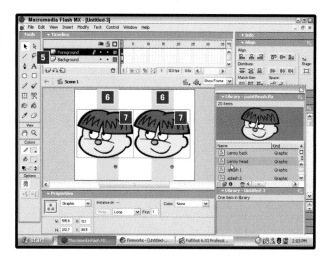

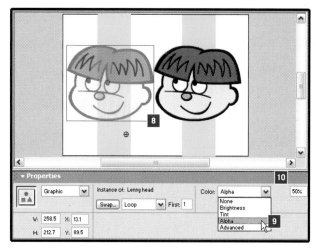

Tutorial
» Changing Tints

Besides changing the transparency and brightness level, you can change colors as well. One way to change color is to change tints of an instance. When you change the tint, you can also change the amount of change, and so you have color changes on two parameters. By moving the mouse over swatches in the Color|Tint popup menu in the Properties panel, you can watch what changes are taking place in a selected object on the stage. Then, in the same way, you can change the amount of tint to adjust the color to get just what you want.

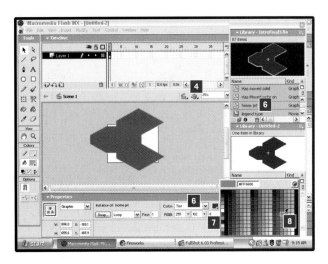

1. **Open the IntroFinal3.fla file.**

2. **Select Window→Library from the menu bar or press Ctrl+L/Cmd+L to open the Library panel.**

3. **Select File→New from the menu bar to open a new movie.**

4. **Set the stage magnification to 25%.**

5. **Open the IntroFinal3.fla Library panel and drag an instance of the "home jet" symbol to the stage.**

6. **Select the instance and choose Tint from the Color popup menu in the Properties panel.**

7. **Click the color well to open a swatch panel.**

8. **Move the mouse pointer over the swatch panel and select orange (#FF6600).**
   Note how the object changes colors while you drag the pointer over the swatches. Note the RGB windows that allow you to set RGB decimal values for tint colors. The original symbol in the Library window remains unchanged, indicating that only the instance is affected by the tint.

9. **Open the Tint slider to the right of the Tint color well.**

10. **Drag the slider so that the value is 20%.**
    Now the color has changed from orange to maroon. By experimenting with the tint RGB values and the Tint slider, you can have just the effect you want. The Tint slider changes the saturation from transparent (0%) to fully saturated (100%). When you plan a movie that animates changes in an instance's tint, you can set the tint to the desired color, and then base the change on the saturation level.

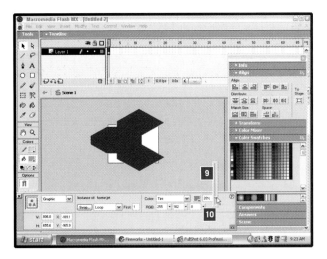

Tutorial
» Working with Advanced Color Values

The final type of Color Style is Advanced. Suffice it to say that this is one of the better named elements in Flash MX because it is indeed advanced. This tutorial shows different things you can do to a bitmapped graphic wrapped in a symbol.

1. **Open the IntroFinal3.fla file.**

2. **Select Window→Library from the menu bar or press Ctrl+L/Cmd+L to open the Library panel.**

3. **Select File→New from the menu bar to open a new movie.**

4. **Select the "color boxes" graphic symbol in the IntroFinal3.fla Library panel and drag an instance of it to the stage.**

5. **Double-click the "color boxes" object twice so that you see the "hand draws box" object on your screen.**
   You could have selected the larger symbol or have double-clicked the object once again to go to an even deeper level in the movie.

6. **Select the instance on the stage and unlock the layer if it's locked.**

7. **Choose Advanced from the Color Styles popup menu.**

8. **Click the Settings button.**

9. **In the left column of popup menus use the settings (from top to bottom), 100%, 50%, 50%, and 70% and in the right column, set the values to 255, 120, 64, and 55.**
   The effect is to put an orange, ghostly glow to the hand object.

10. **With the object still selected, in the left column of popup menus use the settings (from top to bottom), 0%, –40%, –50%, and 100% and in the right column, set the values to 0, 255, 255, and 255.**
    The negative values in the left column tend to reverse color, giving them an x-ray or photo negative appearance.

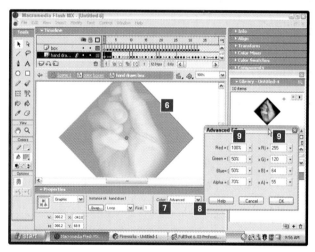

<NOTE>

The Advanced Effect panel consists of two sets of RGB and Alpha values. Those on the left have values from –100% to +100%, and those on the right from –255 to +255. You can determine the Advanced Color value based on this formula:

color=(percent * color) + color value

Thus, if you set Green left to 25% and the right setting to 255, you would calculate:

green=(.25 * 255) + 255 = 318.75

The value 318.75 is not particularly important. Just remember this panel gives you the ability to make subtle changes.

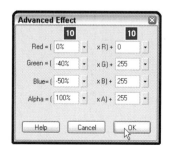

Tutorial
» Editing Button Symbols

The process of editing instances of button symbols is a little different from other instances. The main reason for the difference is the presence of the four button states: Up, Over, Down, and Hit. You can add keyframes to each of the frames with the different button states, and you can even add more layers. Whatever you add in a keyframe will appear on the screen when the button state is achieved. The last of the four states, Hit, is where you can increase or decrease the area that counts as a "hit." For example, if you have very small buttons, you may want to add a larger area around the button that will be detected as a "hit" event. Or you can even make the hit area an unusual shape. However, nothing you draw in the keyframes under the Hit button ever appears on the screen. The drawing simply makes that area "alive" to the button you are editing. Of course you have to be careful that the hit areas of your buttons do not overlap.

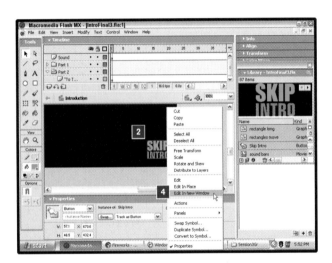

1. **Open IntroFinal3.fla and select the Introduction Scene.**

2. **Select the Skip Intro button in the lower-right corner of the stage.**

3. **Right-click (Windows) or Control-click (Macintosh) the mouse.**

4. **Select Edit In New Window.**
   The button will appear in the Symbol Editing Mode in a separate window.

5. **Select Show All in the magnification window.**
   The full button appears in the center of the screen. Note the timeline with four frame labels. Up, Over, Down, and Hit.

6. **Drag the playhead to the Over frame.**

   The colors in the word SKIP and INTRO are reversed. This can be accomplished using the Paint Bucket tool.

7. **Drag the playhead to the Down frame.**

   The colors in the word SKIP and INTRO are now changed to all blue, again using the Paint Bucket tool.

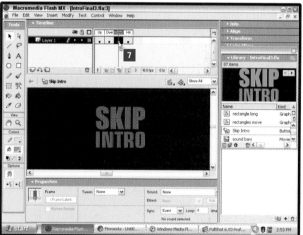

8. **Drag the playhead to the Hit frame.**

   The blue rectangle represents the hit area. In other words, it specifies the area where the mouse pointer becomes sensitive to the button. It can be much larger or smaller than the visible portion of the button. In this case, the hit area is roughly the same size as the SKIP INTRO message. The image in the hit area is always invisible to the user. It simply defines an area sensitive to the mouse.

9. **Click the black X in the upper-right corner to exit the Symbol Edit Mode.**

   When you use the Symbol Edit Mode in a new window, you need to close the window to return to the stage.

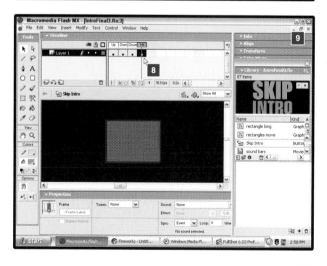

Tutorial
» Changing Lines

Once you draw a line, you can change it, as well as its fill. You have seen how to change lines using different tools such as the Subselection and Pen tools. You can also use the Arrow tool and menu selections. When looking at these changes, you need to think about how to animate them. Use your mind's eye to picture the smooth changes taking place from the initial drawing to the changed ones you will see. Starting with the Arrow tool, you see that whenever the pointer shows a half-circle or right-angle with the arrow pointer, the tool is ready.

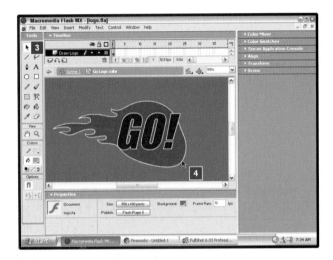

1. **Open logo.fla and drag the playhead to Frame 36.**

2. **Double-click the symbol instance on the stage to enter the Symbol Editing Mode.**

3. **Select the Arrow tool and place it near the front and bottom of the drawing.**
   You will see a little half-circle appear near the pointer.

4. **With the half-circle showing on the arrow pointer, drag the line downward and to the right.**
   The distorted line is followed by the fill. (Remember, once you've changed a shape, using the Ctrl+Z/Cmd+Z or selecting File→Undo from the menu bar will restore it for you.)

5. **Restore the drawing using Ctrl+Z/Cmd+Z.**

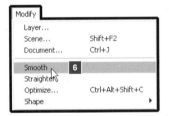

6. **Select the drawing and then select Modify→Smooth from the menu bar.**
   Some minor smoothing occurs because the drawing was fairly smooth to begin with. However, if the drawing had more irregular lines, you would find that it would be far smoother and somewhat less defined.

7. **Restore the drawing using Ctrl+Z/Cmd+Z.**

8. **Select the drawing and then select Modify→Straighten from the menu bar.**
   You will see significant changes in the drawing. Any line that was not fully curved has been straightened, leaving straight lines in both the text drawings and tail of the fireball. (Remember to undo the distortions before closing the FLA file.)

Tutorial
» Optimizing Lines

When you optimize a line, you actually optimize a curve within a line. The optimizing refines the curved lines by using a smaller number of elements to define the curve. This means it takes up less bandwidth because the file is smaller. This tutorial uses logo.fla to show you how optimizing lines works.

1. **Open logo.fla and drag the playhead to Frame 36.**

2. **Double-click the symbol instance on the stage to enter the Symbol Editing Mode.**

3. **Select the drawing.**

4. **Select Modify→Optimize from the menu bar.**
   The Optimize Curves dialog box appears.

5. **Move the slider to the right, half-way between the middle and the far left side, select Use multiple passes (slower) and Show totals message and press OK.**

6. **When you see the Flash MX alert box, click OK.**
   The alert box shows you the original number of curves and the optimized number of curves in the new drawing. Obviously, you only want to use this tool when reducing the number of curves will make the drawing look better. By optimizing curves, you also reduce the size of the file.

7. **Examine your new drawing and decide if the effect is the desired one, and if not press Ctrl+Z/Cmd+Z.**
   The distortions give the fireball a ghostly look, and if this is the effect you want, you could make an interesting animation of the changes in the fireball logo going from this ghostly look to the final fireball image.

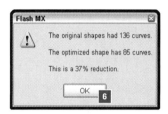

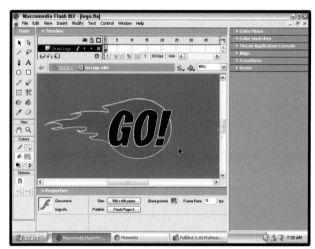

Tutorial
» Converting Lines and Changing Fills

Converting lines to fills and expanding and softening fill edges can produce some interesting shape changes. Whenever you work with lines and fills, only the fills can accept gradient or radial fills. By converting the lines (strokes) to fills, you can use gradient and radials in the converted lines. This allows you to create interesting effects using radial line fills generating a "glow" effect. The focus of this tutorial is on converting lines to fills and then changing the fills in interesting ways.

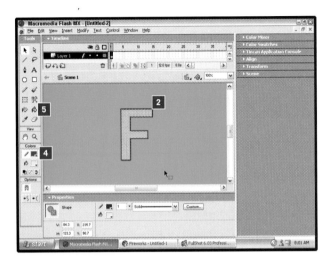

1. **Open a new window and set the background color to a light cream green.**

2. **Using the Text tool type a yellow 200-point Verdana F.**

3. **Select the F and select Modify→Break Apart.**

4. **Select blue in the stroke color well in the Properties panel.**

5. **Use the Ink Bottle tool to color the line around the F blue.**

6. **Select the F.**

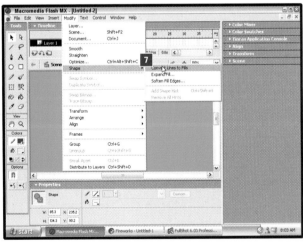

7. **From the menu bar, select Modify→Shape→Convert Lines to Fills.**
   Now, all of the drawing elements that make up the F are fills.

8. **From the menu bar, select Modify→Shape→Expand Fill.**

9. **In the Expand Fill dialog box, type** 4 px **for the Distance.**

10. **Click the Expand radio button, and then click OK.**
    The line around the F is expanded 4 pixels.

11. **Select the line fill around the F.**

12. **Open the Fill color well in the Properties panel.**

13. **Select the red radial color from the bottom of the available swatches.**
    A red "glow" appears around the F.

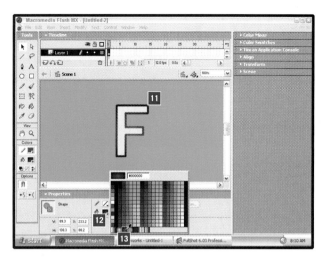

14. **From the menu bar, select Modify→Shape→Soften Fill Edges.**
    The Soften Fill Edges dialog box appears.

15. **Type** 4 px **in the Distance text window and** 4 **in the Number of Steps text window.**

16. **Click the Expand radio button.**

17. **Click OK.**
    Now you can see a widened "glow" around the F. You can make further adjustments using the Fill Transformation tool so that you get the right effect you want.

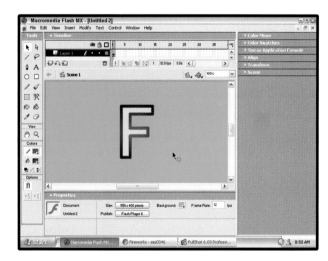

Tutorial
» Making Transformations

With all of the tools and special effects the menu provides, you can find still more ways to change your drawings using the Transform submenu. The Free Transform menu works the same as the Free Transform tool in the Toolbox, but some of the other transformations allow you to make several kinds of adjustments to drawings that you may find useful when making movies. To see the types of effects, the next tutorial again makes use of the GO! fireball object in the logo.fla movie. (You will notice that some of the Transform menu options were skipped. This is because they are fairly self-explanatory and/or because tools from the Toolbox can perform the same function. However, take note of the other Transform options when opening the ones used in the tutorial.)

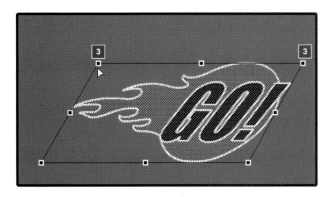

1. **Open the logo.fla file, move the playhead to Frame 36, and double-click the fireball object to enter the Symbol Editing Mode.**

2. **Select the drawing and then select Modify→Transform→Distort from the menu bar.**

3. **Drag the upper right corner to the right and push the upper-left corner to the right.**
   A parallelogram appears around the object and it has been distorted in a lean-forward manner. The distortion gives it an even more pronounced moving appearance.

4. **Restore the drawing to its original state by pressing Ctrl+Z/Cmd+Z.**

5. **With the fireball object selected, select Modify→Transform→Envelope from the menu bar.**

6. **Push and pull on the different points and tangent handles to modify it into different interesting shapes.**

7. **Restore the drawing to its original state by pressing Ctrl+Z/Cmd+Z.**

8. **With the fireball object selected, select Modify→Transform→Flip Horizontal from the menu bar.**
   The object is reversed in a horizontal position. You can also flip it vertically.

Tutorial
» Changing the Center Position on a Symbol

The ability to change the center position is essential for making the chart bar in the Preloader in IntroFinal3.html. The chart begins at the left and then using changes in scale expands to 100 percent. By having the center point on the far left side, rather than expanding left and right from the default center position, the bar chart expands to the right. Only by having the ability to move the center point can the design include the desired change in the chart movement.

1. **Select the Rectangle tool and open the Color Mixer panel.**

2. **Select no color for the stroke and mix a purple with the values R=255, G=0, B=255, Alpha=62% for the fill color.**

3. **Draw a rectangle with the dimensions W=200 and H=16.**
   You can check the size in the Properties or Info panels.

4. **Select the rectangle and press the F8 key to open the Convert to Symbol dialog box.**

5. **Select Movie Clip for the behavior and preLoadChart for the symbol name, and then press OK.**

6. **Double-click the new MC to enter the Symbol Editing stage.**
   You will see the cross-hair icon indicating the center position. You need to move that icon to the far left.

7. **Magnify the stage to 200%.**

8. **Select the rectangle.**

9. **Using the right-arrow key (or shift + right-arrow), move the rectangle to the right until the cross-hair icon is at the far-left side.**
   You cannot drag the center from this mode, and so you must move the rectangle.

10. **Click the scene icon to return to the main timeline.**
    On the main timeline of the completed movie clip, you can still see the center icon of the chart bar on the far left. In the project movie, you will see the chart object beneath a quartered grid showing load progress. When the scale is reduced to 0, and bar disappears to the left, and as the scale is increased, the bar expands to the right.

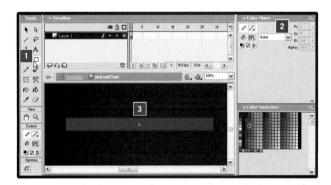

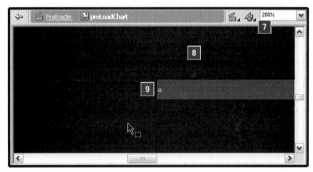

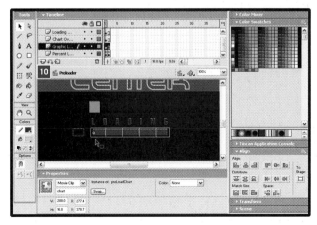

Tutorial
Pivoting on an Offset Center Point

Besides moving a center point to scale from someplace other than the default center, you may find that you need to move a center as a pivot point. In animation, joining pivot points at the natural joints in a body is essential to a natural-looking animation. In addition, you can move pivot points on symbol instances by dragging them using the Free Transform Tool. In this tutorial, you learn how to move a center point on an object from IntroFinal3.fla to see how to move it and what the rotation effects are of doing so.

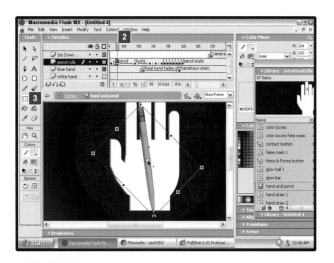

1. **Open IntroFinal3.fla and drag the playhead to Frame 363 of the Introduction scene.**

2. **Double-click on the hand object to open the hand and pencil graphic symbol and drag the playhead to Frame to 98.**

3. **Select the Free Transform tool from the Toolbox and click the pencil.**
   The pencil is a symbol within the hand and pencil symbol, but you want the center point from the combined symbol. The open circle is the object's center point.

4. **Drag the open circle center point to the tip of the pencil.**

5. **Drag the playhead back and forth between Frames 98 and 104.**
   The open circle is the pivot point, and so instead of pivoting on the center of the object, it will pivot on the pencil's point.

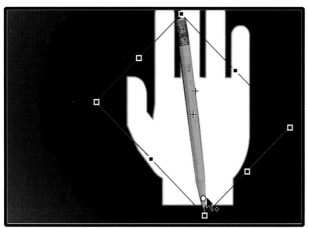

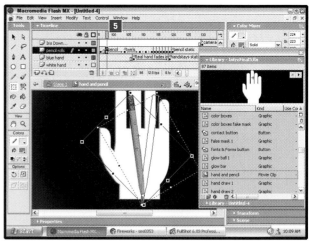

» Session Review

1. What are the differences between symbols and drawings? (See "Tutorial: Understanding Drawings and Symbols.")

2. What advantages and disadvantages are there to vector and bitmapped graphics? When is the best time to use bitmapped graphics and vector graphics? (See "Tutorial: Bitmapped and Vector Graphics.")

3. How many different color wells does Flash MX have when all of the panels are on the screen? What are the different ways to mix colors in Flash MX? (See "Tutorial: Coloring Objects in Flash.")

4. How do you create a color palette in the Swatches panel? (See "Tutorial: Setting a Color Palette.")

5. What different mixing schemes do Windows and Macintosh computers have? Which has CMYK and what does CMYK stand for? (See "Tutorial: Understanding the Differences between Windows and Macintosh Coloring.")

6. Gradients and radials are both fills and cannot be put into line components of drawings. What method can you use to put gradients and radials in lines? (See "Tutorial: Converting Lines and Changing Fills.")

7. Using the Subselection or Pen tool allows you to bring out the different anchor points in a drawing. What other methods are available to create alterations in lines using other tools and menus? (See "Tutorial: Making Transformations.")

» Additional Projects

» Create a drawing of your own or use one from the project. Select the drawing, and try the different options available in the Modify menu. As you gain skills in Flash, you will find that knowing what submenus are available for modifying your drawing will both save you time when creating animated movies and provide you with many creative options that you may not think of unless you know of their availability. Remember, if you use a drawing from the project files, you can always restore it to its original state by making another copy from the CD-ROM.

» Surf the Web and find a site with a color scheme you really admire. See if you can duplicate that color scheme by creating a color palette with the same set of colors. (Hint: Look at the source code in the browser for the color values, and put those values into the Color Mixer panel.)

» Create a drawing, convert it to a movie clip symbol. First, see how many different changes you can make to the instance of the movie clip without changing the basic symbol. Then, make changes to it that will affect all instances of the symbol and the symbol itself.

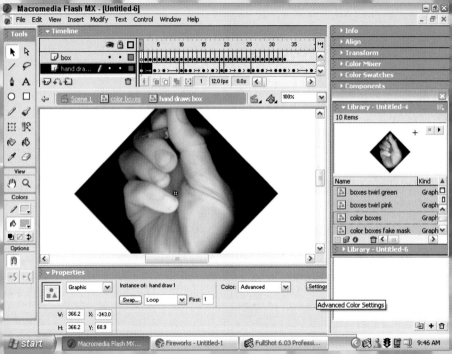

Part III:
Moving and
Changing Objects

Session 4

Animation from Cels to Digital Frames

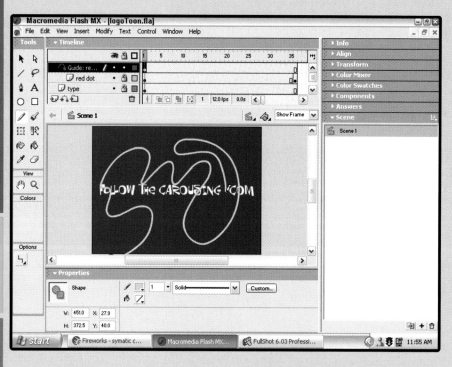

Session Introduction

Flash MX uses frames, keyframes, and blank keyframes. You can make changes in position or appearance only in a keyframe. Blank keyframes bring a halt to any series of drawings or symbols in a layer. Frames can be empty or contain tweened materials. A tweened element in a frame is the state of an object between two keyframes that have been tweened.

The metaphor of examining a strip of film frame by frame does not always work in Flash. Change occurs only in keyframes and regular frames cannot accept a changed object. However, if you roll out a strip of film, you can note change in every single frame, whether the frames are animated or not. But in Flash, suppose you have five frames. Only Frame 1 is a keyframe. If you move the playhead to Frame 5 and make changes on the stage, those changes will be reflected in all five frames, including the first. However, if you have five keyframes and make changes in any keyframe, each frame will be different.

To make matters even more mysterious, if you create a tween between two keyframes and move the playhead between them, each of the intervening frames shows the object changing. So it might make sense to add a fourth type of frame category, a "tweened frame," or one in which a tweening takes place between two keyframes. An object in a tweened frame cannot be selected and altered in any way, even though each frame changes as you move the playhead. So if a tween is taking place between a keyframe at Frames 10 and 20, you can move the playhead to Frame 15 and note the changes, but you can't make changes to the object in the frame. The next section on tweening explains why a tweened frame works as it does.

You can create a movie by inserting a keyframe into every single frame, but think of yourself as the master cartoonist who only has to insert drawings into keyframes. As in the old-fashioned hand-drawn cartoons, all of the in-betweening work is done by someone else. What you must envision are key points of change, place those points on the timeline, and let the tweening process do the rest.

TOOLS YOU'LL USE
Toolbox, Align, Info, Transformation, Color Mixer, Color Swatches, and Properties panels

MATERIALS NEEDED
From the accompanying CD-ROM you'll need the IntroFinal3.fla, paintBrush.fla, logo.fla, logoToon.fla files.

TIME REQUIRED
120 minutes

SESSION OUTCOME
Applying Animation Concepts to Flash MX

PROJECT PORTION
Tween the Animation Studio Section

Tutorial

» Working with Frames

To effectively work with Flash MX, you need to understand how the different types of frames work. Keyframes are the master frames where you add and change different shapes, text, and symbol instances. The frames between the keyframes are automatically filled by tweened images. The tweened images can be viewed, but they cannot be changed directly. Only an object in a specific keyframe on a specific layer, on a specific timeline can be altered by changing the object itself. Inserting a blank keyframe has the effect of removing objects to the left of the blank keyframe. In the following tutorial, you will examine a series of different frames in the project to see how they affect a movie.

1. **Drag IntroFinal3.fla from the CD-ROM and open it in Flash MX.**

2. **Drag the playhead to Frame 270 in the Introduction scene.**

3. **Click the movie clip with the outline text TO THE.**
   In selecting the MC on the stage, look at the Properties panel to see that the correct object is selected. You will see "Instance of: TO THE build on" below the middle of the stage on the Properties panel.

4. **With the "TO THE build on" MC selected, right-click the mouse (or Control+click on the Macintosh).**
   You will see a popup menu.

5. **Select the menu option Edit In Place.**
   You are now in the Symbol Editing Mode and in the MC's timeline.

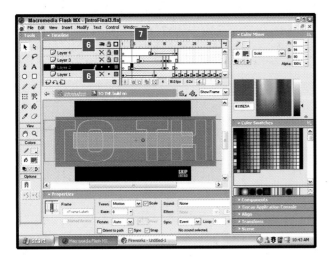

6. **Click the Eye column for Layers 4, 3, and 1 to hide those layers.**
   Hiding layers you're not working with helps you better see what's going on.

7. **Drag the playhead to Frame 4 and click Frame 4 to select it.**
   Now you can see the object TO THE in green outline. It is the first object in a two-object sequence that is tweened.

8. Drag the playhead to Frame 9.

Note that when you drag the playhead to Frame 9, the "TO THE" shrinks in size. Frame 9 is a normal frame, but it is in the middle of a motion tween where Flash automatically changes the images between two keyframes.

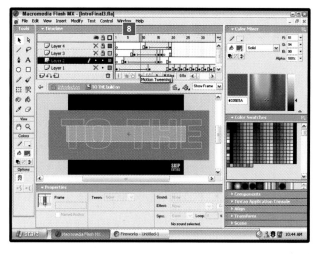

9. Drag the playhead to Frame 15.

Because Frame 15 is a keyframe, it contains the final shape and position of the tweened object. The tween began in Frame 4, and the frames between the keyframes contained all of the degrees of change between Frames 4 and 15. Because tweening is automatic, you cannot make any changes to the object in the frame itself, but if you change either of the keyframes in a tweened set of keyframes, the tweened images change.

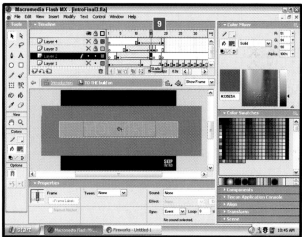

10. Drag the playhead to Frame 16.

Frame 16 is a blank keyframe. The object disappears from the stage. You do not need to include a blank keyframe after a tween. Use blank keyframes in a layer only to remove the object from the stage you no longer need.

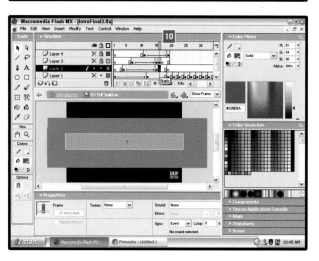

Tutorial

» Creating Keyframe Changes

Before learning how to tween objects, you should realize that keyframes play an important role in animation without the tweening process. In fact, if you want, you can insert keyframes into every frame in a movie and make changes in your drawing without having to make any tweens at all. You may have noticed in the previous tutorial that several keyframes (indicated by a black dot on the timeline) were spaced along the timeline without any tweening at all. The next tutorial shows how to use individual frames to animate processes where sharp changes are expected — such as splashing paint on a canvas.

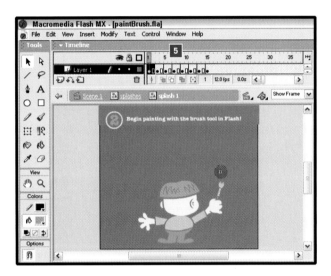

1. **Open the paintBrush.fla movie.**

2. **Drag the playhead to the last keyframe.**

3. **Double-click the instance named splashes.**
   You are now in the Symbol Editing Mode.

4. **Select the first frame in the "splashes all" layer.**

5. **Double-click the graphic instance splash1.**
   You will now see a single layer (Layer 1) with eight keyframes.

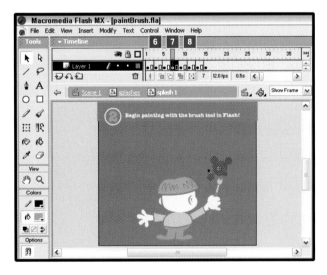

6. **Drag the playhead to Frame 3.**
   A slightly different splash of paint is on the canvas.

7. **Drag the playhead to Frame 5.**
   The paint splash changes again.

8. **Drag the playhead to Frame 7.**
   The paint splash has grown again.

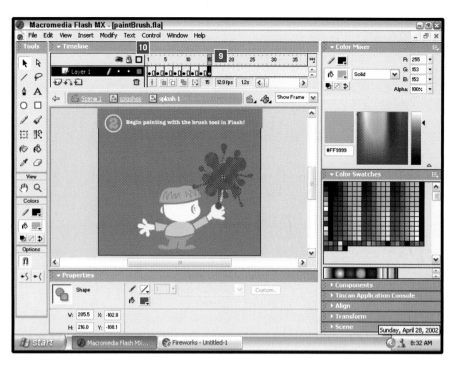

9. **Drag the playhead to Frame 15, stopping at all of the key frames in between Frames 7 and 15.**

10. **Drag the playhead back to the first frame and press the Enter/Return key to play the timeline.**

    When you play the timeline, you see the paint splash grow from a dot to a large splatter. The effect is not a smooth one, but rather, as the designer intended, one of quickly flinging paint on the canvas.

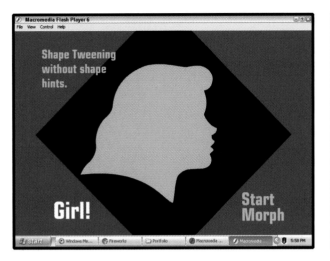

To prepare for the next tutorial on Shape tweening, look at this sequence of images to see how one image can change to its opposite using Flash and a little imagination. The effect of one object transforming into another is called *morphing*.

The movie begins with the image of a girl's profile. The pink image in the center of the movie is a drawing that is to be morphed.

Five frames into the morphing process, we can still see the girl looks like a girl, but some changes have begun to occur.

By 10 frames into the shape tween, you can barely see the eye, nose, and mouth, but it's still a girl's profile (sort of). The pink is starting to fade to a muddy color.

At Frame 15, you can begin to see the beginning of a muddy green, and hair above the forehead has a flip in it.

At Frame 20, you can see a more decided green, and the girl's eye has become the bottom of another creature's nose, and the nose, the top of a lip.

By Frame 25, the green is still more pronounced, the hair in the back is now flattened, and the girl has totally been replaced by someone more sinister-looking (a tele-marketer?).

It's Frankie! Two drawings in keyframes along with a shape tween generated an entire series of drawings that nicely animate and morph of the girl into the monster.

Tutorial
» Creating a Shape Tween

The most powerful tool in Flash is its ability to tween. A tween instruction is placed in the first keyframe of a tweening pair. The tweening pair is made up of the first object in the keyframe where the tween instruction is placed and the next keyframe in the same layer. The two types of tweens, Shape and Motion, both involve changes. Shape tweens change drawings and Motion tweens change symbol instances, groups, and text.

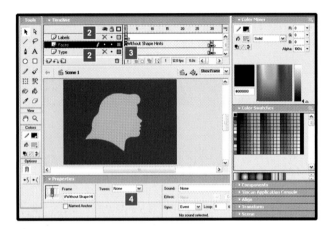

1. **Drag a copy of shapeTween.fla from the CD-ROM to the desktop and double-click the file icon to open it and Flash MX.**

2. **In the Eye column, place an X on the Labels and Type layers to hide them.**
   The Fake Hints layer should be renamed Labels.

3. **Click the first frame of the Faces layer.**

4. **In the Properties panel, open the Tween popup menu and choose None.**
   The light green background and tween arrow disappear from the layer. You will be putting it back later, but to see how the tweening process works, you must start with nothing but a drawing.

5. **Drag the playhead to the keyframe in Frame 30.**
   This is where the second drawing goes. Note that the drawing is both a different color and shape.

6. **Drag the playhead back to the first keyframe in Frame 1.**

7. **In the Tween popup menu in the Properties panel select Shape.**
   An arrow appears between the first and second keyframes indicating a successful tween. Further, the background in the tweened area turns a light green, indicating a Shape tween. (Motion tweens show a blue background.) You're all done. Remember, all you have to do to create a Shape tween is to draw two shapes on keyframes on the same layer. The command for the Shape tween goes in the first keyframe only. Just open the Tween popup menu and choose Shape, and you're all done.

< N O T E >
The terms "Shape" and "Motion" are not literal — that is, Shape tweens only change shapes and Motion tweens only change position. Shape tweens are used with drawings where one drawing is tweened into another drawing. Sometimes the change in shape has a "morphing" quality. With its root meaning in metamorphosis, morphing is the animated gradual change from one image to another — like the girl morphing into a monster. This next tutorial shows how to create a Shape tween that also happens to be a morph. Using shapeTween.fla, some steps have been removed so that you can see how to build them up yourself.

Tutorial
» Making a Morph Using Shape Hints

Sometimes a Shape tween generates a jumbled mess between the beginning and the ending of the tween. This can be especially disconcerting when you are attempting to generate a smooth morphing effect between the first and second keyframes. To help smooth the transition, Flash MX provides Shape Hints. These hints point to the areas where shapes should coincide to best smooth the process. For example, the nose of one figure should be linked to the nose of the second figure in the tween. Then, the nose simply changes to a different nose rather than becoming an eye or a mouth!

1. Drag a copy of shapeTween.fla from the CD-ROM to the desktop and double-click the file icon to open it and Flash MX.

2. In the Eye column, place an X on the Labels and Type layers to hide them.

3. Click Frame 35 of the Faces layer to move the playhead to that frame position.

4. Click the drawing to select it.
   When drawings are selected they take on a "dotty" appearance.

5. Select Modify→Shape→Add Shape Hint from the menu bar.
   A red "a" dot (a shape hint) appears in the middle of the drawing. You will be able to drag the shape hint anywhere you want on the drawing. All shape hints are sequentially alphabetized, and they are all initially placed in the middle of the drawing.

6. Drag the shape hint from the center of the drawing to the forehead just beneath the hairline.

7. Create three more shape hints and place them on the nose, the lips, and the chin.
   Place the shape hints where you have prominent features that can be linked to prominent features on the second drawing.

8. Move the playhead to Frame 66.

9. Place shape hints in the corresponding position in the face of the second drawing.

10. Remove the X from the Eye column of the Labels and Type layers.
    Your work is complete. The morph between the two drawings was very smooth to begin with, but the added shape hints will make it even smoother.

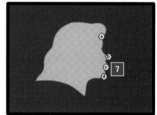

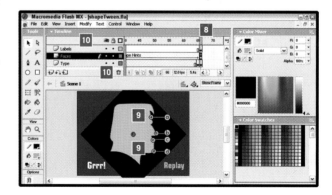

Tutorial
» Creating a Motion Tween

Creating a Motion tween is almost identical to creating a Shape tween. However, instead of using drawings, you use symbol instances, text blocks, or groups. Motion tweening implies changing positions, but you can change rotation, shape, tint, advanced color, and alpha (transparency), as well as position. You can change any aspect of a symbol instance, text block or group, but only certain kinds of changes will be tweened. Tweening means that all of the intermediate elements of a change between two keyframes are implemented as opposed to the abrupt change seen when one configuration replaces another at a new keyframe.

The easiest objects to use are symbol instances. The shape of an instance will be tweened if the changes in the shape are those made in the Info, Transform, or Properties panel but not in the Symbol Editing Mode. (Besides, if you change an instance in the Symbol Editing Mode, all instances and the symbol itself will be changed.) So when considering changes for instances, the easiest path is to stick with the Properties panel. If the color or shape change can be made in the Properties panel, the change will be tweened from one keyframe to another. You will find the Transform panel and Free Transform tool invaluable as well for making instance changes that are fully tweened.

Using the Motion tween with text is a different kettle of characters. If you move a text block from one position to another in a tween, you will get full tweening. If you change text color, style, or size using the text Properties panel, you do not get full tweening. For example, if you want a block of text to move across the screen and gradually decrease in size, you cannot use changes in the font size to tween the change. Instead, to gradually change the size, you would use the Transform panel to reduce the percent size (scale) of the text block in the second keyframe. (When you make changes in the Transform panel that involve changing scale, be sure to check constrain so that the proportions are maintained.) Think of Motion tweening in terms of larger blocks rather than the contents within the blocks. That will help you better remember what to use when making changes to text blocks.

Groups are fused drawings, text blocks, and/or instances. When making changes to group blocks, use the same consideration you would for a text block. If you enter the Symbol Editing mode to change drawings or text in a group, you get an abrupt change. However, if you use the Info or Transform panels or the Free Transform tool to make the changes, like text blocks, groups will be fully tweened.

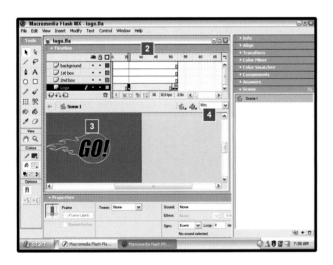

1. Open the logo.fla movie.

2. Drag the playhead to Frame 36 and click it to select it.

3. Select None in the Tween popup menu in the Properties panel. Select the fireball object.

4. Set magnification to 50%.

5. **Drag the playhead to Frame 51.**

6. **Drag the fireball object off the right side of the stage.**
In the movie, you will see that this has been done already. Just note the position of the fireball. You can make an object disappear from sight by the simple expedient of dragging it off the stage.

7. **Drag the playhead back to Frame 36 and click Frame 36 to select it.**

8. **Select Motion from the Tween popup menu in the Properties panel.**
As soon as a successful Motion tween is complete, you will see a blue background and a tweening arrow appear. The tweening arrow is between the initial keyframe and the concluding keyframe of a tween. You only set the tween in the first frame of a tweening keyframe pair.

9. **Select Control→Test Movie from the menu bar.**

Tutorial
» Using Motion Tweens on Multiple Layers

When working with tweens, whether Shape or Motion, chances are you will be using multiple objects. In fact, you can have a Shape tween on one layer and Motion tween on another layer within the same area on the timeline. This next tutorial shows how to coordinate different objects in the same movie clip using two Motion tweens and a set of keyframes to create the effect of a pencil drawing a line from the beginning of the project movie.

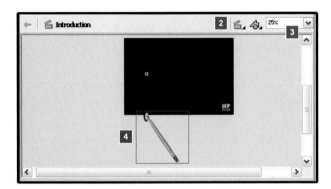

1. **Open the file IntroFinal3.html.**

2. **Open the Introduction Scene.**

3. **Set the magnification to 25%.**

4. **Using the Hand tool, move the stage up so that you can see the pencil/glow object beneath the stage.**

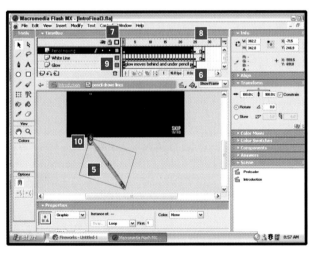

5. **Double-click the pencil.**
   As soon as you double-click the pencil, you will see it is actually two objects — a glow object and the pencil. You will see a new timeline belonging to the instance.

6. **Change the magnification to Show Frame.**

7. **Select the first frame in the Pencil moving layer and in the Tween popup menu select None.**

8. **Move the playhead to Frame 25 in the Pencil moving layer and select None in the Tween popup menu.**

9. **Repeat step 7 but select the first frame in the Glow layer.**
   All of the motion tweens are now removed.

10. **Select the pencil and glow object and position them where you want them at the beginning of the tween.**
    In developing the movie from the very beginning, you would need to change the position, but they are now correctly positioned. Also, the middle layer with all of the keyframes contains line segments to create a line following the glow.

11. **Move the playhead to Frame 25.**

12. **Move the pencil and glow object to the new position.**

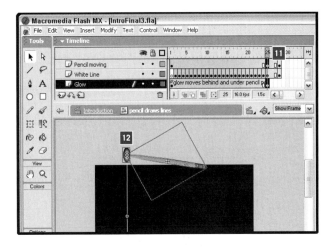

13. **Move the playhead to Frame 28.**

14. **Move the pencil object to its new position.**
    The pencil is now in the final position for the movie clip. The glow point has disappeared because the layer with the glow point terminated at Frame 25.

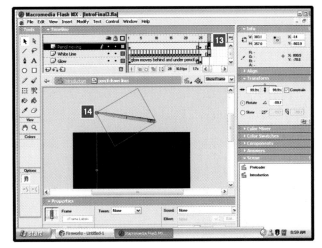

15. **Move the playhead back to the first frame and click on the Pencil moving layer.**

16. **Open the Tween popup menu in the Properties panel and select Motion.**

17. **Select the Glow layer and repeat step 16.**

18. **Move the playhead to Frame 25, select the keyframe in the Pencil moving layer, and repeat step 16.**
    You will see that you can create a second motion tween in a keyframe where another tween ended. Linked tweens can be as long as you need for an animation.

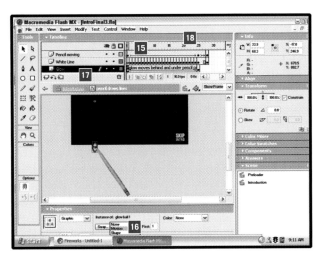

Tutorial
» Moving an Object Along a Path

When an object is tweened to go from point A to point B, it moves in a straight line. Wouldn't it be nice if you could lay out a path between two keyframes for an object to follow? Using a path guide layer, you can make any kind of path you want, and your object will follow the path. You use the pencil or paint brush to create the path in the path layer, and then in the layer with the motion tween, you put your object that follows the path. You then put the object at the beginning of the path in the first keyframe. Then, all you have to do is to place the object at the end of the path in the second keyframe. When you run your movie, instead of going directly from the first to the second point, the movie follows the path from the first to second movie. The best part is that the path automatically becomes invisible when you run the movie.

To see how to move objects along a path, you will use a *logotoon*. A logotoon is an animated logo, just like the logo.fla movie you have seen in previous tutorials. This logotoon, however, uses a path to put a very big dot in a dot.com. Also, this tutorial shows you how to make the movie from scratch.

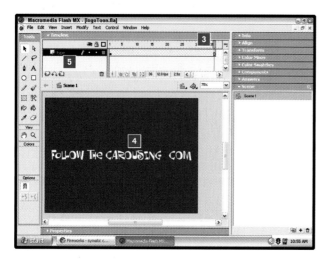

1. **Open a new movie.**

2. **Select Modify→Movie and select a nice navy blue for the background color.**

3. **Click Frame 36 and press the F5 key to add active frames to Frame 36.**

4. **Using the Text tool type out in large letters,** Follow The Carousing [space] Com.
   Use an interesting font. The one in the example is HiHat from www.flashfonts.com.

5. **Rename Layer 1** type.

6. **Insert a new layer and name it red dot.**

7. **Draw a red circle near the bottom of the stage with a diameter of about 21 pixels using the Oval tool.**

8. **Select the circle, and press the F8 key to open the Convert to Symbol dialog box.**

9. **Choose Graphic for the behavior.**
   This red dot will be following a path.

10. **Click the red dot layer to select it.**

11. **Click the Add Motion Guide button beneath the layers column.**
    It's the middle button between the Add Layer and Add Folder buttons.

12. **Lock the type and red dot layers.**

13. **Select the Guide layer, and using the Pencil or Paint Brush tool, draw your path line beginning at the bottom of the stage near the red dot object.**
    It can be as crooked as you want.

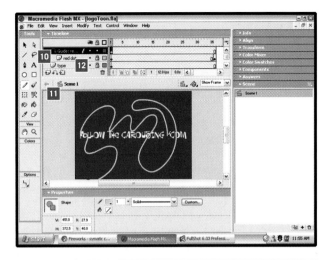

14. **Click the Snap to Objects button at the bottom of the Toolbox.**
    It's the button with the magnet.

15. **Make sure the playhead is at the beginning of the movie, and drag the red dot to the beginning of the path line.**
    A little open circle should appear in the middle of the red dot, and place that circle right on the tip of the path line.

16. **Drag the playhead to the last frame.**

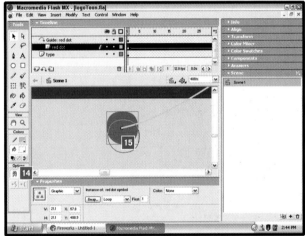

17. **Insert a keyframe in the last frame of the red dot layer.**

18. **Drag the red dot and place it at the other end of the path line.**
    It too should lock in place when you get it near the tip.

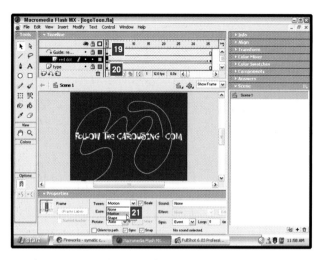

19. **Drag the playhead to the first frame.**

20. **Select the first frame in the red dot layer.**

21. **Open the Tween popup menu and select Motion.**
    You now have a Motion tween between the first and second keyframes in the red dot layer. You should see a blue background to the frames in the layer and a tweening arrow.

22. **Select Window→Actions from the menu bar or press F9.**
    The Actions panel appears. This is where you place ActionScript.

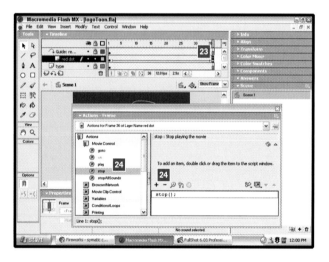

23. **Click on Frame 36 on the red dot layer.**

24. **In the left pane of the Actions panel, select Actions→Movie Control→stop and then click the add (+) button in the right pane.**
    The stop(); action appears. That will stop the movie after the dot has wound its way to the final stopping place. You're all finished, and you've got a logotoon of your very own making!

As the red dot is launched from its starting position, rather than making a beeline to the final stopping point, it heads upwards well to the left of the space between "carousing" and "com."

Rising above the line of text, the red dot looks like it's headed for outer space.

Following the path, instead of heading off the stage, the dot comes back around and positions itself so that Carousing.com has a point. And did you notice that the path is invisible? Whenever you create a path in the Guide layer of a movie, it is automatically invisible. If you want a visible path, you need to cut and paste-in-place an identical path on another layer.

Tutorial

» Using Alpha and Motion Tweens to Create Fades

In a previous session, you saw how to change an object's alpha (transparency) level. In just about every motion picture you will see at the theaters, you will see fades. A fade occurs when the pictures on the scene gradually disappear. Gradual disappearances are called *fade-outs*. When a picture gradually fades into sight, it's called a *fade-in*. With Flash you can do both. One way to create a fade is to place a black rectangle over the entire stage. Beginning with 0% alpha (fully transparent) for the rectangle in the first keyframe, a motion tween to 100% alpha (fully opaque) in the second keyframe generates a fade-out. You may remember seeing the fade-out in the paintBrush.fla movie. Now you will see how it was done.

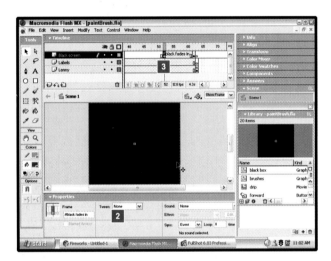

1. **Open the paintBrush.fla file, move the playhead to Frame 52, and lock the Labels and Lenny layers.**
   Please add the label names **Black screen**, **Labels,** and **Lenny** as shown in the figure. (During revisions, they were incorrectly left unlabeled.)

2. **In the Black screen layer, remove the Motion tween from Frame 52 by selecting None from the Tween popup menu.**

3. **Select the invisible black box overlaying the stage by clicking the Black screen layer and then clicking the stage.**

4. **Open the Color popup menu and, in the Alpha Amount box, change the alpha value from 0% to 100%.**
   All of the first four steps set the stage for seeing how the fade-out is created.

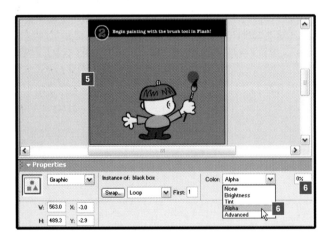

5. **Select the black rectangle over the stage.**

6. **From the Color popup menu, select Alpha, and in the Alpha Amount window, type** 0%.
   This essentially reverses what you did in step 4. However, when starting from the beginning of a fade-out, you would begin with a solid black screen that would have to be made fully transparent in the first keyframe where the tween began.

7. **Drag the playhead to Frame 62.**

8. **Check to make sure that the black rectangle graphic Alpha's level is 100%.**

9. **Move the playhead back to Frame 52.**

10. **Click Frame 52 in the Black screen layer and select Motion from the Tween popup menu in the Properties panel.**

Now the effect is complete. Drag the playhead back and forth between the two keyframes to see fade-out when moving to the right and fade-in when moving to the left. A blank keyframe gets rid of the screen when it's done with the fade.

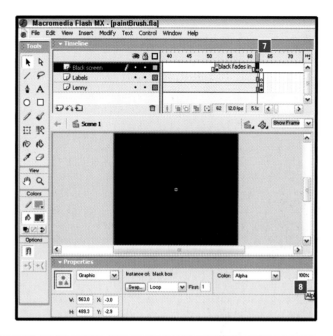

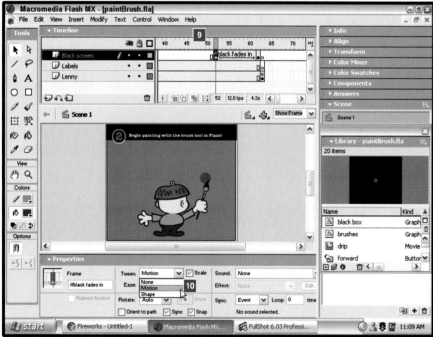

Tutorial
» Altering Size with Motion Tweens

Changing the size of an object has several applications. For example, to make an object appear to be moving closer to the viewer, a small object in the upper-right corner is moved to the lower-left corner and scaled to a larger size. Likewise, a pulsing effect is possible using a tweened object made larger and smaller. In the introduction to the course project, the artist put the size tween to a very creative use. He created an object that when fully expanded is a double-rectangle colored with a gradient from purple to white. The bottom rectangle has a gradient from purple to white with purple on the bottom while the top rectangle has purple on the top with white on the bottom. The effect is a "glow bar" with a purple border and white center. The combined rectangles make up a symbol rectangle, and by changing the vertical height of the rectangle, it has the effect of opening and closing a "glow box." This next tutorial shows you how to create it.

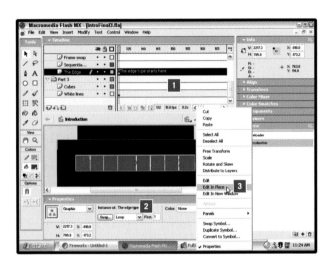

1. **Open IntroFinal3.fla and move the playhead to Frame 132 of the Intro scene.**

2. **Select the object named The edge type.**
   Sometimes it can be tricky getting just the right object. In the Properties panel you should see "Instance of: The edge type" when you have it correctly selected.

3. **Right-click (Control+click on the Macintosh) to open the Context menu and select Edit In Place.**
   Sometimes using the Context menu is easier than double-clicking an object to edit it. Using either technique, you should be in the Symbol Editing Mode. Also, take note of the new timeline in the edited object.

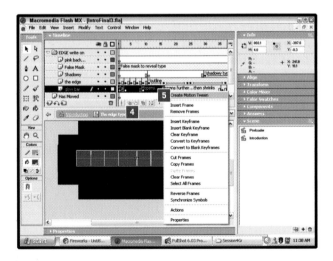

4. **Press down the Shift key and select the keyframes in Frames 1, 3, 9, and 16 in the glow bar layer.**
   When you need to select multiple keyframes, simply hold down the Shift key and click each one.

5. **Right-click (Control+click on the Macintosh) to open the Context menu and select Create Motion Tween.**
   In the movie, these tweens will have already been made, but were you starting from the beginning you would need to put in motion tweens in those keyframes. You can create tweened frames prior to putting in the objects that will be tweened.

6. **Drag the playhead to the first frame.**

7. **Select the instance of "The edge type."**

8. **In the Info panel, change the height to 4.**
   The instance will appear like a blue line on top of the underlying object. You can also make changes in the Properties panel that affect size.

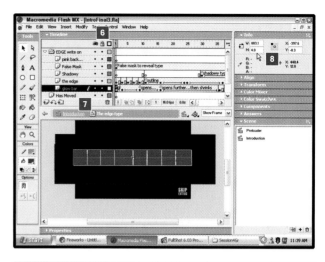

9. **Drag the playhead to Frame 3.**

10. **Change the value of H in the Info panel to 36.3.**
    A wider white glowing line appears. Also, as part of another movie clip in the background you can see the phrase THE EDGE beginning to rotate.

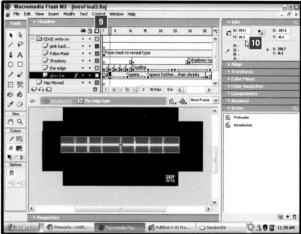

11. **Drag the playhead to Frame 9.**

12. **Change the value of H in the Info panel to 133.1.**
    A wider white glowing line appears. Also, as part of another movie clip in the background you can see the phrase THE EDGE beginning to rotate.

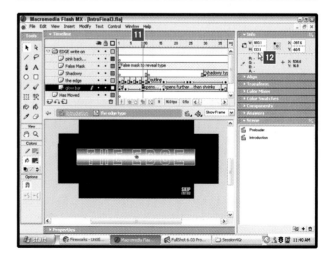

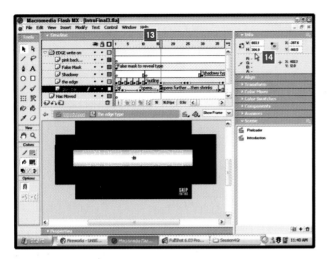

13. **Drag the playhead to Frame 16.**

14. **Change the value of H in the Info panel to 304.9.**

    Whoaaa! It should be clear that the object is not over 300 pixels wide. What's going on? The project has a false mask in the False Mask layer. Click the Eye column in the False Mask layer to hide the mask and to reveal how big the object really is. In further sessions, you will learn about masks and false masks.

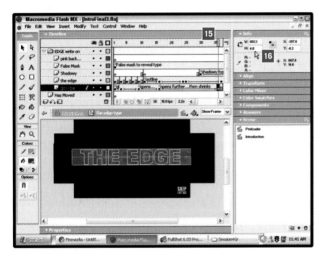

15. **Drag the playhead to Frame 36.**

16. **Change the value of H in the Info panel to 4.**

    Now the object shrinks to a line 4 pixels high. Then in two frames it disappears altogether because the layer runs out of frames. (If more frames were needed for the tween, a blank keyframe would have been used to get rid of the object.)

Tutorial

» Using Multiple Coordinated Tweens

Often when you play a Flash movie, more than one tween occurs at the same time. The tweens can be on the same timeline or on different timelines. When multiple tweens occur in a movie, you must take special care to coordinate them. In a single motion tween, you can simultaneously change the size, shape, and position of a symbol instance and one color element — tint, alpha, brightness, or advanced color combinations. Multiply that by more than a single tween, and you have your hands full. This next tutorial shows you how part of the introduction was designed using multiple coordinated tweens. You will also learn how to change the size of frames you are viewing.

In this tutorial, you will see the different steps where three objects are coordinated using changes in position and size. As the vertical value of two rectangle objects change and their Y positions change as well, a third object, a hand, moves upwards. The goal is to create a movie segment where the hand appears to shove the objects upward and compress them.

1. **Open the IntroFinal3.fla file and drag the playhead to Frame 362 of the Intro scene.**
   You will see three layers with motion tweens. These tweens are coordinated to create the effect you see.

2. **Click the Frame View Button and select Medium.**
   You will see the three tweened layers and the comments in the layers more clearly. Use the Frame View Button for expanding or contracting the size of the frames to get the view you need.

3. **Open the Info panel if it is not already open.**

4. **Click the first frame of the "To The" clip layer.**
   Note the H and Y positions of the objects in the Info panel.

5. **Hold down the Shift key and select the first frame in the Frame swap layer.**

6. **Selection Motion from the Tween popup menu in the Properties panel.**
   Both keyframes are set for Motion tweening. (In the complete movie, this step has been done already.)

7. **Move the playhead to Frame 363 and select the keyframe in the Sequential Multiple clips layer.**

8. **Use the Magnification popup menu to change the view to 25%.**
   You can now better see what the three tweens are coordinating. Also, in Frame 363, the hand and pencil instance first appears. Note the Y position of the hand in the Info panel.

9. **Select Motion from the Tween popup menu in the Properties panel.**

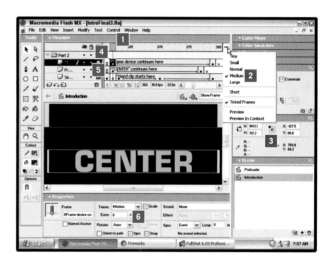

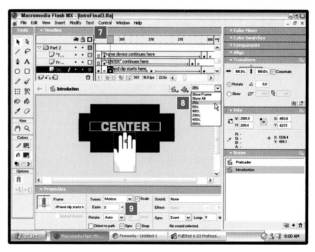

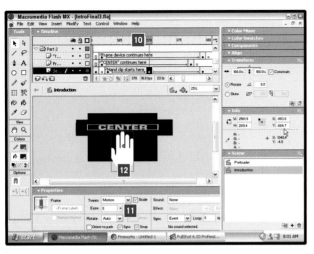

10. **Move the playhead to Frame 370 and select the keyframe in the Sequential Multiple clips layer.**

    Notice how the word CENTER on the stage has become narrower, and note the changed position of the "Y" value in the Info panel. The position of the hand and the vertical position and scale of the "Center" object must be coordinated so that it appears that the hand is pushing the object upward and at the same time making it narrower.

11. **Select Motion from the Tween popup menu in the Properties panel.**

12. **Select the hand object and, using the vertical arrow keys, reposition it so that it just touches the bottom of the CENTER block.**

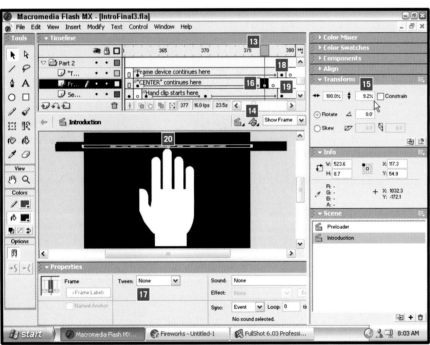

13. **Move the playhead to Frame 377 and select the keyframe in the Frame swap layer.**

14. **Change the magnification to Show Frame.**

15. **Open the Transform panel if it is not already open.**

    Note the percent of the object. By changing the percent of the vertical size of the object, you can make changes as a percent of the full size.

16. **Click Frame 377 in the "To The" clip layer and press F6 to insert a keyframe if one is not there.**

17. **Select Motion from the Tween popup menu in the Properties panel.**

18. **Press the period (.) on the keyboard to move the playhead one position to the right.**

    To move the playhead one to the right, use the period on your keyboard and press the comma (,) to move the playhead one to the left.

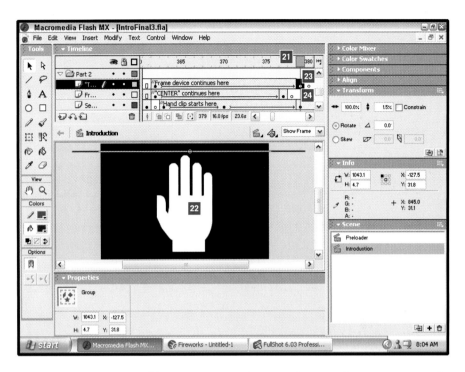

19. **Insert a blank keyframe if none is there.**
    The blank keyframe removes the objects from the blank keyframe to the next keyframe in the layer containing objects.

20. **Select the hand object and, using the vertical arrow keys, reposition it so that it just touches the bottom of the CENTER block.**

21. **Move the playhead to Frame 379 in the "To The" clip layer and press F6 to insert a keyframe if one is not there.**
    The remaining object is now a line.

22. **Select the hand object and, using the vertical arrow keys, reposition it so that it just touches the bottom of the line that represents the last vestiges of the black box object.**

23. **Press the period (.) on the keyboard to move the playhead one position to the right.**

24. **Insert a blank keyframe if none is there.**

Tutorial
» Changing Color Elements with Motion Tweens

Besides changing the alpha level, you can change the other color elements associated with Motion tweens — brightness, tint, and advanced color. The tweening process fills in all of the different degrees of color and brightness between two keyframes. To see how to use these other color elements in a Motion tween, this next tutorial uses logo.fla and adds some interesting characteristics that it does not originally have. You will see how you can add a whole new dimension to an existing movie.

1. **Open logo.fla, drag the playhead to Frame 20, and click Frame 20 in the Logo layer to select it.**

2. **Insert a keyframe in Frame 20 by pressing the F6 key.**

3. **Select the keyframe in Frame 20 and select Motion from the Tween popup menu in the Properties panel.**
   You will see a tweening arrow between Frames 20 and 36. This little tween is where you will test your movie using different color elements for objects.

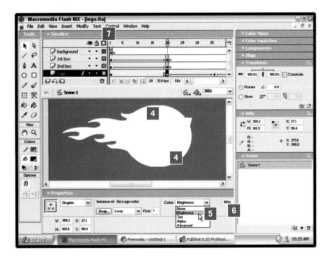

4. **Select the fireball object (Go Logo color instance).**

5. **Select Brightness from the Color popup menu in the Properties panel.**

6. **Change the Brightness level to 100%.**
   The fireball has turned white.

7. **Select Control→Play from the menu bar or press Enter/Return.**
   When you test it, it will fade in to its original color. Using a white background, you could create a fade in or fade out using the brightness attribute.

8. **Click on Frame 20 of the Logo layer to select it.**

9. **Choose Tint from the Color popup menu in the Properties panel.**
   When you select Tint or one of the other Color attributes, the previous one is negated. So you'll see that the Brightness attribute has disappeared.

10. **Set the color in the color well next to the popup menu to green.**

11. **Set the Tint Amount to 50%.**
    Using tint on top of existing colors gives different results depending on the underlying colors and the amount of tint used. The white outlines show a fuller green while the black and red undertones show different results. Using 100% Tint Amount over any colors wholly covers the existing colors.

12. **Repeat step 7.**
    The tint is tweened into the full original colors.

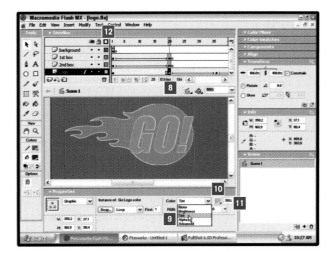

13. **Click Frame 20 of the Logo layer to select it.**

14. **Select the fireball object and select Advanced from the Color popup menu in the Properties panel.**

15. **Click the Settings button that appears once Advanced has been selected.**

16. **In the Advanced Effect dialog box, set all of the values on the left to 100%, and set the G value on the right to 255.**
    The background of the fireball object becomes yellow and the text a bright green. You may have noticed that when you first opened the Advanced Effect dialog box, the green tint at 50% is the same as advanced colors with RGB set to 50% and G set to 128.

17. **First drag the playhead right and left to see the interesting combination of colors the tween has, and then repeat step 7 to see the animated color change.**
    Frame 28 shows a dark green text and rich orange background.

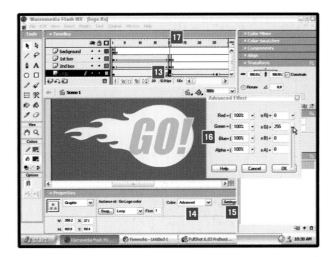

» Session Review

1. What are the different kinds of frames and what effect does each have on a movie? (See "Tutorial: Working with Frames.")

2. How are frames in a tween affected by changes in other keyframes on either end of the tween? (See "Tutorial: Creating Keyframe Changes.")

3. What are the two types of tweens and what objects are used with each? What attributes can be changed in different tweens? (See "Tutorial: Creating a Shape Tween.")

4. What is a "morph" and how do you create a morphing effect in Flash MX? (See "Tutorial: Making a Morph Using Shape Hints.")

5. What types of objects can be used with Motion tweens and what elements of the objects can be changed? (See "Tutorial: Creating a Motion Tween.")

6. Why is it important to place objects on different layers when creating multiple Motion tweens? (See "Tutorial: Using Motion Tweens on Multiple Layers.")

7. How do you create a Guide layer? What do you use a Guide layer for when creating movement along a path in a Motion tween? (See "Tutorial: Moving an Object Along a Path.")

8. How can you make fade in and fade out effects using Motion tweens and changes in an object's alpha level? (See "Tutorial: Using Alpha and Motion Tweens to Create Fades.")

9. What "shapes" can be changed in a Motion tween? What tools and panels are used when creating a change in a symbol instance's shape (including skew and scale)? (See "Tutorial: Altering Size with Motion Tweens.")

10. What happens when the brightness, tint, or advanced color of an instance is changed in a Motion tween? (See "Tutorial: Changing Color Elements with Motion Tweens.")

» Additional Projects

» As has been noted several times throughout the different sessions, the way to learn Flash MX is to experiment, and this first project should be a lot of fun for the sheer possibilities of experimentation. Set up two keyframes about 50 frames apart. In the first of the two keyframes, place a Motion tween. Create a simple Graphic symbol and place instances of the symbol in both keyframes. In the second keyframe, see how many changes you can make to the instance without changing the symbol. Hint: Use the Info and Transformation panels and the Color popup menu options for changing Brightness, Tint, Alpha, and Advanced Color.

» This next project is one for children to learn the alphabet, but you'll learn a lot about using Shape tweens and morphing. It's called the "Morphing Alphabet." The project's goal is to create an alphabet that morphs from one letter to another using Shape tweens. You use only a single layer with one tween following another on the timeline. Each letter of the alphabet is spaced 20 frames apart in a separate keyframe. Select all but the last keyframe and select Shape in the Tween popup menu. In each of the 26 keyframes, place a big (96 points) letter of the alphabet. Transform the text letters into shapes by selecting a letter and then selecting Modify→Break Apart or pressing Ctrl+B/Cmd+B. To improve the morphing effect from one letter to another add Shape Hints. (By the time you're finished with this project, you'll be able to put together just about any kind of interesting animated message you can imagine.)

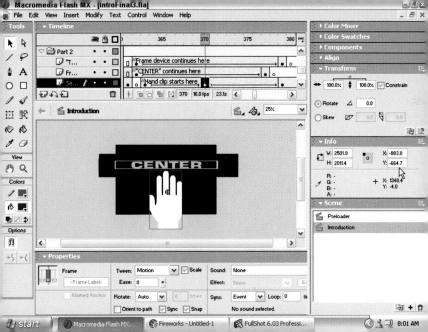

Text and Forms

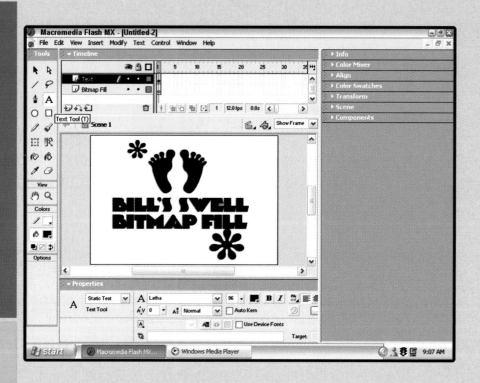

Session Introduction

This session is dedicated to text and text fields. Beginning with text based in your computer system's font collection, you can add special effects using Flash, and a good deal of this session shows some interesting effects. All of the effects are created as movie clips so that you can create them once and then use them in different movies. Furthermore, most of the special effects use text that has been broken into graphic shapes so that you can use the same techniques for them as you use for creating any other graphic animation.

You also can create a number of special effects using text blocks that have not been broken apart into graphic shapes. The best part is that your font information is embedded in SWF files. So if you want to use a specialized font, it means that you can do so even if the viewer's computer does not have that font. However, if your viewers don't have the font in their system, they will not see the same font. Therefore in the examples in this session, you learn how to create animated text movies using text blocks instead of graphic fonts.

Text fields have three formats: static, dynamic, and input. For the most part, you will be using static text to create animations. Static text is essentially printed words on the stage that you need for labels or animated banners. Dynamic text fields are used to receive text generated in a Flash MX movie or imported from an external text file or server-side script. Finally, input text fields are used as forms in Flash. The user can enter text into a dynamic text field.

TOOLS YOU'LL USE
Properties panel, Text tool, color panels, drawing tools

MATERIALS NEEDED
From the accompanying CD-ROM, you'll need the TypeTrixMenu.fla and contact.fla files.

TIME REQUIRED
120 minutes

SESSION OUTCOME
How to control text and create and use text fields

PROJECT PORTION
The "Fonts and Forms" in the Portfolio section

Tutorial
» Using the Text Properties Panel

This tutorial is part refresher and part introduction. By this point you've been involved in several different uses of the Text tool and different fonts. However, this tutorial takes a close look at the Text Properties panel itself, what all of the different options mean, and what happens when you use them. To save time later and to be aware of the different options you have available to you, take a little time now to run through this little review of the mighty Text Properties panel.

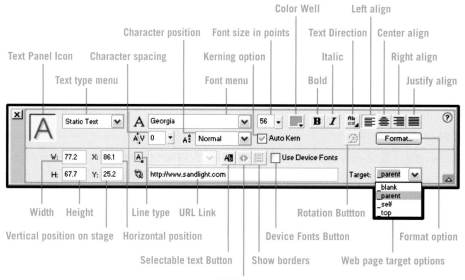

1. **Open the Properties panel and select the Text tool to activate the Text Properties panel.**
   As soon as it's activated, you will see the Text Panel icon.

2. **Select the type of text you want from the Text type menu.**
   Static Text is used for labels and for animated banners. Input Text allows users to enter text into the field, and Dynamic Text is used for creating fields where text messages can be dynamically added.

3. **Select a font from the popup Font Menu.**
   All of the fonts in your system will appear. You can choose any font you want, and its information is stored in the Flash MX SWF file. That means you don't have to worry about a viewer not having the font in her system.

4. **Select the Kerning option.**
   Font sets have special kerning information about how to space different characters horizontally. Depending on a character's

shape, a specific amount of space is placed between that character and the adjacent character. Text using kerning information generally looks better than text that does not. Moreover, you have no bandwidth "cost" associated with the kerning information. If you turn off the Auto Kern, you can set your own kerning.

5. **Select the text or the text box and use the Font Size slider to establish a font size.**
   Once you have written all of your text on the stage, use the pointer tool to select the text block and then change the text to best fit the stage and your design.

6. **Select the text block and choose a color from the Color Well (Color Box) swatches.**
   Using a color palette makes it easier to select the right color for your text.

7. **Select Bold and/or Italic fonts.**

   Depending on the size and type of font you're using, the results of either or both of these options will vary. Flash MX uses anti-aliasing to smooth the text. Essentially, it blurs the text, and if you add Italic or Bold styles to some fonts, especially very small ones, you can easily blur your text so that it is hard to read.

8. **Use the pointer tool to select the text box and select Text Direction→Vertical, Left to Right.**

   Your text block changes to a vertical alignment with each letter on top of the one below it.

9. **With the text still in the vertical position, click the Rotation Button.**

   The text now rotates on its side but is still vertically aligned.

10. **Press Ctrl+Z/Cmd+Z twice to return the text to the original position.**

11. **Select the text block with the pointer tool and press the Left, Center, Right, and Justify align buttons.**

    You will see the text shift its position depending on which alignment you use. Most body text is left aligned, but headers are generally centered aligned. You can line up numbers using right align as long as the decimal places are the same.

12. **Select the text block with the pointer tool and change the Width (W) and Height (H) values.**

    Unless you make proportional changes, the text becomes distorted. If you want to make a text block larger and keep the width and height proportional, use the Transform panel with the Constrain option selected instead of the Text Properties panel. When tweening text blocks, you can use the W/H values to create a smooth tween. However, two text blocks in keyframes will not tween font sizes — only text block sizes.

13. **Select the text block with the pointer tool and type the X (horizontal) and Y (vertical) positions on the stage.**

    You can type any value within the dimensions of the movie. When you want precision in placing text blocks, use the X and Y values rather than dragging the text blocks. Text blocks tween nicely from one position to another using the X/Y values to position the block.

14. **With the text block selected, open the Character spacing slider and drag it up and down.**

    You will see the text expand and contract. Unfortunately, you cannot tween character spacing. Instead, you will have to insert several keyframes and sequentially change the spacing to generate an animated spacing effect using text.

15. **Select a group of characters in a text block and in the Uniform Resource Locator (URL) link window, type a linking URL.**

    If you're familiar with links in HTML where underlined text indicates a link, you will find a similar connection in Flash MX. When you select text in a block and enter a URL, a dotted underline appears beneath the text associated with a link. The underline shows up only while you're editing the movie. So if you plan to include a link in your movie, be sure to make it clear that the text you want to be a link is clearly linked text. Changing the color of the text from non-linking text is one strategy.

16. **In the Target popup menu, select the target for your URL link or type the target name.**

    This particular popup menu is also a text box. You can choose either a general target provided in the popup menu by simply clicking it, or use the name for the target in a frameset. If you choose _blank, a new window appears leaving your movie in place while bringing up the linked page.

17. **Select the Text tool and, using a 24-point text, type 10th and H2O.**

18. **Select the th in 10th and select Superscript from the Character position popup menu, and then select the 2 in H2O and choose Subscript from the same menu.**

    Your text now reads 10th and H_2O. Rather than making separate text blocks for super- and subscripts, use the Character position menu to both change the position and size of the text. The size change is always relative to the size of the text in the text block.

19. **Select a text block and click the Selectable text button.**

    When your movie runs, the viewer can select the text in static and dynamic text blocks. (Input text blocks are always selectable.) If you have a block of text that you want the viewer to be able to cut and paste from your movie, for example, use the Selectable text option.

20. **Click the HTML button with a selected text block of dynamic text to preserve rich text formatting.**

    When you want to preserve any text formatting, such as that found in hyperlinks and forms with HTML tags (for example, `<a href="url">`), use this option.

21. **With either an input or dynamic text field selected, click the Show borders button.**

    With input text this option is especially important because it shows the user where to type text in input text fields. With dynamic text fields it shows the text block area. Generally, design considerations will dictate whether to use this option, but almost always you will need it with input text fields.

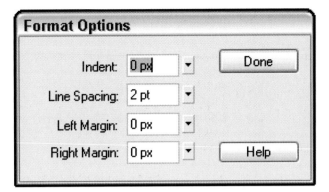

22. **With a text block selected choose the Device Fonts option.**
When you type text in Flash, a certain amount of font information is preserved in the SWF file to duplicate the font when
you use it in your movies. Naturally this adds file size to your
movie. If the font appearance is not important or file size is an
overriding concern, use this option. Instead of the font information being sent with your SWF file, your SWF file looks for
the closest font on the host system. Generally, the font will be
the generic sans serif, serif, or monospaced font. A small SWF
file of 768 bytes (less than 1KB!) is reduced to 194 bytes
when the Device Fonts option is selected. However, the saving
is only a one-time saving for a single font. The font information in the SWF file is the same whether using a lot of that
font or a little. Thus, a page full of a single font has the same
added "font weight" as a single line of a font. Moreover, you
can mix device fonts with regular fonts. For example, if you
have a large block of text with instructions, you can use a
fairly generic font like Arial or Times and have that block
option as device, and then use a special font for headers but
not use device fonts. One additional advantage of using device
fonts is that when using smaller fonts, device fonts provide a
more legible reading.

23. **Type some text on the stage and click the Format button on the
Text Properties panel.**
The Format Options dialog box opens.

24. **Type** 15 px **for Indent,** 20 pt **for Line Spacing, and** 20 px **for Left
Margin and Right Margin.**
You will see your text with 20 pixel margins around the text
block, a 15-pixel indent, and 20 points (not pixels) line spacing. This little formatting dialog box should not be overlooked
for getting your text blocks just like you want them.

Tutorial

» Creating Micro-Animations with Text

Now that you've had a guided tour of the Text Properties panel, it's the time to put it to work. This next tutorial shows you one of several different animated text effects from TypeTrixMenu.fla. All of the different type effects you will see are movie clips that are part of the larger movie with the menu. Each is treated as a separate movie to make it easier for you to see how to create the effect. (A larger extended movie, TypeTrix.fla, which containts all of the effects along with the artist's comments, is also available on the CD-ROM.) This first effect using text, though, is special because it is the only one that does not rely on text that has been filled with bitmap images or broken apart into shapes. It is pure text dancing around the stage for you.

1. **Open a new page in Flash MX and select black for the background color.**

2. **Select Modify→New Symbol or press Ctrl+F8/Cmd+F8.**
   You are now in the Symbol Editing Mode. You will build your movie from here so that it can be saved as a movie clip that you can use easily in other movies.

3. **Choose Movie Clip for behavior, type the name** EZ type clip, **and click OK.**

4. **Drag the playhead to Frame 164 and insert a new frame by clicking the frame and pressing the F5 key.**

5. **Select the Text tool, choose Arial from the font popup menu, and choose Static Text from the Text type menu.**
   Helvetica or _sans are acceptable substitutions. The plan is to use a font you will most likely have on your system.

6. **Use the Font size slider to create a 48 point font.**

7. **Select a dark yellow (FFCCOO) from the Color Well and type a capital** F.

8. **Move the playhead to Frame 4.**

9. **Press the F6 key to insert a new keyframe.**

10. **Type** R **next to the F.**

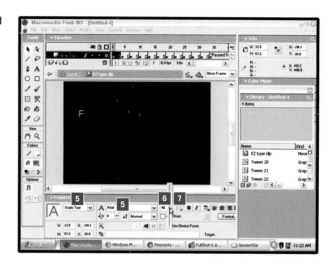

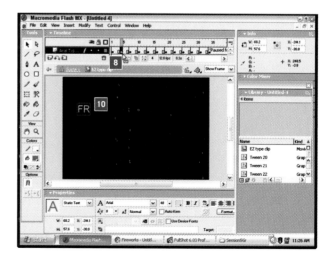

11. **Repeat steps 8–10 inserting a keyframe every third frame.**
    Insert keyframes in Frames 4, 7, 10, and so on.

12. **With each new keyframe, add a letter to the phrase FRAME BY FRAME until you have completed the entire phrase.**
    The last character in the phrase will be on Frame 34.

13. **Add keyframes to Frames 47–54 by selecting each frame and pressing the F6 key.**

14. **Select the text block.**

15. **Use the Character Spacing slider in Frame 48 to change the character spacing to 2.**

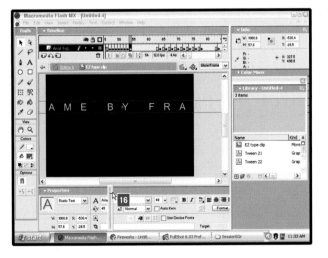

16. **Repeat step 15 in Frames 49–54 using the following spacing, respectively: 5, 9, 15, 22, 33, and 45.**
    By Frame 54, the text should be spread so that it is off the stage.

17. Insert a keyframe in Frame 64.

18. Move the playhead to Frame 66, insert a keyframe, and change the character spacing to 22.

19. Move the playhead to Frame 68, insert a keyframe, and change the character spacing to 7.

20. Move the playhead to Frame 72, insert a keyframe, and change the character size to 54.

21. **Repeat step 20 inserting keyframes every other frame beginning with Frame 74 and changing the character size to 60, 68, and 74, respectively, at the keyframes.**
First make a change in the keyframes and then add another keyframe to the right. (For a more gradual transition you can add a keyframe in Frame 70, and change the size to 50.)

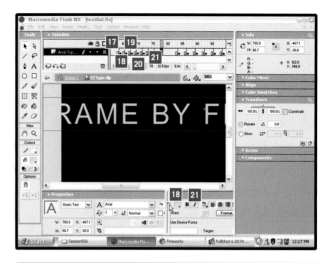

22. Move the playhead to frame 84 and insert a keyframe.

23. Select the text block and choose the color red from the Color Well.

24. Move the playhead to Frame 87.

25. Insert a keyframe, and change the color back to yellow.

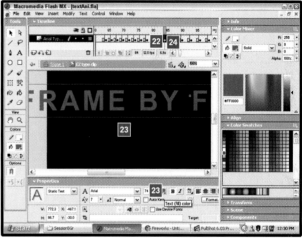

26. **Repeat steps 23–24 every third frame alternating the text colors between red and yellow up to frame 117.**
Frame 117 should be back to the golden yellow color you began with.

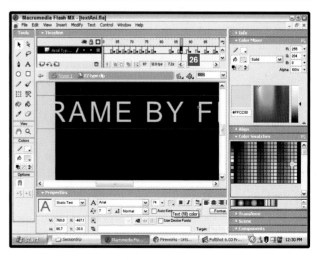

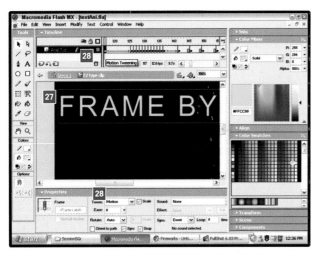

27. **Position the text block against the left side of the stage in Frame 117.**

28. **Select Frame 117 and choose Motion from the Tween popup menu.**

29. **Insert a keyframe in Frame 126 by selecting the frame and pressing the F6 key.**
    You should now see the tweening arrow and the blue background indicating a motion tween.

30. **Move the text block to the left off the stage.**
    Text blocks work well with motion tweens where the text blocks change position.

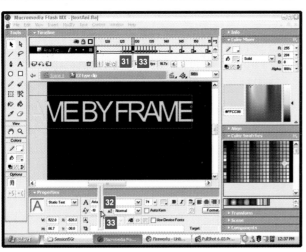

31. **Add a keyframe in Frame 127.**

32. **Select the text block and use the Character space slider to change the spacing to 1.**

33. **Repeat steps 31–32 for Frames 128–136 with the following respective character spacing: –5, –10, –21, –36, –36, –21, –10, –5, and 1.**
    The animated effect of this is an accordion squeeze with the text first compressing in on itself and then expanding out again.

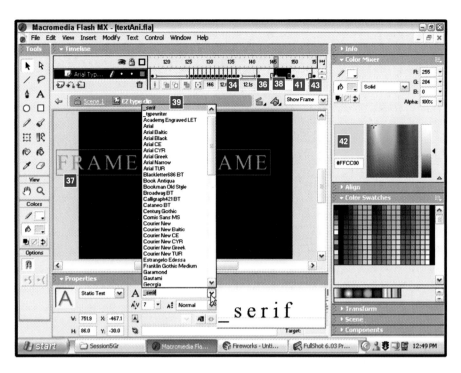

34. **Insert a keyframe in Frame 137 by selecting the frame and pressing the F6 key.**

35. **With Frame 137 selected, add a motion tween by selecting Motion from the Tween popup menu in the Properties panel.**

36. **Move the playhead to Frame 142 and insert a keyframe by pressing the F6 key.**

37. **Drag the text block to the right so that the first R is partially on the stage and partially off.**

38. **Select Frame 146 and insert a keyframe by pressing the F6 key.**

39. **Select the text block and choose the _serif font from the Font popup menu on the Properties panel.**

40. **Change the font color to an olive green (EODFE3).**

41. **Select Frame 150 and insert a keyframe by pressing the F6 key.**

42. **Change the font and color back to Arial and golden yellow.**

43. **Repeat steps 38–42 with frames 155, 159, and 164.**
    The effect is an alternating text type and color.

44. **Press the F9 key to open the Actions panel.**

45. **Click Frame 164 and in the left pane of the Actions panel select Actions→Movie Control→Stop. Click the plus (+) button above the right pane to add a** stop(); **action.**

46. **Click Frame 165 and press F7 to insert a blank keyframe.**
    Your movie is complete. Save it and take it out for a test drive.

Tutorial
» Transforming Text with Bitmapped Fills

One of the more interesting options available in Flash is the use of bitmap fills. A bitmap fill is like any other color fill in Flash, but instead of using a solid color, gradient, or radial, you use a bitmap image. The process is quite easy. First, you create the bitmap image using a graphic program like FreeHand, Illustrator, Photoshop, or Fireworks — any other handy graphic editing program will do just as well. Then, save the graphic as a bitmapped one such as JPEG, GIF, or BMP. (You can even create a bitmapped graphic using Flash MX by drawing a shape and then exporting it in a bitmapped format.) When you select the Bitmap option from the Color Mixer Fill Style popup menu, either you are shown a collection of bitmapped objects in the library or, if none are there, an Import to Library dialog box appears and you select one from your computer. Then when you select a shape, you can use the bitmap image as the fill just like filling any other object. (This tutorial uses an extra temporary layer to place the bitmapped graphic on the stage. You can use bitmapped images without having to go through this extra stage. It was included simply to help illustrate the bitmapped graphic that was used.)

However, because this session focuses on what you can do with text objects, this tutorial shows how to use bitmapped fills with text blocks that have been transformed into shape objects.

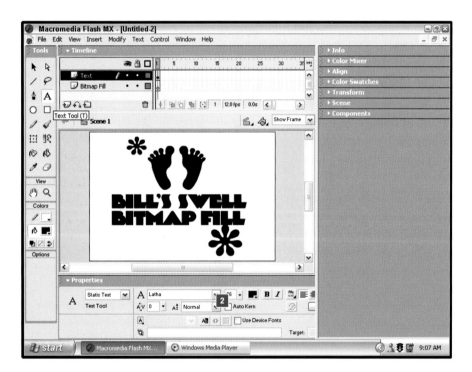

1. **Open a new file.**

2. **Choose any font you want, make it about 48–96 points in size and type on the stage.**
   The sample illustration uses a combination of Kobalt and some dingbats from a font called Love — a hippie 1960s font.

   Use large fonts and font sizes so there will be plenty of room for your bitmapped fill. The size of the font will depend on the font's shape.

3. Select the text blocks.

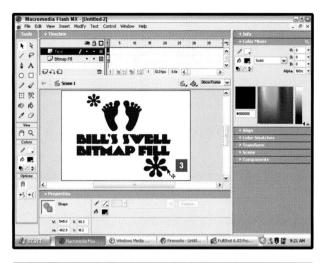

4. Select Modify→Break Apart from the menu bar or press Ctrl+B/Cmd+B twice.

First the text blocks are broken apart and then the individual letters are.

5. Add a layer and name it Bitmap Fill.

6. Create a graphic design and save it in JPG format.

Use any program you want to create the bitmap. Programs like Photoshop and Fireworks work fine as well as any other drawing program that allows you to save the graphic as a JPEG file.

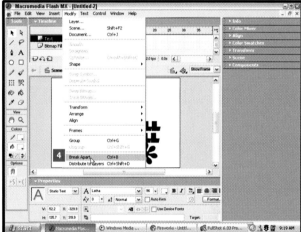

7. Select the first frame in the Bitmap layer and select File→Import to Library from the menu bar.

The graphic will appear in the library. You can import it directly to the layer by choosing Import instead of Import to Library.

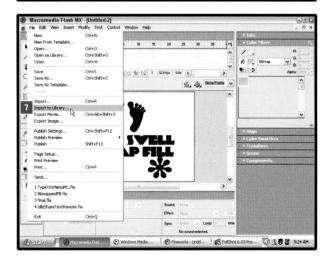

8. **In the Import dialog box, select the file you want to import and press the Open button.**

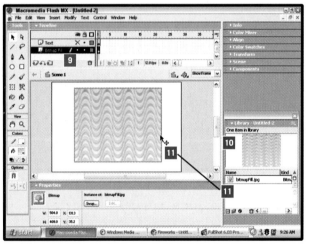

9. **Select the Bitmap Fill layer.**

10. **Open the Library panel by pressing Ctrl+L/Cmd+L.**

11. **Drag the image from the Library panel to the stage.**

12. **Click the Eye column for the Bitmap Fill layer.**
    This will get the bitmap out of the way for now while you work on the text.

13. **Click the first frame in the Text layer to select all of the broken apart text.**

14. **In the Color Mixer panel, select Bitmap in the Fill Style popup menu.**

15. **Click on the thumbnail image in the bottom pane of the Color Mixer panel.**
    Voila! Your text shapes are filled with your bitmapped pattern.

16. **Delete the Bitmap Fill layer.**
    Actually, you never needed the layer. It was placed in the example to help you better see the process. However, having an extra temporary layer can be handy when you're using bitmap fills.

Tutorial
» Blinking Cursor with Text Graphic Images

The first of several effects using graphic text is creating a blinking cursor that simulates the kind of reversing effect you get when you select text. You may have noticed that when you select a text character in Flash MX, the selection reverses the color of the text. For example, if you select a black set of characters, the selected characters reverse to white. Likewise, selected green text reverses to magenta. To simulate this effect, a blinking cursor reverses a red character to black. (Normally, red reverses to blue, but when you control the design, you can make it any color you want. In this case the designer wanted black.) The overall effect is one of a typewriter, Teletype, or word processor typing going on. It's a good attention-getter without being overbearing.

1. Open a new page, select black for the background color, and select Insert→New Symbol from the menu bar.

2. Choose Movie Clip for Behavior, name it cursor blink, and click OK. You are now in the Symbol Editing Mode.

3. Select the Rectangle tool, and draw a red rectangle with the dimensions W=32, H=4.

4. Click Frame 5 and press the F5 key to insert frames.

5. Click Frame 4 and press F7 to insert a blank keyframe. By having the rectangle appear for three frames and disappear for one frame, you create a blinking effect.

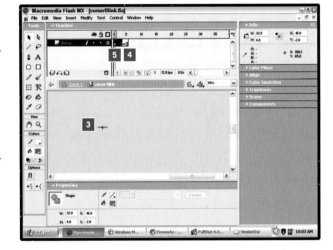

6. Click Scene 1 to return to the main timeline and select Insert→New Symbol from the menu bar.

7. Choose Movie Clip for Behavior, name it block cursor, and click OK. You're back in the Symbol Editing Mode.

8. Press Ctrl+L/Cmd+L to open the Library panel and drag an instance of the cursor to the stage.

9. Over the cursor blink instance, use the Rectangle tool to draw a W=30, H=42 red rectangle.

10. Select Layer 1 and press the Insert Layer button to add a new layer.

11. Rename the top layer Type and the Bottom Layer Cursor

12. Click Frame 101 on either layer and drag the pointer vertically so that both layers are selected and press the F5 key. Both layers should have frames out to Frame 101 now.

13. Insert a keyframe in Frame 28 of the Cursor layer.

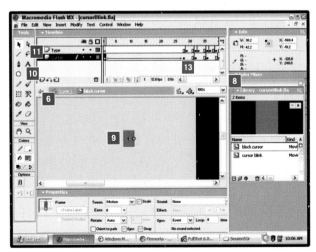

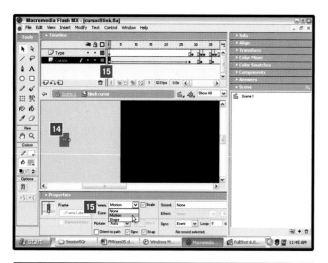

14. Select the block cursor object and drag it off the stage to the left.

15. Click the first frame of the Cursor layer and choose Motion from the Tween popup layer in the Properties panel.

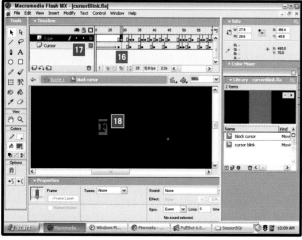

16. Insert a keyframe in Frame 29 of the Type layer by selecting the frame and pressing the F6 key.

17. Lock the Cursor layer, and type a black 42-point F directly on top of the red cursor.

18. Select the letter F and press Ctrl+B/Cmd+B or select Modify→Break Apart from the menu bar.

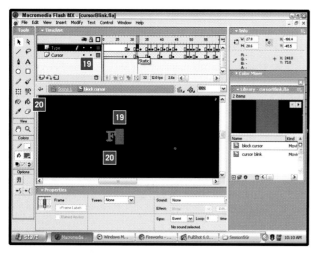

19. Unlock the Cursor layer and move the red rectangle and cursor blink objects to the right of the letter F.

   When moving the red rectangle and cursor blink objects, use the arrow keys instead of trying to drag them with the mouse. By selecting the objects and using the right arrow key, you can keep the objects on the same vertical line.

20. Use the Paint Bucket tool to change the fill color of F to red.

21. **Add a keyframe to Frame 33 in the Type layer and lock the Cursor layer.**

22. **Type a black letter I over the cursor block using the Text tool.**

23. **Select the I and press Ctrl+B/Cmd+B to break it apart.**

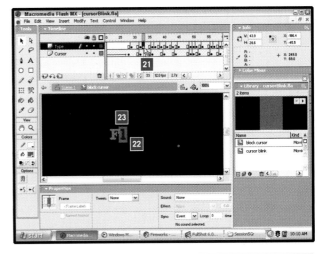

24. **Insert keyframes in both layers of Frame 36 and unlock the Cursor layer.**

25. **Move the red rectangle and cursor blink object to the right of the letter I.**

26. **Use the Paint Bucket tool to change the color of the letter I to red.**
This repeats the sequence used with the first letter of the phrase "Flash Write Ons" — "F." The rest of the movie is a repeat of that sequence.

27. **Repeat steps 21 to 26 to spell out "Flash Write Ons."**

28. **Insert a keyframe in both layers of Frame 80 by selecting the frames and pressing the F6 key.**

29. **Select Frame 80 in the Cursor layer, and choose Motion from the Tween popup menu in Properties panel.**

30. **Click Frame 100 in the Type layer and press the F6 key.**

31. **Open the Actions panel by pressing F9 and select the stop action from the Actions toolbox in the left pane.**
This step is optional; you can remove the stop action when you use the movie clip.

32. **Add a keyframe (press Ctrl+F6/Cmd+F6) to the Cursor Layer and a blank keyframe (press Ctrl+F7/Cmd+F7) in Frame 101.**

33. **Select Frame 101, and move the red rectangle and cursor blink object to the right of the stage.**

Tutorial
» Creating a Laser Effect with Graphic Text

This next effect is an interesting one because you do it backwards! You will learn how to begin with the "completed" side of an effect and progressively work backwards to the beginning. Artist Leslie Cabarga created this next graphic text effect by making a text block in an ending frame and then erasing parts of the broken-apart text block in descending keyframes.

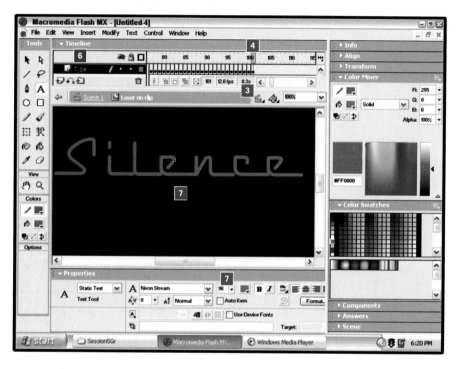

1. **Open a new page, select black for the background color, and select Insert→New Symbol from the menu bar.**

2. **Choose Movie Clip for Behavior, name it** Laser on clip, **and click OK.**
   You are now in the Symbol Editing Mode. You will be creating the entire movie as a movie clip and remain in the Symbol Editing Mode until the project is complete. Then you can place in it in a larger movie wherever you want.

3. **Select the Arrow tool, click Frame 101, and press the F5 key to insert a frame.**

4. **Click the first frame, hold down the Shift key and click Frame 101.**
   All of the frames between Frame 1 and Frame 101 are selected. If they are not, do it again until they are.

5. **Press the F6 key.**
   All of the frames between 1 and 101 are now keyframes.

6. **Rename the Layer** Type **and then click Frame 101 to select it.**

7. **Select the Text tool, and in a 96-point sans-serif font, type** Silence.
   The example uses a neon font called Neon Stream from flash-fonts.com. One of the other effects you will see is a sputtering neon that seem to be the hallmark of cheap motels.

8. **Click the text block and press Ctrl+B/Cmd+B twice to break it apart.**

   Now your text is a graphic shape after both the block of text is broken apart and the individual letters are as well.

9. **Click Frame 101 to select the entire frame.**

10. **Select Edit→Copy from the menu bar or press Ctrl+C/Cmd+C.**

11. **Click Frame 100 and then select Edit→Paste in Place.**

12. **Select the Eraser tool from the Toolbox and erase the tip of the last "e" in Silence.**

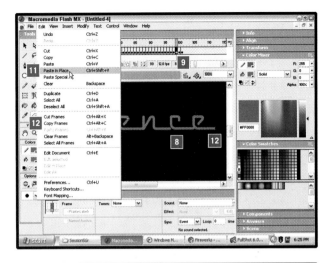

13. **Continue cutting and pasting each new section of the word Silence, erasing a little with each frame.**

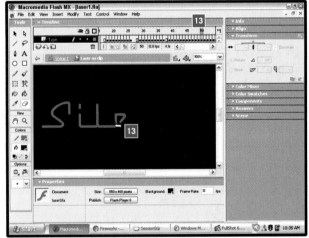

14. **When you reach Frame 2, erase the last remnants of Silence.**

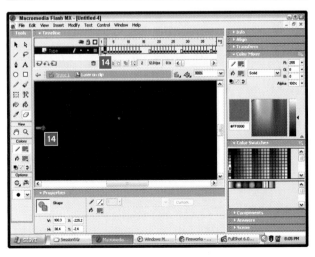

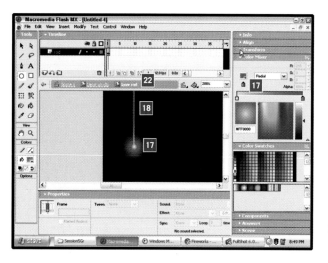

15. **Click the Insert Layer button and drag the new layer beneath the Type layers.**

16. **Rename the layer** Laser Line **and click the first frame of the layer.**

17. **Use the Oval tool to draw a circle with a radial fill consisting of a yellow center and red outer gradient.**

18. **Use the Line tool to draw a 2.25 point stroke red line that's 574 pixels in length.**

19. **Drag the circle to the bottom of the red line.**

20. **Select both drawings and then select Modify→Group from the menu bar or press Ctrl+G/Cmd+G.**
    Grouping drawings makes them easier to work with.

21. **Select the group and press the F8 key to open the Convert to Symbol dialog box.**

22. **Choose Movie Clip for Behavior,** laser rod **for the name, and click OK.**
    The new movie clip is inside the Laser on clip MC.

23. **Click Frame 1 in the Laser Line layer, and position the laser rod object at the forward part of the first part of the letter "S" in Silence.**
    The laser rod is supposed to appear to be burning in the characters, and so it should lead the letters being etched.

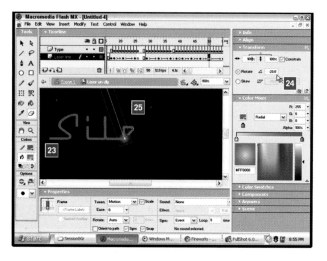

24. **Open the Transform panel, and select the laser rod movie clip and change the angle to –2 in the Rotate window.**
    The rotation change makes the laser source appear to be a single point. For example, by Frame 50, the angle should be about –20.

25. **Repeat steps 23–24, pressing the F6 key to insert keyframes, and through the movie increase the angle of rotation with each new keyframe.**
    When you encounter a straight line in the characters, you can use a Motion tween to move the laser rod object between keyframes.

26. **In Frame 99, place the laser rod object at the end of the word Silence.**

27. **Use the Transform panel to set the rotation to –37.**

28. **Click Frame 101 of the Laser line layer and press the F6 key to insert a keyframe.**

29. **Select the laser rod object and then press Ctrl+X/Cmd+X to delete the laser rod.**

30. **Use the Line tool to draw a 2.25 stroke red line angled above the last segment of the last "e" in Silence.**

    The laser beam is still visible but the "burning arc" from etching the word Silence is gone.

31. **Insert keyframes in Frames 103–105, and reduce the size of the line until it is gone at Frame 105.**

    The laser beam appears to recede back to its source.

Gallery

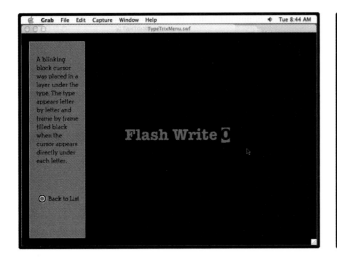

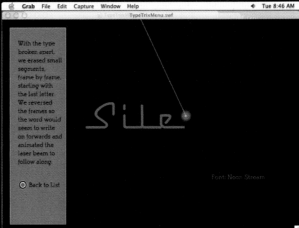

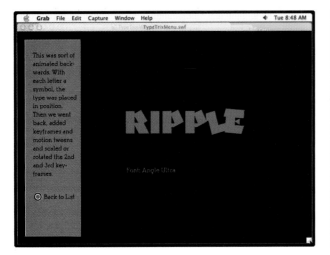

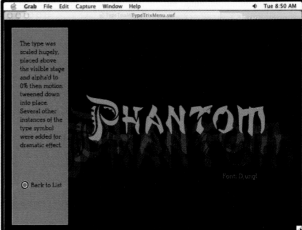

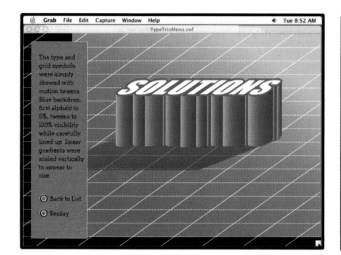

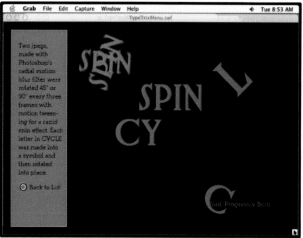

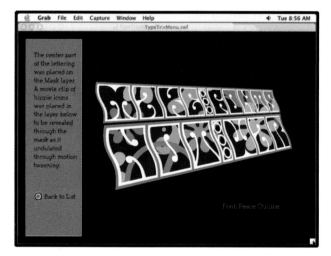

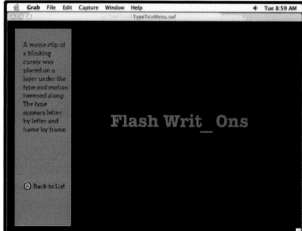

Tutorial
» Working with Input and Dynamic Text Fields

Every Web site needs a good contact page. The one provided uses one of the most important and overlooked features of Flash MX — the ability to handle dynamic text in both Input and Dynamic text fields. Static text fields do not change in the course of a Flash movie, but both Input and Dynamic text fields do. Input text fields accept typed text by the user who is viewing the movie. Dynamic text fields can have their contents changed in the course of a Flash movie by an action initiated by ActionScript. We're getting just a little bit ahead of ourselves with this movie because you will need to understand some ActionScript that is discussed in Session 10. Here, however, we'll keep the code simple. Also, this movie shows how to use Flash MX's new UI components, and they require ActionScript as well; so we'll be tickling two birds at the same time. (I don't like killing birds!)

The next movie contains yet another trick with text. As you saw elsewhere in this session, you can use bitmapped images as fills for graphic text. However, you can also create masklike overlays by cutting out text graphic fills revealing an underlying pattern. First, though, look at the use of Dynamic and Input text fields.

1. **Open the movie contact.fla.**

2. **Test the movie by pressing Ctrl+Enter/Cmd+Return.**

3. **When the movie opens, fill in all of the areas with white backgrounds.**

4. **Press the button marked Press to Send.**

   A message appears when you press the button. The message is in a Dynamic text field. All of the areas where you typed in text are Input text fields. A little ActionScript takes the first name of the user and sends it to the Dynamic text field when the UI component button is pressed. The ActionScript for the UI component is associated with the first frame of the top layer. This overview will help you understand creating the rest of the tutorial.

5. Open a new movie by selecting File→New from the menu bar.

6. Click the stage and in the Properties panel set the background color to black and the size to 750 X 500 pixels.

7. Press the Insert Layer button twice to add two new layers.

8. Rename the layers, from top to bottom, Nav Bar, Text Fields, and Background.

9. Select the Background layer, the Rectangle tool, a blue fill color #6633FF, and no color for the stroke from the Properties panel.

10. Draw a rectangle with the dimensions W=487, H=417.

11. Bottom-align the rectangle with the stage, in the horizontal middle of the stage using the Align tool.

12. Draw a second rectangle using green #01C201 with dimensions W=166, H=96 and X=414, Y=180.

The second rectangle will serve as a backdrop to the Dynamic text field and a reference point for the input fields to the left and below it.

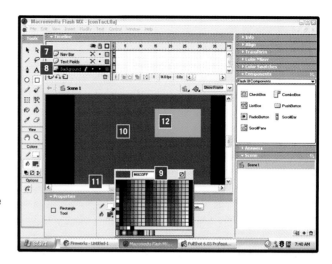

13. Lock the Background layer and select the Text tool.

14. Choose Input Text from the Text Type popup menu in the Properties panel, click the Show Border Around Text option, and click the stage.

The default width of an Input text field is 104 pixels. That size is fine.

15. With the text field selected, position it at X=144, Y=185 using the X and Y windows in the Properties panel.

16. Type the text fname in the Instance Name window below the popup menu showing Input text and select an 11-point black Verdana font.

fname (for first name) is the Input Text field object's name. Providing instance names for text fields is new to Flash MX. The variable associated with any text field's instance name is referenced as a property called text. In the ActionScript further on in this tutorial, you will see a reference to fname.text. That reference is to this first Input text field.

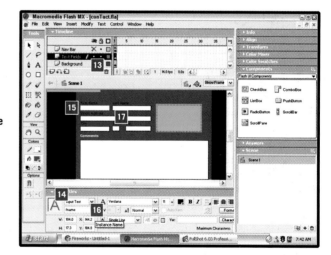

17. Repeat steps 14 to 16 for input fields for last name (lname), address (address), city (city), state (state), and ZIP (zip).

The names in quotations are the instance names to be used with each of the input fields.

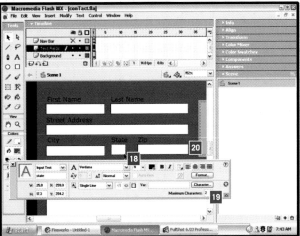

18. **Select the Input text field for State.**

19. **Type** 2 **in the Maximum Characters box.**
    By typing the maximum number of characters, the user cannot type more characters than you may want for a particular field.

20. **Repeat steps 18 and 19, but select the ZIP text field and 5 for the Maximum Characters window.**

21. **Use the Text tool to create an Input Text field near the bottom center of the stage.**

22. **Select Multiline from the Line type popup menu in the Properties panel.**

23. **Type the word** Comments **in the Instance name text box below the Text type popup menu.**

24. **Position the text field at X=150 and Y=315.**

25. **Drag the lower-right corner to size the text field to W=425, H=120.**

<NOTE>
Do not use the text boxes to establish the size of the text field. Doing so causes the type to be distorted. Only use the square pull tab in the lower-right corner to change the size, and then read the size in the W and H value boxes in the Properties or Info panels. Changing text fields using the values in the W/H boxes can be used in tweening text blocks from one size to another, but they are a disaster to use when you want to establish a text field using the font sizes established in the Font Size box.

26. Lock the Background layer, and in the Text Fields layer, use the Text tool to create a text field over the green rectangle.

27. Choose Dynamic Text from the Text type popup menu in the Properties panel, and use the name reformat for the instance name.

28. Change the font color to white by selecting the white swatch in the popup color well in the Properties panel.

29. Deselect Show Border Around Text option.

30. Select Multiline from the Line type popup menu in the Properties panel.

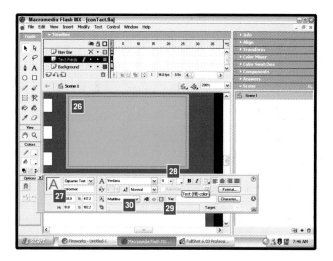

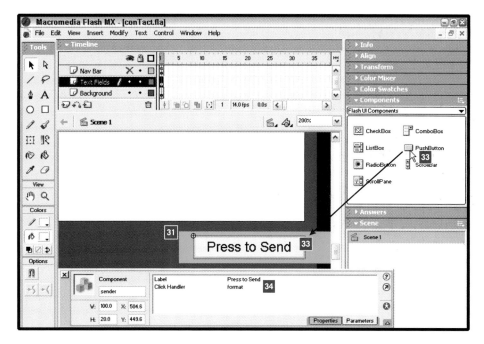

31. Unlock the Background layer and draw a green #01C201 rectangle with the dimensions W=262 and H=28 positioned at X=292, Y=446.

The rectangle should be beneath the lower-right corner of the comments overlapping the blue rectangle and black background of the stage.

32. Lock the Background layer and select Window→Components to open the Components panel.

33. Select the Text Fields layer and from the Components panel drag an instance of the PushButton UI component positioned on top of the green rectangle beneath the comments text field.

The Properties panel shows the label PushButton and beneath Label you will see Click Handler. If you don't see that, click the Parameters button in the lower-right corner of the Component panel.

34. Click the label "PushButton" and rename it "Press to Send" and beneath "Press to Send" type the word format.

The Click handler named "format" will be added in ActionScript in the Actions panel.

Tutorial
» Moving Text to Dynamic Text Fields

The last tutorial for this session continues what was started in the previous tutorial. Here, you will write the magic script that makes the materials entered by the user appear in a different part of the stage. The point of doing this is more to demonstrate how text in input fields can be passed to other places. As you become more experienced, you will find that the text can be moved into a database or into middleware that can send it to another computer. The final part of the tutorial places the colorful logo into place.

35. Click the first frame of the Nav Bar layer and press the F9 key to open the Actions panel.

36. From the View Options popup menu in the upper-right corner of the Actions panel, select Expert Mode.

37. Type the following script:

```
function format() {
    _root.reformat.text=fname.text + ", " +
newline + "Thanks for your comments."
}
```

The second line of the code should be one continuous line without using carriage returns (pressing Enter or Return). The Dynamic text field named reformat will be sent whatever is in the Input text box with the instance name of fname.

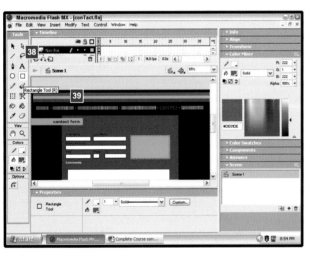

38. Lock the Text Fields layer and Background layers and select the Nav Bar layer.

39. Use the Rectangle tool to draw three parallel colored bars across the top of the stage using pink (#DE01DE), green (#01C201), and blue (#6633FF).

The heights of each rectangle will vary. The blue will be H=12.9, green H=12.5, and pink H=12.6. Use the H window in the Properties or Info panel to get the size right.

40. Select all three rectangles and select Modify→Group to create a group.

You will find grouping drawings has the advantage of keeping them separate from other drawings on top of them in the same layer.

41. Use the Rectangle tool to draw a black rectangle that completely covers the three colored rectangles.

42. Using a 54-point sans-serif font, type the words FLASH DESIGN CENTER over the black rectangle covering the colored rectangles.

The color of the font is not important other than you don't want a black font that will disappear when you type over the black rectangle. I used a red font.

<TIP>

When you are writing or drawing over another drawing, you may find it easier to draw or type off the stage and then drag the text block or shape over the existing shape.

43. Select the text block and press Ctrl+B/Cmd+B twice to break apart the text block.

Be sure to break up the text block twice so that the text is a graphic shape.

44. Select the Ink Bottle tool and white from the color well and then click each of the graphic letters so that they all have a white outline.

Be sure to click the interior line areas as well, such as the interior loop in the D.

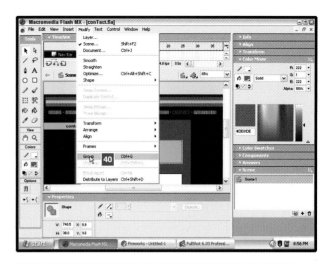

45. Select the Arrow tool and click each fill area of the letters and then press Ctrl+X/Cmd+X to delete the fill areas.

As soon as you delete the fill area, you will see the colored strips behind each letter. When you place an ungrouped shape on another shape they fuse. So, when you turned the text into graphics, they fused with the black background rectangle covering the grouped colored band of rectangles beneath. Thus, when the fill areas of the letters were deleted, they deleted the portions of the black underlying rectangle.

46. Use the Text tool with Static text to label the different input text fields.

Also add a green rectangle near the top of the blue rectangle and type the label "contact form." The menu bar is discussed in another session.

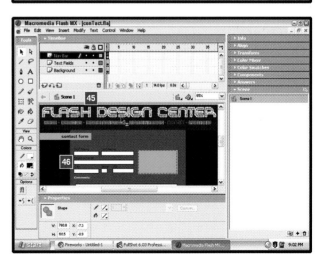

> **191**

» Session Review

This session covers text used in animation, as information labels, and as an animated object. Both text blocks and broken apart graphic text can be animated in many different ways.

1. How do you change the spacing between characters in a text block in the Properties panel? (See "Tutorial: Using the Text Properties Panel.")

2. How do you rotate text blocks using the Properties panel? How many different elements can be rotated? (See "Tutorial: Using the Text Properties Panel.")

3. How can text be linked to a URL and how do you designate a target at the URL? (See "Tutorial: Using the Text Properties Panel.")

4. What text formatting options are available in the Format dialog box? How do you open the Format dialog box? (See "Tutorial: Using the Text Properties Panel.")

5. Because you cannot use tweening with character spacing, how do you animate different character spacing effects using text blocks? (See "Tutorial: Creating Micro-Animations with Text.")

6. What has to be done to motion tween and animate changes in the size of a text block? (See "Tutorial: Creating Micro-Animations with Text.")

7. How can text be filled with bitmapped images? (See "Tutorial: Transforming Text with Bitmapped Fills.")

8. In creating a "blinking cursor" using broken apart text, how was it possible to reverse the color of the individual characters as the cursor passed over them to make them look like selected text? (See "Tutorial: Blinking Cursor with Text Graphic Images.")

9. What technique was used with the laser "etching" to animate the forward animated "drawing" of the text? (See "Tutorial: Creating a Laser Effect with Graphic Text.")

10. How was the "laser beam" created and animated to appear to etch the text into the page? (See "Tutorial: Creating a Laser Effect with Graphic Text.")

11. What are the different types of text fields and what is each used for? (See "Tutorial: Working with Input and Dynamic Text Fields.")

12. How is text changed dynamically in Dynamic and Input text fields? (See Tutorial: "Working with Input and Dynamic Text Fields.")

» Additional Projects

The following is a list of projects that relate to this session and can help you refine your expertise in working with text in Flash MX.

» Look at the different examples in the Gallery section and try recreating them. (Use the examples on the CD-ROM to help you.)

» Take different techniques from this session and re-combine them to create your own special effects with text animation.

» Animate graphic text with bitmapped fills.

» Take two very different font shapes, such as a fancy display font like Neon Stream and another such as Times. Break them apart and then, using Shape tweens, morph one of the fonts into the other. Begin with two keyframes. In one keyframe type one text block, and in the other keyframe, type the other. Break them both apart, and then simply select Shape from the Tween popup menu in the Properties panel.

» Place several UI Component push buttons on the stage, change the function names for each one, and give each one a different label. Then, using the script in the tutorial "Working with Input and Dynamic Text Fields," using unique function names for each push button, have different messages appear in a dynamic text field.

Macromedia Flash MX - [conTact.swf]

File Edit View Control Debug Window Help

FLASH DESIGN CENTER

HOME · ABOUT US · ANIMATION STUDIO · FONTS & FORMS · CONTACT · PORTFOLIO

contact form

First Name
Bill

Last Name
Sanders

Bill,
Thanks for your comments.

Street Address
123 Flash Design Center Drive

City
Bloomfield

State
CT

Zip
06002

Comments

These comments can be placed into a database, an email or analyzed by middleware and automatically send a reply to the user. However, you need to use more advanced programming to do so.

Press to Send

start

Fireworks - Untitl...

Macromedia Flas...

FullShot 6.03 Pro...

Session5Gr

8:59 AM

Session 6

Enhanced Animations

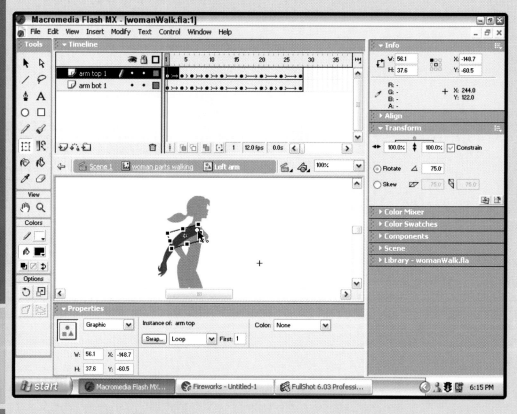

Tutorial: **Breaking Down Complex Projects into Simple Steps**

Tutorial: **Layers and Independent Motion of a Compound Object**

Tutorial: **Multiple Modifications of Movie Clips**

Tutorial: **Moving and Changing Movie Clips**

Tutorial: **Replicating Human Motion**

Tutorial: **Creating Animated Characters**

Tutorial: **Building a Background**

Tutorial: **Using Masks**

Tutorial: **Multiple Tweens and Masks**

Session Introduction

This session goes to the next level of sophistication in Flash MX, where actions take place not only on different layers, but in different scenes and even in different timelines in movie clips (MCs).

As Flash MX movies become more complex, they also increase the realm of possibilities for designers. Because of the larger number of objects, the interaction between them requires planning and organization at the outset. In most respects, you organize a Flash movie as you would organize any movie.

The first step is to create a story and then a script that breaks the story into discreet parts to be created with Flash. Once the script is prepared, you need a storyboard to provide a visual aid to see all of the parts of the story in sequence. Using the storyboard as a guide, compile a list of all of the graphic and textual elements that are needed for each page of the storyboard. Build each of the objects. The drawings you need may be done in FreeHand, Illustrator, Fireworks, Photoshop, or some other drawing program, and so each of those needs to be created and then imported into Flash. Once you have all the objects in Flash, you need to prepare them in the format you plan to use for each. The final step is to put the objects where they belong in the movie. If everything is organized, the job becomes a matter of following the script using the appropriate parts. Not only does this save a considerable amount of time, the time you do spend on the project is used more effectively. If you need to make changes, you can see where the changes will have a ripple effect and make the necessary adjustments to those areas as well. A little planning up front saves a great deal of time.

TOOLS YOU USE
Properties panel, Text tool, color panels, drawing tools

CD-ROM FILES NEEDED
From the accompanying CD-ROM you'll need the TypeTrixMenu.fla, IntroFinal3.fla, and animation.fla files.

TIME REQUIRED
120 minutes

SESSION OUTCOME
How to coordinate the different parts of a Flash Movie

PROJECT PORTION
All of the Movie Clip objects and Masks

Tutorial
» Breaking Down Complex Projects into Simple Steps

This tutorial takes the multiple graphics and objects in the movie introduction and shows how to break them down into component parts. Then it explains how to reconstruct them as part of the Introduction scene in the IntroFinal3.fla movie file. This deconstruction shows you how to isolate different movie elements, take them apart and see what makes them tick. At the bedrock level of the objects is some kind of drawing or shape. The shapes are either made in Flash MX or imported bitmapped objects.

1. **Open IntroFinal3.fla.**

2. **Press Ctrl+L/Cmd+L to open the Library panel.**

3. **Select File→New to open a new file.**
   Even though you open a new file, the Library panel remains on the stage or in the dock. However, the Library panel for IntroFinal3.fla is minimized, and so you have to click the arrow on the minimized panel to open it. Also, IntroFinal3.fla remains open.

4. **Select BG moving from the IntroFinal3.fla Library and drag it to the stage.**
   Now that the object is isolated, you can see in the new file that the graphic object contains a bitmapped object.

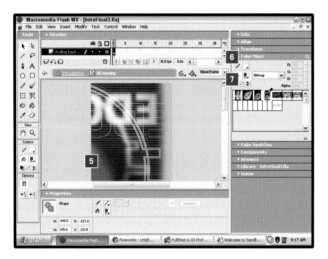

5. **Double-click the object on the stage to enter the Symbol-Editing Mode.**

6. **Open the Color Mixer panel.**

7. **Select Bitmap from the Fill Color popup menu.**
   You see all of the bitmapped images in the movie. Because the Library panel from the larger movie is still available in the dock, all of the bitmapped images in the movie are displayed in the window below the Fill Color popup menu. As you can see, the BG Moving graphic symbol is made up of a single bitmapped image. By creating a symbol out of it, not only can the designer use it multiple times with no additional bandwidth cost, but he also can use Motion tweens to move it without morphing distortions. Likewise, a bitmapped graphic in a graphic symbol can be changed dynamically using coloring changes associated with symbols—tint, alpha, brightness, or advanced color.

8. **Select Window→IntroFinal3.fla.**
   You have to scroll to the bottom of the Window menu.

9. **Select the White lines layer.**

10. **Drag the playhead to Frame 54 and click the frame.**

11. **Click the white line at the top of the object on the stage.**
    You see that the Properties panel indicates that the object is a Group. The comment indicates that a second white line and false mask make up the group. The false mask is a rectangle that has a changing alpha level.

Tutorial

» Layers and Independent Motion of a Compound Object

One of the key elements of understanding effective Flash MX movies is understanding how independent timelines work. In this tutorial, you see a very simple movie that is part of a more complex one. Once the movie is complete, it is placed in a corner of a larger movie and is one of the sideshows of the main event running on the main timeline. However, the exact same techniques for creating a movie on the main timeline are used with movie clips that are placed within other movie clips or on the main timeline. At the same time, you see how five independent objects are animated on four different layers.

1. **Select Open→IntroFinal3.fla.**

2. **Press Ctrl+L/Cmd+L to open the Library panel.**

3. **Select File→New from the menu bar.**

4. **Open the IntroFinal3.fla Library and drag an instance of the movie clip sound bars to the stage.**

5. **Click the stage and select Black for the Background color in the Properties panel.**

6. **Double-click the instance on the stage to enter the Symbol-Editing Mode.**
   As soon as you enter the Symbol-Editing Mode you see five layers with a series of keyframes. Note the layer named Top & Bottom. Two different rectangles are controlled by the one layer. When using individual keyframes to create changes, having all objects on a different layer is not as important as it is for tweened materials. Nevertheless, having separate layers for each object is a good practice.

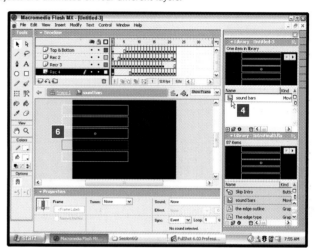

7. **Drag the playhead to Frame 16.**
   You can see how the designer changed the sizes of the rectangles.

8. **Select any of the rectangles.**

9. **In the Properties panel, change the W value.**
   When you change the W value, the rectangle's width changes.

10. **Move the playhead to Frame 20.**
    Note how the rectangles have changed.

11. **Select Control→Loop Playback.**

12. **Press Enter/Return.**
    You can see the in-and-out effect of the rectangles in the movie clip. To re-create the clip, all you have to do is to add a new keyframe at every frame and change the W (width) of the rectangles. You can make the changes sequentially so that each rectangle has a tweening effect of moving in and out, or you can make random width changes within the limits of the maximum rectangle size for a different effect. In this movie clip, the designer used a sequential movement.

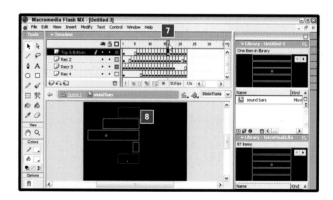

Tutorial
» Multiple Modifications of Movie Clips

The main value of creating symbols from drawings is that instances of the same symbol can be used more than once and in different configurations. In this tutorial, you see how a simple movie clip of a moving rectangle is used in two very different instances. One instance is magnified almost five times and rotated in a positive direction. The other instance of the same symbol is left at its original size and rotated with a negative value. The result is the appearance of two different-looking animated objects adding an abstract motion graphic to the movie.

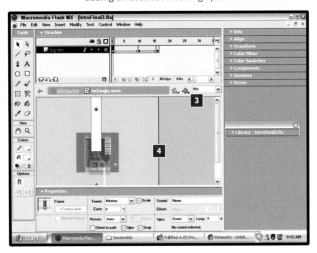

1. **Select Open→IntroFinal3.fla and select the Introduction scene.**

2. **Drag the playhead to Frame 65 and click on the frame in the Vertical rectangles layer.**

3. **Set the magnification to 15%.**
   You see a larger rectangle extending up over the top of the stage and a smaller one extending downwards and below.

4. **Double-click either of the two white vertical rectangles.**
   You might be surprised to find that both go to an identical timeline in Symbol-Editing Mode. If you select the larger of the two rectangles on the main timeline and open the Transform panel, you see it is magnified to 465%. You also see that it has been rotated 90°.

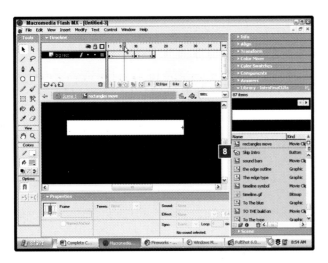

5. **Press Ctrl+L/Cmd+L to open the Library panel.**

6. **Select File→New from the menu bar.**

7. **Select Black from the Background color well on the Properties panel.**

8. **Drag an instance of the "rectangles move" Movie clip from the IntroFinal3.fla Library panel to the stage.**
   On the stage, you see a horizontal rectangle. However, on the main timeline, both rectangles were vertical. The larger of the two was rotated +90° and the smaller one to −90°. Regardless of rotation angle, the movie clip operates on the basis of the movie clip's own timeline.

Tutorial

» Moving and Changing Movie Clips

In the same vein as the previous tutorial, you see a second instance of the same movie examined in a previous tutorial in this session. (See "Tutorial: Breaking Down Complex Projects into Simple Steps.") You see it is introduced in the introductory movie as a second bitmap. However, it is the same bitmap, but the designer has added a blue tint and rotated it 180° which makes it appear as a reverse mirror image of the original. The good news is that the designer was able to use the same symbol and not add to the weight of the design.

1. **Select Open→IntroFinal3.fla.**

2. **Set the magnification to 15%.**

3. **Open the Transform and Properties panel.**

4. **Drag the playhead to Frame 71 and click the frame in the Background moving layer.**

   In the Transform panel, you would set the Rotate value to 180, flipping the movie clip on its head (BG moving). In the Properties panel, the Color menu has selected Tint and blue (#E0DFE3) and the alpha to 58%. The result is an entirely different looking object. At this point, you would also add a Motion tween to Frame 71 in the Background moving layer.

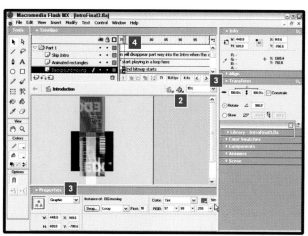

5. **Drag the playhead to Frame 100.**

   At this point, the instance has slid over the other instance of the same symbol (BG moving). Note on the right side of the instance, you can see the rectangles discussed in a previous tutorial in this session. (See "Tutorial: Layers and Independent Motion of a Compound Object.")

6. **Drag the playhead to Frame 123.**

   By the time the tween is complete, the instance has moved to the middle of the stage. However, at the same time, much more has been going on. On the Animated rectangles layer, several different rectangles have come on the stage while the motion tween was in progress. A dark pink rectangle with 60% alpha has screened over the blue tinted instance, adding to the coordinated effect of multiple change. However, when looking at any one of the objects on the different layers, you find relatively simple instances being moved.

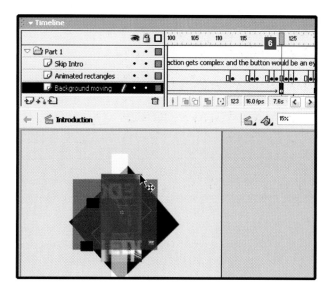

Tutorial
» Replicating Human Motion

The study of human motion still used in animation today can be traced back to an 1872 argument between Leland Stanford and a fellow horse-breeding enthusiast over whether all four hooves of a trotting horse ever left the ground simultaneously. (Mr. Stanford is best known as founder of Stanford University.) To settle the argument, Stanford hired a photographer named Eadweard Muybridge to photograph his horses in motion hoping to capture the horse completely off the ground during a trot. Because movie cameras had not been invented at the time, Muybridge rigged a series of cameras that were sequentially triggered as the horse trotted by. After experimenting with a number of different cameras, shutter speeds, backgrounds, and even a new film he invented, Muybridge was able to capture the sequence of movement that did indeed show a trotter's hooves all in the air at the same time.

In the process of his experiments, Muybridge became interested in animal motions, which later led him to study human motion. He perfected using a battery of 12 cameras and photographed people in motion to create not only a record of human movement but also of 19th Century life. Later, to show his sequential photographs as live movement, he developed the zoopraxiscope, which rotated his pictures through a light source. Unfortunately, finding a handy zoopraxiscope today may be a bit difficult, but you can turn Flash MX into your own zoopraxiscope using Muybridge's photographs in GIF and JPG format.

Two movies, Muybridge1.fla and Muybridge2.fla, use 12 GIF files to create a Flash zoopraxiscope. The first (Muybridge1.fla) of the two movies shows a woman walking. When you run the movie you see a simple walk in front of one of Muybridge's signature backdrops that helps measure movement. You notice very little arm movement in the walk, but you can get an excellent sense of how legs move in human locomotion. The second movie (Muybridge2.fla) shows a woman running and jumping over stones. This simple scene shows how human arms and legs move to maintain balance during motion. In only 12 frames, Muybridge was able to show a wide range of motion that can be used in animating human movement. This tutorial shows how to create these movies, but the emphasis is on how the arms, legs, and torso move.

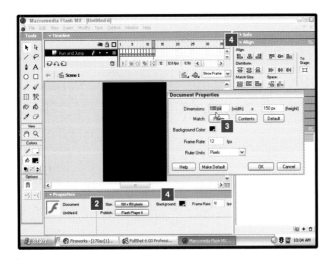

1. Select File→New to open a new movie.

2. Click the Size button on the Properties panel to open the Document Properties dialog box.

3. Set the Dimensions to 100 px (width) by 150 px (height), set the background color to black, and the Frame Rate to 12.

4. Open the Align Panel either by clicking it in the Dock or selecting Window→Align from the menu bar.

5. **Click Frame 12 and press the F6 key to insert a keyframe.**

6. **Click Frame 1, hold down the Shift key, and click Frame 11.**

7. **Press the F6 key to insert keyframes in the remaining frames.**

8. **Select File→Import to Library.**

9. **Select the Muybridge1 folder.**

10. **In the Import to Library window, hold down the Shift key and select all of the images by clicking the top and then the bottom image file.**

    All of these images are selected this way. When you only want to select certain images not in sequence, hold down the Ctrl or Cmd key and make selections.

11. **Click Open.**

    All of these files are sent to the Library panel.

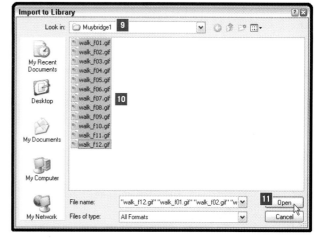

12. **Press Ctrl+L/Cmd+L to open the Library panel.**

    When the Library panel opens you see all of the files you imported.

13. **Click the first frame.**

14. **Drag the file walk_f01.gif to the stage.**

15. **Select the image on the stage.**

16. **In the Align panel click the To Stage button, and then click the Align horizontal center and the Align vertical center buttons.**

    The image should center itself on the stage. It is not a perfect fit, but rather a black border surrounds the image. When you run the movie, you see the entire area filled with black.

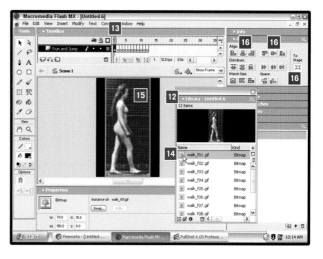

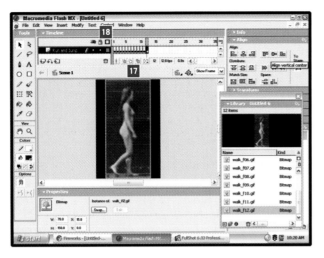

17. **Repeats steps 14 through 16, matching the frame number to the image number.**

18. **Once you have all 12 images in the 12 keyframes, select Control→Test Movie.**
    When you run your movie, you see a woman walking from left to right. The movement seems natural, and while some arm movement is evident, you can see the key movement of taking a step. Notice how the thigh, calf, and foot move and bend.

19. **While testing the movie, select Control→Rewind from the test movie's menu bar.**

20. **Select View→Zoom-in.**
    The figure, while highly pixelated, enables you to see the leg elements' movement in detail.

21. **Press the period (.) key to move one frame forward and the comma (,) key to move back.**
    By moving the enlarged image forward and back frame by frame, you can see the details of the foot and ankle movements and knee, thigh, and calf movements. While walking, the torso remains fairly stable.

22. **Repeat steps 1–21 using the files in the Muybridge2 folder.**
    In this second example from the works of Eadweard Muybridge, you see a far more animated figure (again in 12 frames). Instead of walking, the woman is running and jumping over rocks. Her movement requires far more balance requiring her to move her arms and legs and torso far more. Note how the different parts of her body move in relationship to one another.

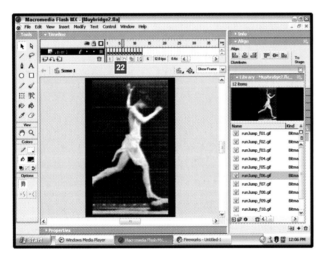

Auto-Sequence of Images

Instead of forcing you to repeat steps 10–17, Flash MX recognizes the beginning of a sequence by a number in the file's title and imports the entire sequence with a single action. By using the edit multiple frames options and selecting all of the frames, the entire set of images can be aligned to the same point on the stage. That saves you a good deal of time.

» Gallery

Beginning in 1872, before the advent of motion picture technology, studies of body movement were carried out by Eadweard Muybridge using a battery of 12 cameras. As a person or animal moved across a special background, 12 cameras were triggered in a sequence. The sequences ranged from less than a second to between two and three seconds. The film in each camera had to be developed separately and then carefully sequenced. For the early animators, Muybridge's work was a godsend because he used so many different types of movement with both humans and animals. When working out the basic movement of arms, legs, torsos, heads, hands, feet, and even wings of different types of animals and people, Muybridge's 12-frame sequences provided the kind of information animators needed. Muybridge created hundreds of his sequences in situations where simple movement (walking) or more complex movement (running and jumping over stones) could be studied for later use in animation.

To experience a very animated collection of Muybridge's works, see the UCR/California Museum of Photography online at: `http://photo.ucr.edu/photographers/muybridge/`.

A collection of Muybridge's works is available in different books as well. *Animals in Motion* and *The Human Figure in Motion* are still available and in print. Likewise, reprints of his original 1887 publication *Animal Locomotion* are available as is *The Male and Female Figure in Motion: 60 Classic Photographic Sequences.*

» More on Muybridge

During the time that Muybridge was gathering proof of levitating horses for his wealthy patron Leland Stanford, he married Flora Shallcross Stone, a young divorcee. In 1874, she gave birth to a son they named Floredo Helios Muybridge. However, Muybridge found that the child was not his own but that of his wife's lover, a many named Harry Larkyns. Chagrined by this turn of events, Muybridge shot and killed Harry. Fortunately for Muybridge, his skilled attorney Wirt Pendegast was able to get him acquitted. Almost immediately after his acquittal, Muybridge headed for Central America until any lingering animosity harbored by friends of the late Harry Larkyns had cooled.

By 1879, though, Muybridge was back in California and demonstrated the zoopraxiscope for the first time in the house of Leland Stanford. By 1880, Muybridge was giving lectures in San Francisco using his photographs and the zoopraxiscope. He later lectured throughout Europe and created a lasting influence on both scientific motion studies and how people and animals in motion are portrayed in art, finding acclaim by both artists and scientists in Paris. Artists such as Degas, Eakins, Whistler, and Vuillard are said to have been greatly influenced by Muybridge's photographs.

While in Europe, Muybridge learned that Leland Stanford published a book, entitled *The Horse in Motion*, giving Muybridge very little credit, even though it was Muybridge who invented the process by which the moving humans and animals could be photographed and made the actual photographs. Losing copyright lawsuits, Muybridge was finished with Stanford.

Fortunately, Thomas Eakins secured support for Muybridge at the University of Pennsylvania, and so Muybridge moved to Philadelphia. While at the University of Pennsylvania he worked with a whole new series of lenses, timing devices, and cameras. He used up to 24 cameras with shots from 30-, 60-, and 90-degree angles. Using this technique, instead of getting only 12 shots, he produced as many as 36 shots of a single motion. In 1887, he published *Animal Locomotion* based on his work at the University of Pennsylvania, and animators still use it today to study how different body movements look broken down into the series of photographs taken by Muybridge.

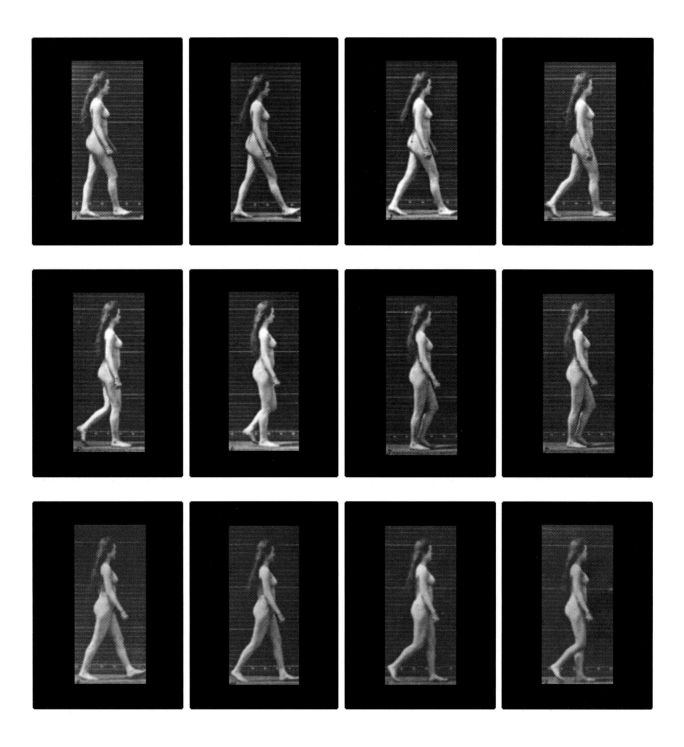

Tutorial
» Creating Animated Characters

After looking at the different movements captured by Eadweard Muybridge, you can begin to see what type of movement considerations you need to make when designing your own animated characters. To both simplify the process and to optimize the use of Flash MX, break down the character into component moving parts. Each of the parts should be treated as a movie clip. Once all of the clips are put together, all that is left is to animate the composite features plus any elements that require more movement to add more realism.

To provide a clear understanding of what you need, the movie, animation.fla, shows you all of the steps required to create animation. Watch the movie several times as Leslie Cabarga takes you on a guided tour spanning three centuries from Muybridge to Flash MX animation. Not a lot has changed in animation other than the technology. However, the technology in Flash MX makes it very easy to create animated characters Disney would have envied. In this next tutorial, you re-create only the animated walking character to see the general principles and techniques for making a movie clip containing an animated character. When you create your own animated characters, all you need to do is to make movie clips and then put them together into a story for your feature length cartoon.

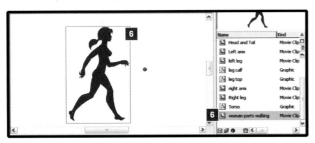

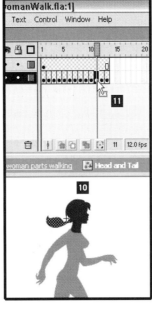

1. **Drag animation.fla from your CD-ROM to your desktop.**

2. **Double-click the movie icon to open it.**

3. **Press Ctrl+L/Cmd+L to open the Library panel.**
   You open a new movie and use a single movie clip, woman parts walking, for this tutorial.

4. **Select File→New from the menu bar.**

5. **Open the animation.fla Library panel.**

6. **Drag the movie clip named woman parts walking to the desktop.**

7. **Close the animation.fla Library panel.**
   As soon as you drag the movie clip to your desktop, you don't need the Library panel from the animation.fla movie.

8. **Double-click the movie clip on the stage to enter the Symbol-Editing Mode.**
   You see several layers and Motion tweens on two layers.

9. **Open the Library panel.**
   Even though you only used a single movie clip from the other movie, that clip is made up of 12 other symbols, including other movie clips.

10. **Double-click the character's head.**
    You are now in the Head and Tail timeline.

11. **Drag the playhead to the left and right to animate the character's ponytail.**
    Each keyframe has a slightly different drawing of the ponytail. Step through each frame to see the changes that have been made. The character's head is a graphic object making it much easier just to change the movement of the ponytail.

12. Click woman parts walking above the stage.

Now you're back up to the character's movie clip timeline.

13. Select Window→Transform to open the Transform panel.

14. Click Frame 4 of the head layer.

In the Transform panel, note the head is rotated 2.5°. These subtle changes give the composite head movie clip a more natural attitude.

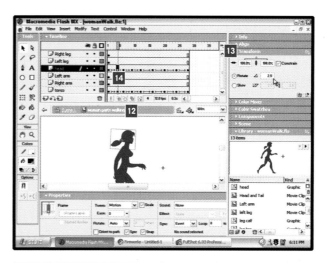

15. Select Window→Info to open the Info panel.

16. Click Frame 1 of the torso layer.

Note the Y value in the Info panel.

17. Click Frame 9 of the Info panel.

Again note the Y value in the Info panel. The Y value has changed from –61.2 to –63.9. This subtle change in the vertical (Y) position of the torso simulates the actual rise in the torso as a person walks. The difference is fewer than 2 pixels, but it doesn't take much to add realism you would lack otherwise.

18. Double-click the Left arm object.

When you select an object, it should highlight in a blue rectangle and its name should appear in the Properties panel. When you enter the timeline for the Left arm, you see two new timelines.

19. Click the upper portion of the arm.

20. Select the Free Transform tool from the Toolbox.

21. Drag the pivot point down to the center of the object and then drag it back to its original position near the shoulder.

Each object has a default pivot point in the object's center. To set the pivot point for an object, simply use the Free Transform tool to drag it to its natural pivot point. In this case, the upper arm's natural pivot point is where the arm connects to the shoulder.

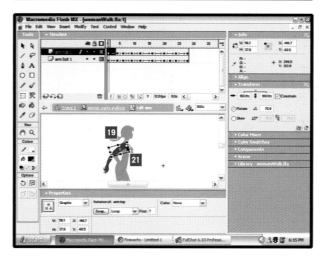

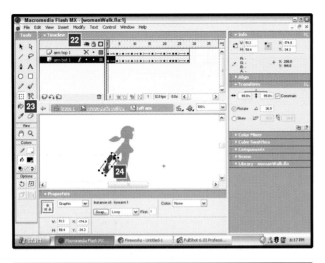

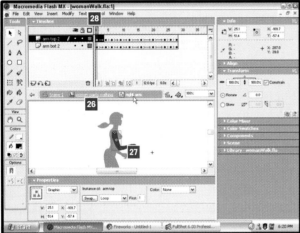

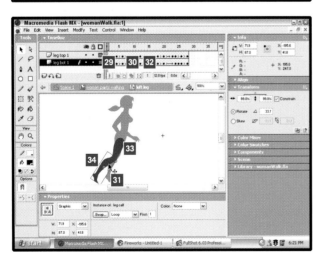

22. **Click the Eye column of the layer named arm top 1 to hide the upper arm.**
    To see the whole lower arm, you need to hide the upper arm. Even if you forget to unhide a feature, it still shows up when you test the movie.

23. **Select the Free Transform tool from the Toolbox.**

24. **Drag the pivot point from the elbow down to the default center indicated by the crosshairs, and then back to the elbow.**
    The upper and lower arm are the only two objects that make up the arm. If a good deal of hand and wrist movement is required, you would want to add a hand and wrist object and move the center point of the wrist position away from the middle of the hand.

25. **Click the Eye layer again to reveal the upper arm.**

26. **Click woman parts walking to return to the timeline with the main character.**

27. **Double-click the right arm to enter that object's timeline.**
    The right arm's timeline looks pretty much like those of the left arm. However, the beginning position is different. The pivot points are the same, but the arm starts with the hand extended forward rather than backwards as it does with the left arm.

28. **Drag the playhead back and forth to see the full motion of the arm.**
    At each keyframe, note the rotation angle and X and Y position of the upper and lower arm object in the Transform and Info panels. To reproduce the movement, you need to use the Free Transform tool to both change the rotation angle of the limbs and move the pivot points.

29. **Move the playhead to Frame 9 and then double-click the left leg to open its timeline.**
    By looking at the leg graphic instance after positioning the larger character's in a frame other then the first frame, you can see the character in relationship to the larger character in different frames.

30. **Drag the playhead to the first frame.**

31. **Click the lower portion of the leg.**
    Note the rotation value in the Transform panel.

32. **Drag the playhead to Frame 12.**

33. **Click the upper part of the leg.**
    Check the Rotate value in the Transform panel. It shows it to be −77.5°.

34. **Click the lower part of the leg.**
    Again check the Rotate value in the Transform panel. It now shows a rotate angle of 5.1°. When recreating the leg and arm movements, the rotation angle is the key to making the movement appear natural.

» Gallery

If you look closely at the lower-left corner of the second group of Muybridge images, you see the numbers he used to keep them in order. This series is numbered as well, but using nine frames instead of 12. However, while Muybridge's models could only simulate 12 positions in all, Flash MX provides movie clips so that you can have full arm and leg movement within independent movie clips with tweens between positions. Look at the similarities between the animated character in these nine shots and the 12 frames in Muybridge's two different sets. You can see the similarities, and unlike Muybridge, you won't need a zoopraxiscope to create the animation!

Tutorial

» Building a Background

To produce the background that moves while the character goes through the walking motions, you need to draw a long background panel that loops behind the walking character. By moving the background in the opposite direction the character is moving, you can simulate the character making headway against a background. In the early days of making films, the film producers created huge wheels with painted background curtains. The camera would remain steady to film the action while the actors either ran on treadmills or went through the motions of pumping arms and legs to simulate movement. All the while the background of a wheeled curtain would spin a series of scenes to make it look like the actors were making progress. This tutorial shows how to make a revolving background against which the animated character can walk.

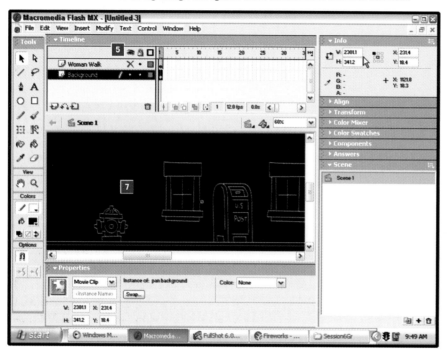

1. **Open the file animation.fla.**

2. **Press Ctrl+L/Cmd+L to open the Library panel.**

3. **Select File→New from the menu bar.**

4. **Click the Insert Layer button, and rename the top layer** Woman Walk **and the bottom layer** Background.

5. **Click the eye column of the Woman Walk layer.**
   Initially, you work with the background, and you won't need the top layer.

6. **Set the stage size to 2550 (width) and 400 (height) and choose black from the Background color well in the Properties panel.**
   This extremely wide stage size is temporary. The color used to draw most of the background is invisible against the off-stage

gray. Having a very wide stage initially allows you to draw a background and see what you're doing. Also, unless you have a wide stage, the background will be off the work area.

7. **Select the background layer and drag an instance of "pan background" from the animation.fla Library panel to the stage.**
   When you get the background object on the stage, you see X=2301.1. It maintains the same vertical (Y) position on the stage and moves horizontally across it in a loop. Were you to create your own background panel, you would be able to create it with plenty of horizontal room. Basically, all you would be doing is drawing a long picture and then animating it across the stage.

8. **Select Edit→Preferences from the menu bar and check Disable Panel Docking in the Preferences dialog box.**

   By disabling the docking, you can temporarily close the panels in the dock and create enough space to see the entire panel.

9. **Set the magnification to 30%.**

   Now you can see the entire panel.

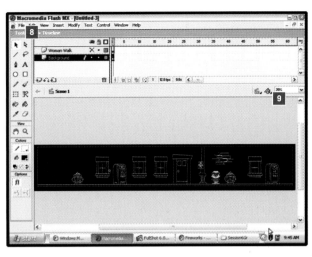

10. **Reset the stage size to 550 (X), 400(Y) and change the magnification to 25%.**

    You want to see where the background panel moves across the stage. The magnification of your computer may be greater than or less than that provided. You want to see as much of the background instance as possible.

11. **Select pan background instance and in the Info panel set the X value to −368.6 and the Y value to 18.4.**

    This is the beginning position of the panel on the main timeline.

12. **Double-click the pan background instance to enter the Symbol-Editing Mode and the pan background's timeline.**

13. **Select the first frame in the Background layer, and in the Info panel set the X value to −642.8 and the Y value to −208.**

    You should see those values if you've used the other values up to this point.

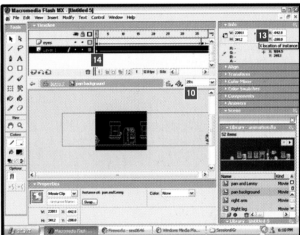

14. **Select the first frame and select Motion from the Tween popup menu in the Properties panel.**

15. **Click Frame 130 and Press the F5 key to add a frame, and then Press the F6 key to insert a keyframe in Frame 130 and select the frame.**

16. **In the Info panel, set the X value to −642.8 and the Y value to −208.1.**

    The pan background drawing jumps to the end. As soon as the playhead passes this portion of the movie, it loops back to the center.

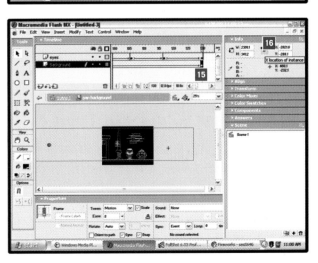

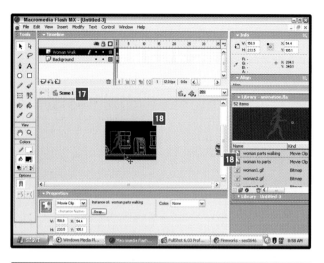

17. Click Scene 1 to return to the main timeline and click the first frame.

18. Drag an instance of "woman parts walking" to the stage, placing it in the lower-left corner.

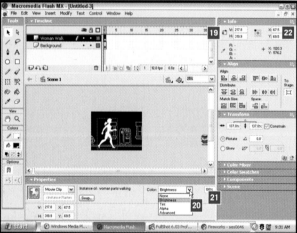

19. Select the walking woman instance and in the Info panel change the dimensions to W=217.8, H=319.9.

20. Open the Color popup menu in the Properties panel and choose Brightness.

21. Type 100% for the Brightness value.
    Now the walking woman is proportionately sized for the background and has better contrast against the background. Note also that all of the different parts that make up the walking woman are changed in size and brightness value.

22. Select the walking woman instance and set the X value to 67.5 and Y to 68.5.

23. Select Control➞Test Movie from the menu bar.
    When the movie runs, you should see the woman jogging down the street. Watch it closely, and if you see any joints out of place, you can edit the movie clip so that all of the parts work optimally with each other. Also make sure that the background slides by smoothly.

Tutorial
» Using Masks

One of the more enjoyable features in Flash MX is its ability to mask layers. Masking takes place in layer pairs. The upper layer is the mask, and the layer directly below it is the masked layer. If you're not familiar with masks, they work like keyholes. In looking through a keyhole, all you can see are the images that pass before the keyhole. Imagine the viewed images taking on a keyhole shape. Masks are the "keyholes" and all you can see on the level directly below on the masked layer are those parts of the layer the keyhole is over. When either the mask or masked layer is animated, what you see changes in the shape of the keyhole. This first mask tutorial shows a very simple application of using the mask and is not from your project. The mask in your project is wonderfully elegant and you learn how to do it in the next tutorial. However, first, to get the fundamentals down, this next little movie focuses on the basics.

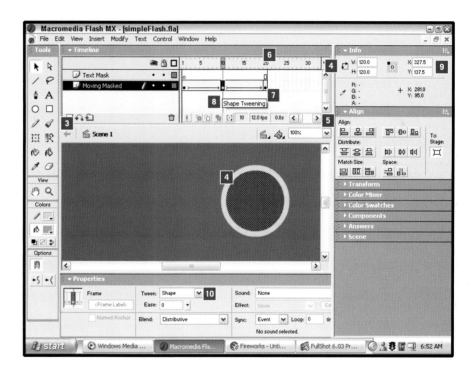

1. **Select File→New to open a new movie.**

2. **Open the Background color well in the Properties panel and use #EODFE3 as the background color.**

3. **Click the Insert Layer button and rename the two layers Text Mask and Moving Mask from top to bottom respectively.**

4. **Choose the Moving Mask layer, select the Oval tool and draw a circle with the dimensions W=120, H=120 with a blue fill and 10-point yellow stroke.**

5. **Position the circle at X=182, Y=138.**

6. **Click Frame 20, drag the cursor to select both frames, and press the F5 key to insert frames out to Frame 20.**

7. **Click Frame 20 and press F6 to insert a keyframe.**

8. **Click Frame 10 and press F6 to insert a keyframe.**

9. **Click Frame 10 and move the circle to X=327, Y=138.**

10. **Click Frame 1, hold down the Shift key and click Frame 10, and select Shape from the Tween popup menu.**
    Test the movie to make sure that that circle bobs back and forth between left and right center of the stage.

11. **Click the Text Mask layer.**

12. **Select the Text tool and Static Text from the Text type popup menu.**

13. **Using a 96-point green Verdana font, type in the word** Flash.

14. **Position the text block at X=176, Y=134 using the Info or Properties panel.**

15. **Click the Text Mask layer.**

16. **Right-click/Control-click to open the Context menu.**
    Interestingly, Flash MX does not have a menu selection for masking a layer. Getting used to using the Context menu can save a lot of time when working with Flash MX, and with masks, you have to use a Context menu.

17. **Select Mask from the Context menu.**

    The top layer is now a mask layer, indicated by the oval icon with a cross-hatch and the bottom layer is a masked layer, indicated by an indented cross-hatch icon.

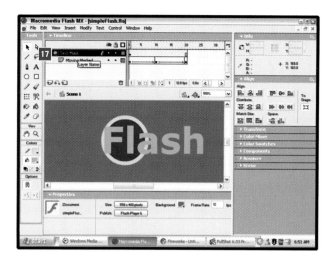

18. **Select the Text Mask layer.**

19. **Right-click/Control-click the layer to open the layer's Context menu.**

20. **Select Show Masking.**

    With the mask on, you can see only those portions of the masked object covered by the word Flash. The green letters (or any other color for that matter) in the word Flash are never seen in the movie — only the colors of the objects in the masked layer. You can only use one object for a masking object. Another way to show the masking is to lock all of the layers.

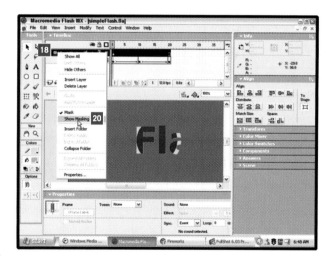

< T I P >

While you can use only a single object to mask a layer, you can create multi-object symbols, or as in the preceding tutorial, you can use a text block for masking an object. In either case, you have multiple objects serving as "peepholes," but only a single object. The text block counts as a single object, but each character in the block has its own mask shape. Likewise, an instance of a symbol is considered a single object to be used as a mask, but it can have multiple shapes within itself.

Tutorial
» Multiple Tweens and Masks

Now that you can see how to create a simple mask, this next one uses multiple effects and tweening in the masked layer object. Taken from the TypeTrix.fla movie, the masked layer moves and changes brightness using motion tween. The mask is made up of a skewed text block that has been broken apart. In order to preserve the text outlines (strokes), the strokes have been cut and pasted on a layer above the mask and masked layer. The effect is a set of "hippie" objects floating and fading in and out beneath a "hippie" font inspired by the 1960s era. The psychedelic effect is fun and drug-free! The next tutorial uses reverse engineering to show you how to create your own font-enhanced mask.

1. **Select File→New to open a new movie and set the magnification to 40%.**

2. **Select Insert→New Symbol from the menu bar, use the name** Piece, **choose Graphic for behavior, and click OK.**

3. Add several layers (six or seven, for example) by clicking the Insert Layer button.

4. **Select the Text tool and a graphic font such as Dingbats, Webdings, or Wingdings and, using different sizes ranging from 24–72 points, type characters on different layers.**
   Place several text blocks on different layers and use a variety of colors.

5. **Use the Free Transform tool to set the text blocks at several different angles.**

6. **Click Scene 1 to return to the main timeline.**

7. **Select Insert→New Symbol from the menu bar, use the name Hippie Clip, and choose Movie Clip for behavior and click OK.**

8. Open the Library panel and drag an instance of the Graphic Pieces to the stage.

9. Click Frame 70 and Press the F5 key to insert a frame.

10. **Click Frame 1, select the Piece object on the stage, select Brightness from the Color Styles popup menu in the Properties panel, and set the brightness to –66%.**
    Using a negative value with the brightness property darkens an object.

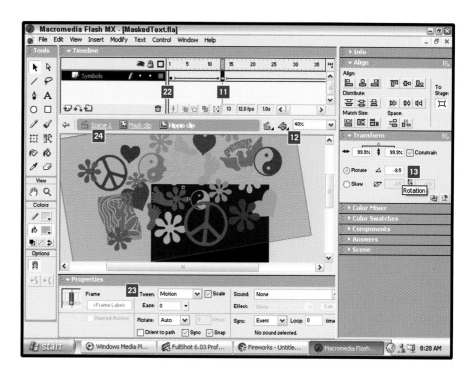

11. **Click Frame 13 and press F6 to insert a keyframe.**

12. **Set Magnification to 40% and select None from the Color Styles popup menu in the Properties panel.**
    Your picture brightens up without any fade in color.

13. **In the Transform panel, change the Rotate value to –9.5°.**

14. Click Frame 50 and press F6 to insert a keyframe.

15. In the Transform panel, change the Rotate value to 13.8°.

16. Click Frame 62 and press F6 to insert a keyframe.

17. In the Transform panel, change the Rotate value to 5°.

18. **Click Frame 69 and press F6 to insert a keyframe.**

19. **In the Transform panel, change the Rotate value to 0°.**

20. **In the Properties panel, from the Color Styles popup menu select Brightness and set the value to –66°.**

21. (Optional) Click Frame 70 and select Insert→Blank Keyframe, open the Actions panel, and add a stop action.

22. **Click Frame 1, hold down the Shift key, and click Frame 62.**

23. **Select Motion from the Tween popup menu in the Properties panel.**

24. **Click Scene 1 to return to the main timeline.**

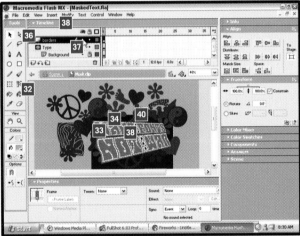

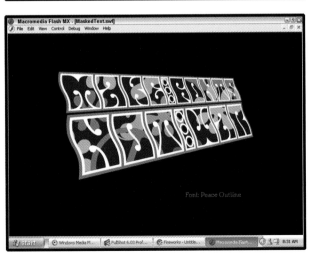

25. Select Insert→New Symbol from the menu bar, use the name Mask Clip, **choose Movie Clip for behavior, and click OK.**

26. **Click the Insert Layers button twice to add two more layers and name them, from top to bottom,** borders, Type, **and** Background.

27. **Select the Background layer, open the Library panel, and drag an instance of the Hippie Clip to the stage.**

28. **Using a 1960s-era font (or any font you happen to have available),** Type MAKE FONTS NOT WAR **centered on two lines on the Type layer.**

29. **Select the text block and press Ctrl+B/Cmd+B twice to break the text into a shape.**

30. **Choose the Free Transform tool and rotate the text upward on the right end slightly.**

31. **With the Free Transform tool, Ctrl+Drag/Cmd+Drag the right corners to narrow the right side of the text.**
The text should appear to be a slightly tilted message angling away from the viewer.

32. **Select the Ink Bottle tool from the Toolbox, choose white from the Stroke color well, and set the Stroke width to 1 in the Properties panel.**

33. **Click all of the letters, including the interior portions, with the Ink Bottle tool.**

34. **Hold down the Shift key and click all of the stroke lines added with the Ink Bottle tool.**

35. **Press Ctrl+X/Cmd+X to delete the stroke lines.**

36. **Select the borders layer, click the first frame, and select Edit→Paste in Place.**

37. **Lock the Type and Background layers.**

38. **Select the graphic outlines in the border layer.**

39. **Select Modify→Shape→Convert Lines to Fills.**

40. **Select the Ink Bottle, a blue stroke color, and click all of the letter outlines.**
By converting the lines to fills, a new line or border can be added to each of the letter outlines in the border layer.

41. **Select Control→Test Movie from the menu bar.**
When the movie plays, the masking letters provide a set of patterns overlaying the underlying patterns in the masked layer. The fade-in and fade-out using the Brightness component of the object adds to the overall effect of the masked moving objects.

» Session Review

This session covers text used in animation, as information labels, and as an animated object. Both text blocks and broken apart graphic text can be animated in many different ways.

1. What is a storyboard and how is it used in planning a Flash MX movie? (See "Session Introduction.")

2. What kinds of computer-based graphics programs can be used with Flash MX? (See "Tutorial: Breaking Down Complex Projects into Simple Steps.")

3. When a movie clip is running on its own timeline, can it be changed in another timeline? For example, can you change the size of a movie clip that is running on its own timeline from the main timeline and tween the change? (See "Tutorial: Moving and Changing Movie Clips.")

4. How did Eadweard Muybridge make sequential photos of movement prior to the invention of the motion picture camera? Was the zoopraxiscope an early version of Flash? (See "Tutorial: Replicating Human Motion.")

5. What tool in Flash MX do you use to move the center point of an object? (By the way, it is a different tool than was used in Flash 5.) (See "Tutorial: Creating Animated Characters.")

6. Why is the Transform panel so important in creating character animation? (See "Tutorial: Multiple Modifications of Movie Clips.")

7. How do you create a moving panoramic background to be used with an animated character movie clip? (See "Tutorial: Building a Background.")

8. What trick is used to make an extremely wide panoramic background that would normally be beyond the horizontal limits of Flash's off-stage area? (See "Tutorial: Building a Background.")

9. Is it possible to animate objects on the mask or masked layers? (See "Tutorial: Multiple Tweens and Masks.")

10. While only a single object can be used as a mask, what trick can you use to have multiple "peepholes" to see the masked layer? (See "Tutorial: Using Masks.")

» Additional Projects

The following projects relate to this session and can help you refine your expertise in working with animation in Flash MX.

» All of Eadweard Muybridge's 12-photo animations are available at http://photo.ucr.edu/photographers/muybridge/contents.html# on the Web. Take one of the animated 12-photo sequences and see if you can duplicate it in Flash.

» Walking involves several different coordinated elements. To focus on the legs, create a torso from an oval. Then attach "stick" legs with pivot points at the top of the thigh, knee, and ankle.

» Go to a used book store or your local library and find a book on pre-computer animation. The techniques artists and art directors used to create natural movement in animation are equally applicable to Flash MX, only with Flash MX, they're much easier to produce.

» Create a two-person animation (you can use stick figures) of people dancing. Because the body moves in so many different ways when dancing, you will learn a good deal about animating body parts. Also, because the animation involves more than one figure, you will have to coordinate your two sets of movement. (Later you can add another layer and a sound track to really give yourself a valuable learning experience.)

Adding Sound to Flash MX

Session Introduction

Before you even think about putting sound files into a movie, you need to understand something about sound on the Internet. Sound files are like graphics files in that they can take up a good deal of memory. In fact, compared to graphics, sounds are monsters. Fortunately, with Flash MX, you can compress sound files as effectively as you can compress graphics and animation files, but you need to know how to do it right.

TOOLS YOU'LL USE
Properties panel, Text tool, Library panels, color panels, drawing tools

MATERIALS NEEDED
From the accompanying CD-ROM, you'll need the IntroFinal3.fla, SoundIdeas.fla, BigWavMono.wav, IntroLoopLong.wav, and ShortMono.wav files.

TIME REQUIRED
90 minutes

SESSION OUTCOME
How to Work with Sound in Flash

PROJECT PORTION
The Flash intro to the Web site

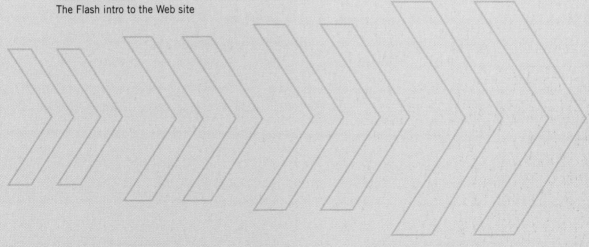

Sound Files: An Overview

Macromedia recommends an optimal setting of 22 kHz with mono sound in Flash. If you use mono instead of stereo, you basically cut the file size in half because you only use a single sound channel instead of two. For example, your project's introduction is 57.8 seconds. The following shows some different values for WAV files that play in that time span.

- » 16-bit stereo 22 kHz — 4.88MB WAV
- » 16-bit mono 22 kHz — 3.06MB WAV
- » 8-bit stereo 22 kHz — 2.44MB AIFF
- » 8-bit mono 22 kHz — 1.22MB AIFF

None of those file sizes are acceptable for the Internet and World Wide Web. The 16-bit stereo takes over 10 minutes to load using a 56.6K modem, and not many people want to wait over 10 minutes to hear 58 seconds of music. Even the smallest size takes about 2 minutes to load on a 56.6K modem.

I'm not suggesting that you give up on using sound over the Web. Rather, if you're going to use sound, learn how to maximize its use and minimize its size. For example, using Flash MX, you can shrink the 4.88MB file into a 116.2KB file — 2.4% of its original size. Besides shrinking files, you have other tricks and methods available to you, and if you use them in conjunction with one another, you can effectively create a movie with great sound without using much bandwidth.

Sound File Types

You use three popular types of sound files with a Flash MX movie:

- » WAV — Pronounced "wave," this is the name of the waveform sound files jointly developed for Windows.

- » AIFF — Audio Interchange File Format created by Apple Computer, Inc. for Macintosh computers.

- » MP3 — The most efficient and effective sound file compression is based on MPEG (Moving Picture Expert Group) Audio Layer 3, or MP3.

If you use both a Macintosh and a Windows computer, you can double your sound collection if you have QuickTime 5 installed on your systems. Although Apple Computer, Inc. created QuickTime 5, it provides free QuickTime 5 players for both Windows and Macintosh platforms. You can use WAV files on your Mac, and AIFF files on your Windows PC. The sound file displays in a QuickTime file icon, but they work just fine. Once you place the files into Flash, you can effectively convert them to MP3 files to reduce file size but maintain quality.

The Web is filled with sources for different sounds. Many are snippets from television shows, some are sound effects, and you can find music of all stripes. Most of the sound sources are free, but some stipulate that you cannot use the sounds for commercial purposes. Others sell different types of sounds for a small fee. For example, one site offers sound effects for $1.25 each. Once you pay the fee, you can use it copyright free on published sites. For professional designers who don't have the time or equipment to develop sounds, the price is a bargain.

I found a few sources that target Flash users and have good collections of WAV and/or AIFF files:

> » www.flashsound.com — High quality commercial and free files

> » www.computerarts.co.uk — Commercial British site with free samples

> » www.flashkit.com — Lots of free music by talented amateurs

> » www.soundshopper.com — Commercial and free WAV and AIFF files

> » www.flash-sounds.com — Commercial only but interesting

Most Flash users know enough to type **WAV** or **AIFF** into a search engine. You can find literally millions of Web sites that way. In looking at a number of these sites, I was never sure whether the sound clips they had were always exactly legal. Sound files from television and movies gave the most pause. The sites featuring WAV files were sincerely dedicated to sharing the host's love of sound. However, were I to use one of the generously offered sound files, I would check out whether the eager sound lover offering it unwittingly clipped it from a copyrighted source.

A major court decision upheld a ruling that it is illegal to swap copyrighted MP3 files over the Web. With music videos now on the Web (many of which were produced with Flash), one might erroneously conclude that if it's out there on the Web, anyone can snatch it, "improve" on it, and use it. You better be careful here, and unless a file is clearly in the public domain, you may find yourself in hot water if you place it on the Web without written permission to do so. Some sites give permission to use a sound on your personal site but prohibit selling the sound or using it in certain commercial endeavors. If you create a Flash music video of your favorite musician or musical group on your computer with your own music CD-ROM, you don't have a problem. However, if you e-mail your Flash music video to a friend, technically, you may have broken the law. If you place the music video you made from a copyrighted song on the Web, you may also have broken copyright laws depending on how you use the site.

Sound Applications

One way (besides getting written permission to use a sound) to be absolutely, positively certain that you don't break the music and sound copyright laws when you are using Flash is to create your own sound. You can write your own songs and music and play them without a problem. (You cannot even sing "Happy Birthday," though, and record it or any other copyrighted song or music without permission and usually a fee.) You may find it much easier to create your own sound effects. Anything that can make a sound can make a sound effect. You can even go to the original source — the airport for jet sounds or your own car for car sounds.

Some computers, such as the iMac, come with built-in microphones and recorders, and with many computers using Windows systems, a microphone is bundled with the other components when you buy your system. If your system does not have a microphone, plenty are available, both online and at just about any computer store. Some of the newer systems, including virtually all of the Macintosh computers to come out since the iMac, require a USB (Universal Serial Bus) for an external microphone. You can also find microphones built into headsets. For example, Telex makes several USB combination headsets with microphones built right into the headset that I tested on both Windows XP and Macintosh OS X. Once you've recorded a sound, getting it to your computer is pretty simple. Most computers come with a sound program hooked into the operating system (Windows 98, ME, or XP or Mac OS 9 or OS X), or you can use programs like Cool Edit (www.syntrillium.com) for Windows or Sound Studio (www.felttip.com/products/soundstudio) for Mac OS.

The easiest way to record sounds is from a CD-ROM in your computer's CD-ROM drive. The downside, of course, is that your CD-ROM is most likely to contain copyrighted materials. You can purchase CD-ROMs with sound effects and then record the sounds from your CD-ROM to your computer or just transfer them from the CD to your hard drive. For truly original sounds, you'll need something more portable, however.

You can record sounds on a portable tape recorder and transfer them to your PC. You need an audio cord (mini stereo) that you can find at stores like Radio Shack for under $10. Attach one jack on the cord end to the line in port on the back of your computer (part of your sound card) and the other end in the tape recorder's earphone jack. Select line in (or equivalent message) on your recording software program. When you play the cassette tape, check to see that the line in is not mute and if it is, click the sound program's mute toggle. You should be able to hear the sounds coming from the recorder (or other sound-generating device) through your computer's speakers. Most recording programs for both Windows PCs and Macs are set up to simulate a hardware recording system. Just click Record to record the sound into your computer, and click Stop when you've recorded all you want. Be careful not to record more than your hard drive or other mass storage device can handle, though. Once you've recorded what you need, save the file in WAV, AIFF, or MP3 format. If your recorder will not make MP3 files, you can convert either WAV or AIFF files into MP3 format once they have been imported into Flash.

One of the more innovative software programs you can use to make legal music and sound effects for Flash is Smart Sound (www.smartsound.com), available for both Windows and Macintosh systems. With Smart Sound software, you have both a series of sound styles and effects from which you can choose, time, and edit. For example, if you want a 15.4-second sound to go with your movie that is exactly 15.4 seconds long, you just select the type of music you want and key in the amount of time for the sound to run; Smart Sound does the rest. Save the sound file as a WAV or AIFF file and place it into Flash, and you're all set. The best part is that the music you create is copyright free in your Flash movies, so you can put them on the Web without having to worry about a lawsuit. Also, you don't have to be able to play even a kazoo to create a wide range of musical scores from Mozart to Techno.

Because you cannot create sounds with Flash, all sounds must be imported. Basically, you can import WAV, AIFF, or MP3 sounds with no additional software. However, if you download QuickTime 4 (or newer) onto either your Windows or Macintosh computer, you can also include the formats listed in Table 7-1.

Table 7-1: Additional Sound Files That Can Be Imported If QuickTime 4 Is On Your System

File Type	System
MP3	Windows or Macintosh
WAV	Windows or Macintosh
Sound Only QuickTime Movies	Windows or Macintosh
System 7 Sounds	Macintosh Only
Sound Designer II	Macintosh Only
Sun AU	Windows or Macintosh

< N O T E >

WAV files also work with Windows machines that do not have QuickTime 4 or newer installed.

< N O T E >

Two windows you may easily confuse are the Library panel and the Library-Sounds.fla window. If you select Window→Common Libraries→Sounds, all of the sounds that come supplied with Flash MX appear in the Library Sounds window. If you select any of those sounds and expect to see them in the Sounds panel pop-up menu, you will be disappointed. Drag the sound you want from the Library Sounds window into the Library panel of your current movie. Once the sound appears in the main Library panel, it will also appear in the Sound panel's pop-up menu.

Tutorial
» Importing Sounds into Flash

Once you have your sound files ready, you're all set to import them into Flash MX and use them in your movie.

1. **Drag IntroFinal3.fla from the CD-ROM to your desktop.**

2. **Double-click the file icon to open Flash MX and the file.**

3. **Select the Introduction scene.**

4. **Select Control→Go To End from the menu bar.**
   You will be at the very end of the Introduction scene on Frame 925. The Elapsed Time window shows you how long the movie runs. In the project Introduction, the time is 57.8 seconds. That doesn't seem long, but a stereo WAV file lasting that long can take almost 5 megabytes — way too big for an Internet file.

5. **Select Control→Rewind from the menu bar.**

6. **Click the first frame of the Sound Layer.**

7. **Press Ctrl+L/Cmd+L to open the Library panel.**

8. **Select File→Import to Library from the menu bar.**
   You can either import a sound file directly to a layer or to the library. You may consider sending the sound file to the library first, and then, if it doesn't work out, deleting it in the library. Once you delete a sound file from the Library panel, Flash removes the sound from all layers and frames where you placed it. (When you import a sound file to a frame in a layer, Flash automatically places the sound file into the Library panel for the current movie; so you can still remove the file from all layers by removing it from the library.) However, by first importing the sound to the library, you can put it in whenever you need it from the Properties panel, and the process is a bit less awkward.

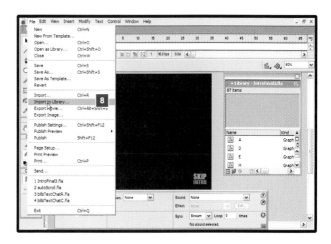

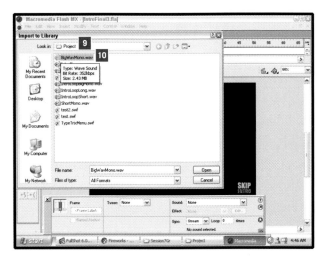

9. **In the Import to Library dialog box, find the Project folder.**

10. **Select BigWavMono.wav.**
    When you select the file, you can see that it is impossibly large for the Web (2.43 megabytes). That will be fixed in due course.

11. **Select BigWavMono.wav in the Library panel.**
    You see a sound wave graphic, and a play button.

12. **Click the play button for the selected sound in the Library panel.**
    Make sure you have the right sound file by first playing it in the Library panel. If it's the wrong one, delete it and try again to import the right one. Because sound files can be very large, you don't want unused ones to add weight to your FLA file.

13. **Click the first frame of the Sound layer to select it.**

14. **If not already opened, open the Properties panel.**

15. **Click the Sound popup menu in the Properties panel.**
    You should see the file you just imported.

16. **Click BigWavMono.wav in the popup menu.**
    As soon as you click the file, you should see a wave graphic in the Sound layer. Drag the playhead to the end of the file. It should end at or very near the end of the movie.

17. **Select Control→Test Scene from the menu bar.**
    The Introduction ran along with the movie until near the end and the movie kept going after the sound quit. The next tutorial shows how to more exactly coordinate a movie with the sound.

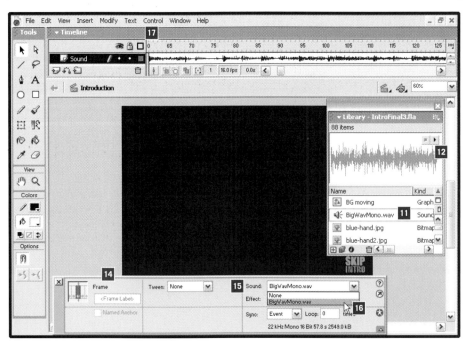

Tutorial
» Using Streaming Sound

Even after setting a 57.8 second movie with a 57.8 second sound file, you found that the coordination was off a bit. To more fully coordinate the frames and the sound, you can use streaming sound. Streaming sounds require enough frames to encompass the entire sound. Streaming sounds start at the first keyframe (where the sound is set) and end when the frames end or the sound goes beyond the last frame.

The pace of the sound, and not the frame rate in the SWF file, drives the animation on the Web. With streaming sound, if the animation drawings cannot keep up with the sound, Flash MX skips frames, leading to a smooth sound but possibly irregular animation as frames are skipped to keep up with the sound track. However, when you make the length of the sound file as close to the size of the movie's time length as possible, you minimize any jerkiness. This next tutorial shows you how to stream the sound with the Introduction movie.

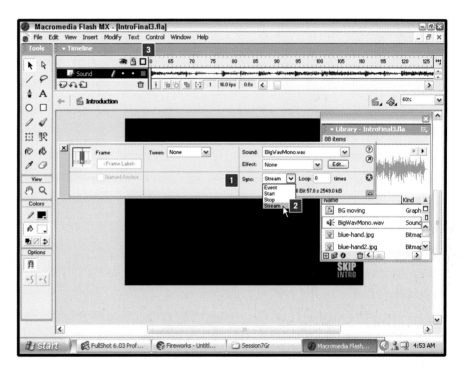

1. **Select the frame where the sound begins and then select the Syn Sound popup menu in the Properties panel.**

2. **Choose Stream.**

3. **Select Control→Test Movie from the menu bar.**
   This time when the movie runs, the sound should end right when the movie ends. Because the frame rate is linked to the sound, you may see a few frames skipped, but chances are all that you will notice is that the movie and sound end together.

Tutorial
» Reducing Sound File Sizes

After coordinating your sound and movie, you still may find it impossible to publish your movie on the Web because the sound file is almost two and a half megabytes (2.44MB). Given the bandwidth speed of even fast DSL and Cable modem links, an added two and a half megabytes in a Flash MX file is just too much to handle. The compression algorithm of MP3 files allows you to reduce your file sizes dramatically, and Flash MX has built-in MP3 compression. So, instead of using the default size of your file, you can reduce it significantly — to only 4.5 percent of its original size. This tutorial shows you how to do that. Moreover, the compression in no way affects the quality of the sound. It's just a more efficient and effective compression algorithm.

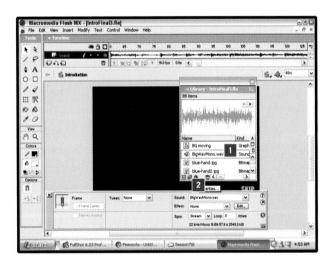

1. **Select BigWavMono.wav from the Library panel.**

2. **Click the Properties button at the bottom of the Library panel.**
   The Properties button is the little white "i" in the blue circle. As soon as you click the button, the Sound Properties dialog box appears.

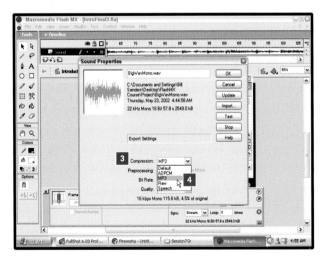

3. **Locate the Compression popup menu.**

4. **Click the menu and select MP3.**
   You will see that the file has been reduced from 2.44MB to only 115.6KB. That is a lot better and you can use a file that size on the Web. The file size in your FLA file will remain the same, but you will see a significant difference in the size of the SWF file. However, it's still pretty big for users with slower Internet connections.

Tutorial

» Using Sound Loops to Reduce SWF Size

Even with the best sound editing tools, you can end up with a big fat sound that weighs down your movie. To avoid this, you can use "sound loops," which are instrumental sounds that cycle so that when the loop repeats itself, it sounds like a continuation of the tune rather than a repetition. The Introduction scene is almost a minute long. Instead of having the single minute tune, a 5-second loop takes ½ the bandwidth weight. The tune can repeat as many times as you want, but it still takes only the single loop to fill in the entire 60 seconds. This tutorial shows you how to use sound loops instead of full tunes.

1. **Select File→Import to Library.**

2. **In the Import to Library dialog box, select IntroLoopLong.wav.**
   Note that the WAV file is only 365KB compared to 2.44MB of the BigWavMono.wav file.

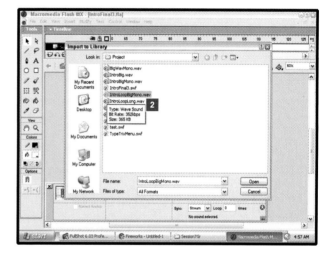

3. **Select the first frame of the Sound layer.**

4. **Select IntroLoopLong.wav in the Library panel.**
   You really do not need this step, but I always like to double-check the Library panel to make sure I got the files I want.

5. **Click the Sound popup menu to open it.**

6. **Select IntroLoopLong.wav.**
   The sound file only goes out to Frame 136 in the Sound layer. You need to fill in about 800 more frames!

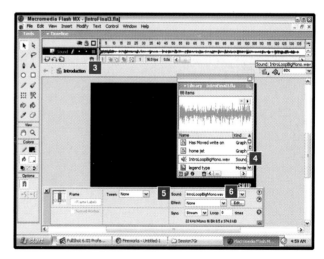

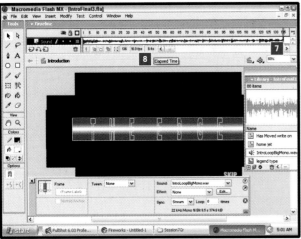

7. **Drag the playhead to Frame 136.**

8. **Write down the value of the elapsed time (8.4 seconds).**
   The entire movie takes 57.8 seconds, so you first need to know how much time the loop takes. You will need the number of loops based on the dividend of the total time divided by the length of the loop. (Total time divided by the time of the loop.) First, though, you will want to reduce the size of the file.

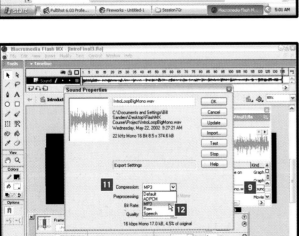

9. **Select the IntroLoopLong.wav file in the Library panel.**

10. **Click the Properties button at the bottom of the Library panel.**
    The Properties button is the little white "i" in the blue circle. As soon as you click the button, the Sound Properties dialog box appears.

11. **In the Sound Properties dialog box, click the Compression popup menu.**

12. **Select MP3.**
    The size has been reduced to 17KB. This size is only imported once because the same file will be used several times.

13. (Windows only) Select Start→Programs→Accessories→Calculator from the Windows Start button.

(Macintosh only) Select Go→Applications→Calculator from the desktop. Depending on the version of operating system you have, your path may be slightly different. As a last resort, you can do a file search for "Calculator" on either system.

14. Use the Calculator to divide 57.8 by 8.4.

You get the result, 6.88.

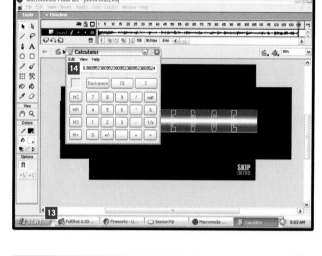

15. Click Frame 1 of the Sound Layer.

16. In the Loop window in the Properties panel, type 7.

The calculated result of 6.88 is rounded to 7. (The total difference between 6.88 and 7 is less than a second in seven loops.)

17. Select Control→Go To End.

Check the last frame to see if the graphic sound wave images go all the way to the end.

18. Select Control→Test Scene.

The sound loop takes up a fraction of what the sound file running the entire movie does because even though the sound takes up the same amount of time depending on the nature of the loop, it may not be noticeable as a sound loop. Good ones are seamless so that a series of loops are indistinguishable from an entire musical piece taking up the entire movie.

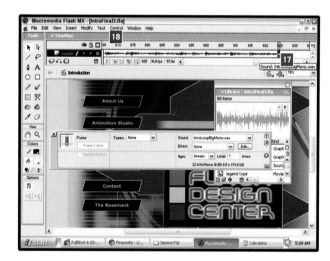

Tutorial
» Editing Sound Length in Flash MX

The great bulk of editing sound files should take place in the sound-editing application you are using. For example, in preparing the sound files for the project movie, I used a program called Smart Sound. In Smart Sound you can select different kinds of sound, mix sound elements, add special effects, and set the length of the sound. However, even using a good sound-editing tool, sometimes after importing the sound into Flash, the sound may not turn out the way you want it. Generally, you would simply have to re-work the sound file in the sound editing application. However, using Flash MX's sound editor, you can make some useful changes. In this tutorial, you import a short loop in the endless quest to make a smaller sound file. The short loop is indeed smaller than the loop you used in the previous tutorial, but it ends too quietly and leaves a sound gap in the loop. To fix this problem, you use the Flash MX sound editor.

1. **Open IntroFinal3.fla.**
    If you have this file open from the previous tutorial, delete the sound in the Sound layer by choosing None from the Sound popup menu in the Properties panel.

2. **Click the first frame of the Sound layer.**

3. **Select File→Import to Library from the menu bar.**

4. **In the Import to Library dialog box, choose ShortMono.wav.**

5. **Click Open.**
    The ShortMono.wav file will now be placed in your Library pane.

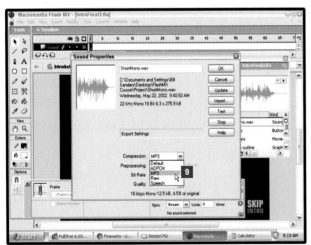

6. **Select Window→Open→Library from the menu bar or press Ctrl+L/Cmd+L.**
    The Library panel opens.

7. **Select ShortMono.wav from the Library panel.**

8. **Click the Properties button at the bottom of the Library panel.**
    The Properties button is the little white "i" in the blue circle. As soon as you click the button, the Sound Properties dialog box appears.

9. **Select the Compression popup menu and choose MP3 as the compression format.**
    The file is compressed to 4.5 percent of its original size.

10. **Select the first frame of the Sound layer.**

11. **Click the Sound popup menu to open the menu.**

12. **Select ShortMono.wav.**
    The graphic wave appears in the Sound layer. The sound file only goes out to Frame 100 in the Sound layer. Note how the end of the sound wave graphic shows a flat line instead of jagged waves in the rest of the file. This flat line contains very low volume sounds that closely resemble silence! This has the effect of leaving a gap in your loop.

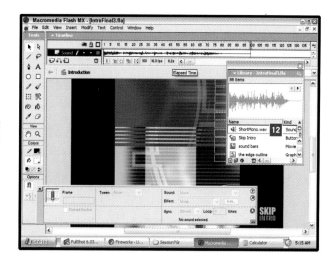

13. **Drag the playhead to Frame 100.**

14. **(Windows only) Select Start→Programs→Accessories→Calculator from the Windows Start button.**
    (Macintosh only) Select Go→Applications→Calculator from the desktop. Depending on the version of operating system you have, your path may be slightly different. As a last resort, you can do a file search for "Calculator" on either system.

15. **Use the Calculator to divide 57.8 by 6.2.**
    You get the result, 9.32.

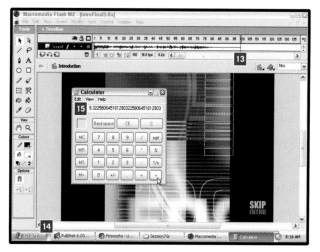

16. **Click Frame 1 of the Sound Layer.**

17. **In the Loop window in the Properties panel, type** 9.
    The calculated result of 9.32 is rounded to 9.

18. **Select Control→Test Scene from the menu bar.**
    When you test the scene, you can clearly hear the gaps between the loops. The length is good, but the gaps sound exactly like loops should not sound — like separate loops rather than one long musical piece.

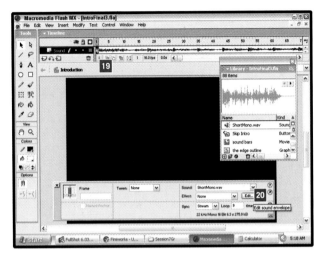

19. **Click the first frame of the Sound layer.**

20. **Click the Edit sound envelope button below the Sound popup menu.**
    The Edit Envelope window appears.

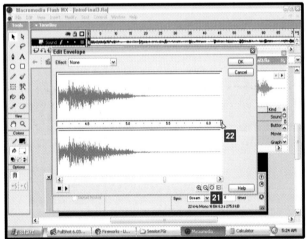

21. **Click the Clock button.**
    The Edit Envelope provides two views — time and frame. By selecting the time view, you will see the time elements listed down the middle of the window.

22. **Drag the horizontal scroll lever to the end of the sound clip.**

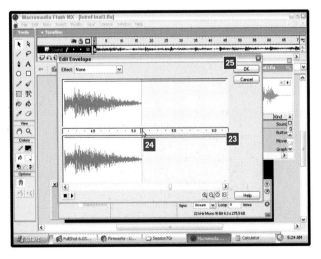

23. **Click the vertical lever on the far right.**

24. **Drag the lever until the long flat wave line is gone.**
    Basically, you're removing the silent gap in the loop.

25. **Click OK to return to the stage.**

26. Drag the playhead to the end of the Sound wave graphic in the Sound layer.

Originally the sound loop extended to Frame 100. Now it only extends to Frame 80.

27. Repeat steps 14–17 using 5.0 to divide the total time of 57.8 seconds.

This time your results are 11.56 which you can round up to 12 without fear of a misalignment of sound and frames. (The difference between the precise and useable is less than half a second.)

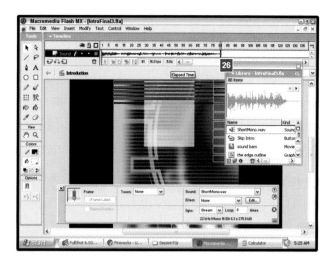

28. Remove 9 from the Loop window in the Properties panel.

29. Type 12 **in the Loop window.**

30. Drag the playhead to the end of the movie to check that the loops cover the range of frames, and then drag it back to the beginning to make sure no gaps exist.

31. Select Control→Test Scene from the menu bar.

This time, the gap between the loop elements should have disappeared and you will hear a continuous uninterrupted stream of music.

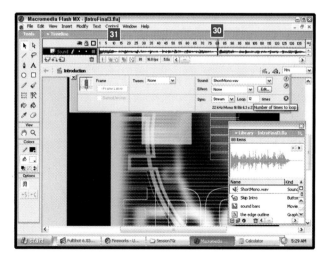

Tutorial
» Creating Fade-in and Fade-out Sounds

Whenever you have sound associated with your Flash site, you can control how the sound begins and ends using a fade-in and fade-out. You can use this technique with a visual fading-in and fading-out as a very effective way to emphasize a transition. Using Flash's Edit Envelope window, you can control different portions of the sound envelope. The top portion of both channels is 100 percent sound, and the bottom portion is 0 percent.

Each channel has a volume line. When the line is pulled up, the volume increases, and when pulled down, it decreases. As you click the sound line, a pull tab appears with up to a total of eight tabs for each channel. By pulling the volume line up and down, you can increase and decrease the sound level for any portion of the movie. This tutorial shows how to create your own fade-in and fade-out effects. You can use one of two methods, and you will see how to use each.

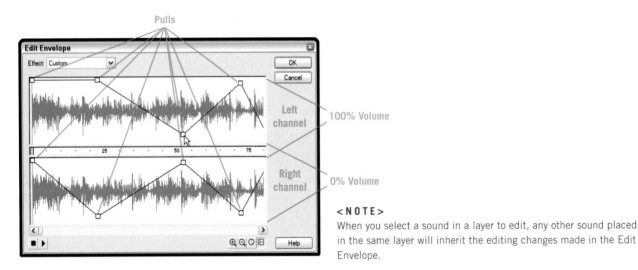

<NOTE>
When you select a sound in a layer to edit, any other sound placed in the same layer will inherit the editing changes made in the Edit Envelope.

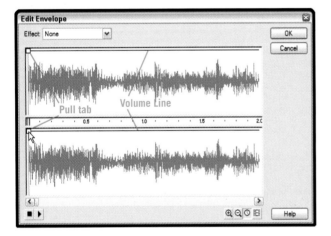

1. Open IntroFinal3.fla.

2. Click the first frame of the Sound layer.

3. Select File→Import to Library from the menu bar.

4. In the Import to Library dialog box, choose BigWavMono.wav.

5. Click Open.
   The BigWavMono.wav file will now be placed in your Library panel.

6. Click the Sound popup menu in the Properties panel and select BigWavMono.wav.

7. Press Edit to open the Edit Envelope window.

8. Click the Clock icon and then click the two magnification buttons until the numbers indicate half-second intervals.
   You will see 0.5 and dots and then 1.0 and more dots and then 1.5.

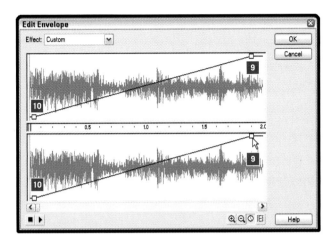

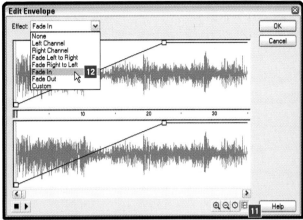

9. **Click the volume line on the right side of the top and bottom channels.**

   When you click the volume line, a pull tab appears.

10. **Drag the pull tabs on the far left side to the bottom of each channel.**

   You should see parallel upward sloping lines in both channels. By moving the pull tabs to the bottom of the channel rows on the left, you turn the sound off. As the sound file plays, both channels' sound increases creating a fade-in sound.

11. **Click the Frame button (to switch from time to frame).**

12. **From the Effect menu, select Fade In.**

   Presto! The same effect was made automatically. However, you cannot set the degree of fade-in, and understand how the process works. Nevertheless, for a quick fade-in, use the Effect menu. You can pull the second tab to made the fade-in more abrupt or gradual.

13. **Drag the horizontal scroll to the end of the sound file.**

14. **Click the volume line slightly before the 54 second marker in both channels.**

   A pull tab appears on the volume line.

15. **Drag the end pull tab on both channels to the bottom of the channel layer.**

   The fade-out takes a little over three seconds, but at 56 seconds, a constant sound line will probably not be heard by most users.

16. **From the Effect menu, select Fade Out.**

   You will see that your fade-out has been replaced by one beginning much earlier in the timeline, providing a more gradual fade-out. You can adjust this manually as with the fade-in effect.

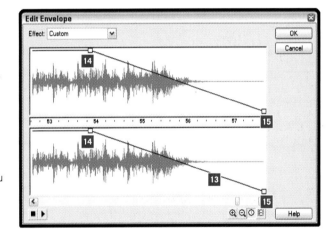

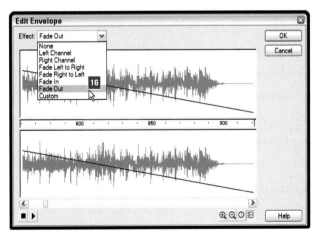

Tutorial
» Customizing Sound Effects

In addition to fading in and fading out, the few other options from the Effect popup menu do not leave too much to do. Therefore, to really use the Edit Envelope, you need to pull the tabs up and down to make your own effects. Limited to eight tabs for each channel, you have to be as creative as possible. One effect you can add to the project movie introduction scene is the ragged sound you get when you alter the volume of a portion of the sound file. To see how to set this up, the following tutorial takes you through the steps to create a bit of cacophony to go with the abstract motion art at the beginning of the movie.

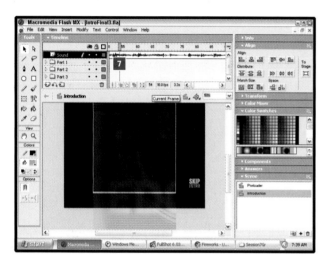

1. **Open IntroFinal3.fla.**

2. **Click the first frame of the Sound layer.**

3. **Select File→Import to Library from the menu bar.**

4. **In the Import to Library dialog box, choose BigWavMono.wav.**

5. **Click Open.**
   The BigWavMono.wav file will now be placed in your Library panel.

6. **Click the Sound popup menu in the Properties panel and select BigWavMono.wav.**

7. **Drag the playhead to Frame 54 and record the number of seconds.**
   This is the beginning of the segment where you will begin your edit.

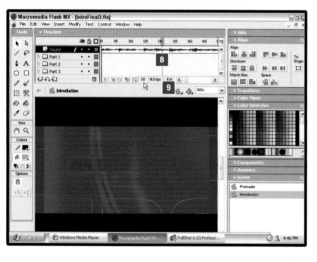

8. **Drag the playhead to Frame 131.**
   This frame is the last frame of the sequence.

9. **Record the number of seconds at Frame 131.**

10. **Press Edit in the Properties panel to open the Edit Envelope window.**

11. **Move the horizontal scroll bar so that you can see Frame 54.**

12. **Click the Zoom-out button until you can see all of the frames between Frame 54 and Frame 131.**

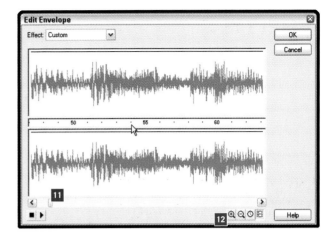

13. **Click the volume lines of both channels as close to Frame 54 as possible.**
    A pull tab will appear.

14. **Pull the tab down to the middle of the volume line.**

15. **Click Frame 78 and pull the line to the top.**

16. **Click Frame 120 and pull the line to the middle of the volume line.**

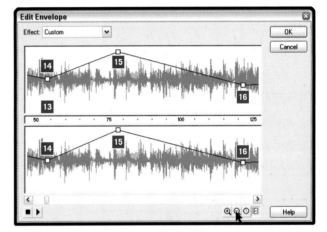

17. **Click Frame 131 and pull the line to the top of the channel.**

18. **Click OK.**

19. **Select Control→Test Scene from the menu bar.**
    You should notice that the sound spikes in the middle of the abstract motion graphics that add to the opening effect.

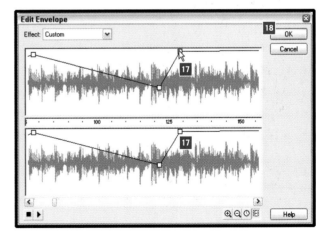

Tutorial
» Using Scripts in Buttons and Event Sounds

One very useful place to put your sounds is in a button's timeline. Then when you click the button, the sound plays. Sound Sync provides for Event Sounds. These sounds play themselves out from a movie event. One such event, obviously, is the click of a button object. By placing the sound in a Down keyframe in a button, as soon as the button is pressed, it triggers the sound in the Down keyframe. It's one of the easiest ways to link sound to actions. This tutorial shows you how.

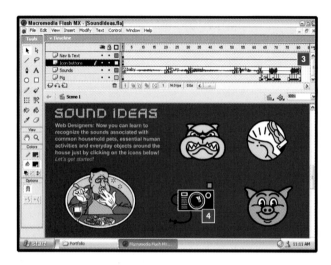

1. **Drag a copy of SoundIdeas.fla from the CD-ROM.**

2. **Double-click the file icon to open it.**
   Once open, you will see five icons representing a dog, a baby's bottom, a gourmand, a camera, and a pig. All of the icons are buttons that emit a sound and associate an action with the sound. Only the pig's nose is a button.

3. **Open the Frame-view popup menu and change the view to Small or Tiny so that you can see all of the frames containing graphic sound images.**
   Most of the sounds were placed in the main timeline. Each keyframe where a sound begins uses a Start sync and a Stop sync where they are terminated.

4. **Double-click the camera button to enter the Symbol Editing Mode.**

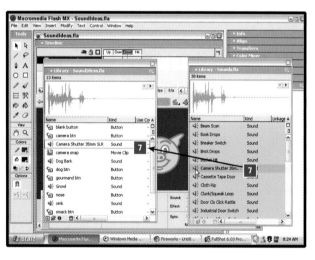

5. **Select Window→Common Libraries→Sounds.**

6. **Select Window→Library.**
   If the two library panels are in the same docking block, drag one to the side.

7. **Select Camera Shutter 35mm SLR from the Library Sounds.fla panel and drag it to the Library panel.**

8. In the Symbol Editing Mode, click Insert Layer and rename the layers "sound" and "icon."

9. Click in the Down frame, select both layers, and press the F6 key to insert a keyframe.

10. In the Up frame of the icon layer, draw a camera without the flash on.

11. Drag the playhead to the Down frame in the icon layer and draw a camera with the flash showing.

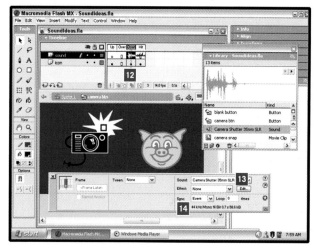

12. Click the Down frame in the sound layer.

13. In the Sound window of the Properties panel, select Camera Shutter 35mm SLR. You will see part of the graphic sound wave in the frame.

14. In the Sync popup menu, choose Event.

   Event is the default, but in case popup menus show something else from other work, be sure to select Event. That's all there is to getting the camera synchronized with the sound.

Tutorial
» Using Start and Stop Sync

Two important and sometimes overlooked Sync options are Start and Stop. Using these two options allows you to set conditions where one a sound begins and another ends. One way to use Start and Stop is to truncate sounds you may have available to coordinate with animated actions, and in this tutorial you learn several examples of how to begin a sound and then stop it when and where you want. All Start sound Sync options occur in keyframes at the beginning of a sound file. You cannot make a file begin in the file's middle. However, you can stop a file anywhere you want when the file is playing. Another way to use the Start and Stop option involves allowing the user viewing your Flash movie to have control of stopping or starting any sound. Your user may find a sound annoying after he or she has heard it more than a few times, and providing this option, you stand a better chance of the user returning to your site.

<NOTE>
You may wonder why you use Start and Stop Sync options to shorten sound clips instead of using the Editor as shown in "Tutorial: Editing Sound Length in Flash MX" earlier in this session. Suppose you need to use the same sound clip in different places for different lengths in the same movie. Once you change a sound length in the Editor, you make all instances of that sound clip exactly the same length. However, using Start and Stop Sync options, you can use the same sound clip as many times as you want at several different lengths.

1. Draw a bulldog, select the image, and press F8 to open the Convert to Symbol dialog box.

2. Select Button as the Behavior and name the button dog btn and click OK.

3. With the dog button selected, open the Actions panel, and select Expert Mode from the View Options popup menu.

4. Type the following script in the script pane:

```
on(press) {
    gotoAndPlay("growl")
}
on(release) {
    gotoAndPlay("bark")
}
```

This script needs to reference two frames, one named "growl" and another named "bark." So that's the next step. In this particular script, when you click the mouse key, the playhead goes to the frame labeled "growl" and plays it. When you release the mouse button, the playhead then goes to the frame labeled "bark" and plays it. So for the price of a single mouse click, you get two sounds.

5. Click in Frame 32 and press F6 to insert a keyframe.

6. In the Frame Properties panel, type growl for the name of the frame.

7. Repeat steps 19–20 in Frame 53 using the name bark.

8. Click in the "growl" frame (32), and in the Properties panel Sound popup menu, choose Growl for the sound, and choose Start for the Sync.

9. Click in the "bark" frame (53), and in the Properties panel select Dog Bark as the sound and choose Start for the Sync.
Then click Frame 52 and press F6 to insert a keyframe.

10. Click the keyframe in the Properties panel, select Growl in the Sound popup menu, and Stop in the Sync popup menu.

11. Repeat steps 9 and 10 with Frame 63 and select Dog Bark.
Now all of the sound files for this button are in place.

12. **Double-click the dog button.**

13. **Select the Down frame and press the F6 key to add keyframes to both layers.**

14. **With the Down frame selected, carefully place a red-orange radial down the middle of the dog's face.**

    The effect adds to the dog's unpleasant attitude and coincides with the growl. So when the button is pressed, the dog growls and reddens and starts barking as soon as you release the key.

15. **Select the first frame of the Sound layer and name the frame "begin" and add the following script in the Actions panel:**

    ```
    stop();
    ```

16. **Insert keyframes in Frames 22, 31, 52, 63 and 81, and enter the following script for each frame in the Actions panel:**

    ```
    gotoAndStop("begin")
    ```

17. **Follow steps 1–14 to recreate the gourmand using the "urp" sound, beginning in Frame 23 (and naming Frame 23 "urp"), and ending in Frame 31 using the following script:**

    ```
    on(press) {
         gotoAndPlay("urp")
    }
    ```

    Instead of turning crimson with anger, the gourmand turns green with nausea. The sound "urp" is actually part of a longer snoring sound. By shortening the series of snores, it was possible to create an "urp" sound. Select the urp sound file in the Library and click the Play button to listen to the entire snore sequence.

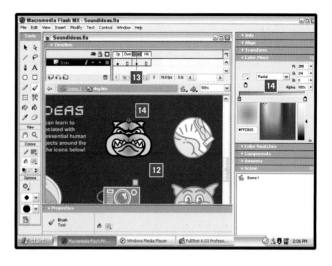

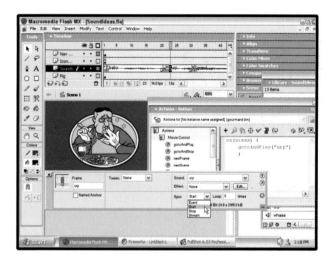

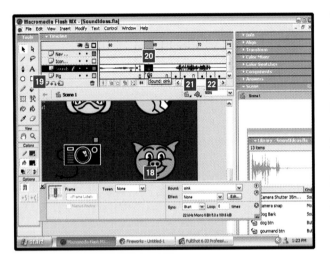

18. You can use steps 1–14 to recreate the oinking pig, but the button is the pig's nose, and not the entire object; so when you draw the pig, select only the pig's nose, press F8, and create a button symbol from the nose drawing.

19. Add a layer to the main timeline and name it Pig.

20. Beginning in Frame 64 on the Pig layer, draw a smiling pig's head, and then in Frame 67, draw a pig opening its mouth.

21. In Frame 68, draw a pig's leaning left with its mouth fully open, and then in Frame 70 rotate the drawing to the right.

22. In Frame 71 and 72, reverse the drawings in step 20.

23. Repeat the sequence in Frames 77–80.

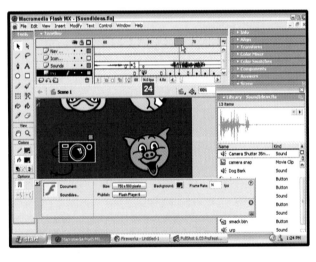

24. Insert keyframes in Frames 64 and 81 of the Sounds layer by clicking the frames and pressing the F6 key.

25. Choose oink in the Sound popup menu and Start in the Sync popup menu in the Properties panel in Frame 64.

26. Choose oink in the Sound popup menu and Stop in the Sync popup menu in the Properties panel in Frame 81.
Notice how the sound wave graphic spikes where the keyframes with the pig's head expression and rotation changed. By looking at both the timeline with the action and the one with the sound, you find it possible to better coordinate movement and sound.

» Session Review

This session covers using, coordinating, and editing sound files used in Flash MX. The synchronization of sound with Flash actions, the ways to reduce the size of Flash files, and how and where to place sounds in Flash MX movies are essential elements in the successful creation of a movie.

1. What are some of the resources for getting sounds for a Flash movie? (See "Session Introduction.")

2. How do you import sound files into Flash MX? (See "Tutorial: Importing Sounds into Flash.")

3. What is streaming sound? What will it do to the speed of a movie? When is streaming sound best used? (See "Tutorial: Using Streaming Sound.")

4. Why is reducing the size of a sound file important? What is the best way to immediately reduce the size of a file? (See "Tutorial: Reducing Sound File Sizes.")

5. What are sound loops? Why are they preferable to a single long sound file? How do you make sound loops loop in Flash MX? (See "Tutorial: Using Sound Loops to Reduce SWF Size.")

6. How do you reduce the size of a sound file in the Edit Envelope? (See "Tutorial: Editing Sound Length in Flash MX.")

7. What elements of a sound file can you edit in the Edit Envelope? How many pull tabs can each channel have in the Edit Envelope? (See "Tutorial: Editing Sound Length in Flash MX.")

8. What are the two ways to create fade-in and fade-out sounds? Why is the easiest method sometimes less preferable? (See "Tutorial: Creating Fade-in and Fade-out Sounds.")

9. What are some of the different ways you can change the way a sound file sounds using the Edit Envelope? (See "Tutorial: Customizing Sound Effects.")

10. How do you trigger a sound using a button? Which ways can this be done with and without having to include ActionScript? (See "Tutorial: Using Scripts in Buttons and Event Sounds.")

11. What happens to a sound when using an Event Sync? How do you set up an Event Sync? (See "Tutorial: Using Scripts in Buttons and Event Sounds.")

12. How do you start and stop a sound using Start and Stop Sync options? Can you stop some sounds and not others using Stop Sync? (See "Tutorial: Using Start and Stop Sync.")

» Additional Projects

The following is a list of projects that relate to this session and can help you refine your expertise in working with text in Flash MX.

» Create a movie with two buttons. When you press the first button, a sound file will start playing and when you press the second button, the sound will stop.

» Use a search engine like Google, Yahoo, or another favorite and see what sounds are available free on the Internet that you can use in a Flash movie.

» Find a sound you like and place it on a layer in a new Flash MX movie. Then, after examining the shape of the graphic sound wave, create a movie that synchronizes with the sound. (Hint: Start with something simple like a bouncing ball.)

» Experiment creating your own sound effects. Use a tape recorder and tape actual sounds that could go with your movie. Also, try your hand at voice narration to go with your movies. Start with simple ones like, "Press button to start" or simply, "Welcome."

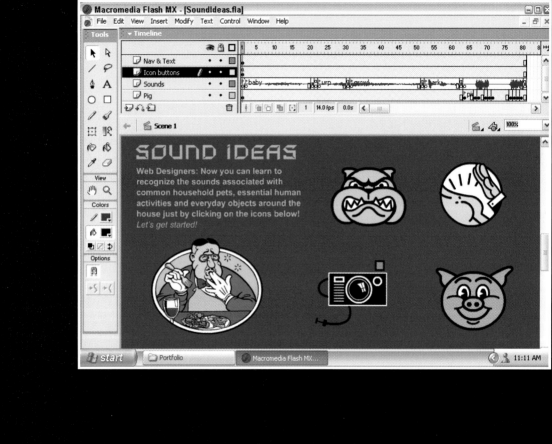

Debugging and Publishing Movies

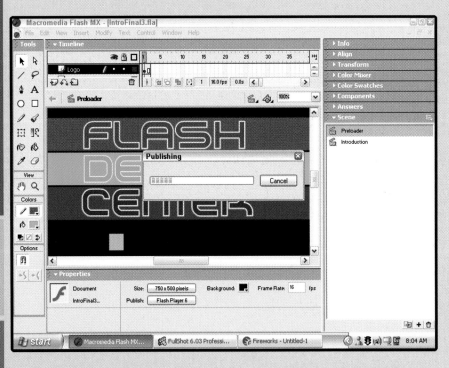

Tutorial: **Publishing a Movie**

Tutorial: **Debugging Controls**

Tutorial: **Viewing a Movie with the Bandwidth Profiler**

Tutorial: **Testing the Speed of Your Movie**

Tutorial: **Using the Publish Formats**

Tutorial: **Selecting Output Options**

Tutorial: **Using Flash Templates**

Tutorial: **Creating Templates for Special Devices**

Preparing for Publication

This session deals with getting your movie ready for publication in two very different ways. First, once your movie is nearly complete, you want to fine-tune it. The greatest culprit to creating a successful movie for the Web is size. Throughout this course, you have seen ways to reduce the size of graphics and sound — the two elements with significant weight problems.

A second important area in preparing for publication is that of setting the publication parameters. While Flash MX is primarily a tool for creating dynamic content for the Internet, it can be used for publishing different types of graphics and movies to be run by "projectors" on a computer's own system and not through a browser.

One shortcut to help prepare for publications can be found at the beginning of a project rather than the end. This is the use of templates to create movies. Flash MX has templates for everything from simple banners to complex quizzes. All you have to do is to fill in the blanks to get a good-looking and working Flash movie completed.

The very first tutorial covers how to publish a movie. One of the reasons that you need to first publish a movie before you debug it is that the Flash MX debugging tools are found in the Flash player. So first you publish your movie, and then, using the debugging tools, you get it ready to launch on the Internet.

TOOLS YOU USE
Properties panel, Text tool, Test Movie window

MATERIALS NEEDED
From the accompanying CD-ROM, you need the IntroFinal3.fla file.

TIME REQUIRED
60 minutes

SESSION OUTCOME
How to use the Flash debugging features and set the Flash controls to publish a movie and use templates

PROJECT PORTION
IntroFinal3.fla

Tutorial
» Publishing a Movie

The best part about publishing a movie is that it's easy. The second step in this tutorial shows you how to do that. What's more, Flash MX is really smart, and when you publish a movie, not only does it create an SWF file (the compiled running movie), but it also generates the HTML that describes the page surrounding the Flash movie. The key element here is the SWF file, which you may have noticed is generated whenever you test a movie. Using other applications, like Macromedia Dreamweaver or Adobe GoLive, you can generate your own HTML page with the SWF file embedded in the file. Sometimes, you want only a part of your HTML page to contain a Flash MX movie. In those cases, you're better off using Dreamweaver or GoLive to set up the framework for creating your HTML file. However, if you want your HTML page to contain your Flash movie and nothing else, all you have to do is publish it from Flash MX and your HTML page is generated for you automatically.

1. **Open IntroFinal3.fla.**

2. **Select File→Publish from the menu bar.**

3. **Observe the Publishing window taskbar.**
   As soon as the taskbar fills the bar window, your movie is published.

4. **Open the folder where your FLA file has been saved.**
   You see two new files. One (IntroFinal3.SWF) is the compiled running version of your movie. You can run it by double-clicking it in the Flash player. The other file (IntroFinal3.html) is the HTML file. It works like an HTML "wrapper" for your Flash movie. Flash MX writes all of the HTML code for you.

5. **Open a text editing tool like MS Windows' Notepad (Start→All Programs→Accessories→Notepad) or SimpleText on the Mac.**

6. Open the file IntroFinal3.html in the text editor.

You see the following HTML listing:

```
<HTML>
<HEAD>
<meta http-equiv=Content-Type
content="text/html; charset=ISO-8859-1">
<TITLE>IntroFinal3</TITLE>
</HEAD>
<BODY bgcolor="#000000">
<!- URLs used in the movie->
<!- text used in the movie->
<OBJECT classid="clsid:D27CDB6E-AE6D-11cf-
96B8-444553540000"
codebase="http://download.macromedia.com/pub/
shockwave/cabs/flash/swflash.cab#ver-
sion=6,0,0,0" WIDTH="750" HEIGHT="500"
id="IntroFinal3" ALIGN="">
<PARAM NAME=movie VALUE="IntroFinal3.swf">
<PARAM NAME=quality VALUE=high>
<PARAM NAME=scale VALUE=noborder>
<PARAM NAME=bgcolor VALUE=#000000>
<EMBED src="IntroFinal3.swf" quality=high
scale=noborder bgcolor=#000000 WIDTH="750"
HEIGHT="500" NAME="IntroFinal3" ALIGN=""
TYPE="application/x-shockwave-flash" PLUG-
INSPAGE= "http://www.macromedia.com/go/get-
flashplayer"></EMBED>
</OBJECT>
</BODY>
</HTML>
```

You don't need to know a thing about HTML scripting to create the code. Flash MX is so smart that it even includes HTML code to detect whether the viewer has the right kind of plug-in. If he doesn't, it redirects the browser to Macromedia's site where he can download the right plug-in. Knowing a little of the generated code helps you understand what parameters you can adjust.

```
<PARAM NAME=movie VALUE="IntroFinal3.swf">
```

This parameter simply identifies the name of the SWF file, naming it "movie." All SWF files have this parameter tag.

```
<PARAM NAME=quality VALUE=high>
```

The quality refers to the amount of anti-aliasing (graphic smoothing) a viewer's processor is required to perform prior to showing a frame on the screen. The trade-off is between playback speed and anti-aliasing. Anti-aliased graphics look better than those that are not anti-aliased. The following list explains what each does:

» Low: Never uses anti-aliasing.

» Autolow: Begins with anti-aliasing turned off and only turns it on if the player determines the processor can handle it.

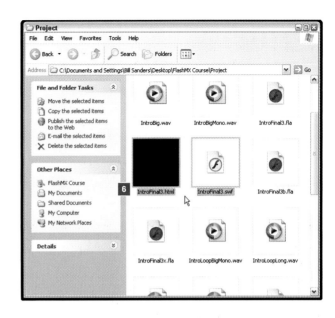

» Autohigh: Attempts to equally emphasize speed and anti-aliasing, but if the processor cannot handle both, it turns off anti-aliasing.

» Medium: Does not attempt to smooth bitmaps but provides anti-aliasing on other graphics.

» High: Emphasizes appearance over playback speed, but does not apply anti-aliasing to animated bitmaps.

» Best: Playback speed is ignored in favor of appearance and applies anti-aliasing to all graphics, including animated bitmaps.

In general, unless you have a good reason to do otherwise, I recommend leaving it at the default high quality.

```
<PARAM NAME=bgcolor VALUE=#000000>
```

This one is interesting. The background color set in the movie is black, or #000000. However, this value is the background color only of the movie, and not the HTML page. The HTML page's background color remains black until the line

```
<BODY bgcolor="#000000">
```

is changed. If you want to have the background color of your page different than that of your movie, all you have to do is to change one or the other. By default, both colors of the HTML page and the Flash MX movie are the same based on what you initially set the color to be in the Flash editor. Fiddling with the HTML code does not change the actual movie itself — just how it is rendered in an HTML page.

Tutorial
» Debugging Controls

Flash MX contains several different tools to help you find possible problems with your movie. When you start writing ActionScript, you will find that most of the problems you encounter are automatically presented in the Output window. However, when you're working primarily without ActionScript, most of the problems stem from the size and speed of the movie. If you have a fast connection, such as a DSL (Digital Subscriber Line) or cable modem, you may think that your movie is just fine. However, if most of the people who are looking at your Web site are running 56K phone modems (that rarely get up to 56K on most phone lines), you need to know how long it takes them to load your movie and what it will look like. This next tutorial shows how to use controls that show you what your movie looks like to people with different modems.

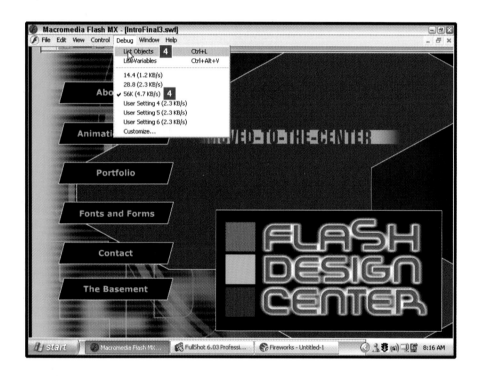

1. **Open IntroFinal3.fla.**

2. **Select Control→Test Movie from the menu bar.**

3. **Click the Skip Intro button to go to the end of the movie.**

4. **Select Debug→56K (4.7 KB/s) from the menu bar.**
   You are now using a different menu bar than the one in the Flash editor. Here, your movie is still running and can be rewound whenever you want. The Debug menu contains the speeds and different objects and variables you can view. The 4.7 KB/s means that it simulates the speed at 4.7 kilobytes per second.

<N O T E>
The project movie for this course is far too big and takes too much time to load for a practical Web application for users with less than a cable modem or DSL line. It was designed to include every trick in the book that we could dream up so that you could pick and choose those aspects of the project that you would like to include in your own movie rather than the ideal for Web usability.

5. **Select Debug→List Objects from the menu bar.**

   An Output window appears on top of the movie.

6. **Drag the vertical scroll bar to the top of the window.**

   You see the different objects listed. The buttons include related target instances. You can also see any labels. Since the movie uses more comments than labels, those labels you see are those that were left as guides to the different objects.

7. **Select Debug→List Variables from the menu bar.**

8. **Drag the vertical scroll bar to the top of the window.**

   Here you see the different variables used in the Preloader ActionScript. When you learn some more ActionScript in Sessions 9–12, you will find this information more useful. For now, though, you know where to find it. For example, one of the variables used was called nowLoaded, which compares the total number of frames loaded (totalLoaded), and when they are they same, it jumps to the Introduction scene.

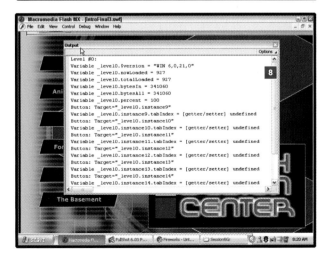

Tutorial

» Viewing a Movie with the Bandwidth Profiler

When you look at a movie running in the player or frame-by-frame in the editor, you can see the different objects on the stage, but what you cannot see is how much bandwidth the different parts take up. The Bandwidth Profiler breaks up the movie into a set of vertical bars that provide a visual scale of what each frame "weighs" in terms of bandwidth. The higher the bar, the more bandwidth it consumes. This next tutorial shows you how to use this handy movie analyzer.

1. Open IntroFinal3.fla.

2. Select Control→Test Movie from the menu bar.

3. Click the Skip Intro button to go to the end of the movie.

4. Select View→Bandwidth Profiler from the menu bar.

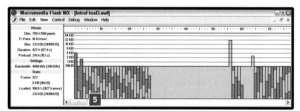

5. Drag the horizontal scroll bar to the far left.

   You see a number of bars beneath a red line with a few bars going above the red line. Each bar represents a frame, and the bars show the amount of "weight" in kilobytes each frame takes. The spikes indicate "heavy" sections in your movie.

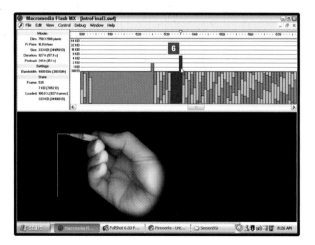

6. Click the bar sticking up in the frame.

   A hand drawing a box appears. The reason the bar is sticking up more than the others is that the bitmapped hand is a relatively "heavy" object taking up bandwidth to display it moving. The bar that sticks up is grouped with several other bars to show the materials associated with it.

Tutorial

» Testing the Speed of Your Movie

If you have been running the main project movie in this course, you have not seen too much of the Preloader. The movie loads right up in the test player and you never get to see the Preloader tick away the percent of the movie loader or watch the bar creep rightwards as it provides a visual indicator of how much of the movie is loaded. By looking at the movie through the eyes of the viewer who has a slow modem, you not only can see your Preloader working away, you can see how long it takes to load the movie. If you test your movie on a cable modem, T1-T3 line, or DSL line from the Web, you cannot see what it looks like to someone with a 56K or 28.8K modem. If your audience has a fast connection like you, you can test it in real time on the Web and with your own system. However, if your audience is typical of the general Web audience, you need to test your movie using the Flash MX Show Streaming view with a 28.8K modem. You'll have lots of time to watch the Preloader at work!

(This tutorial is a continuation of the previous tutorial, so if you're beginning here, take a look at the previous six steps.)

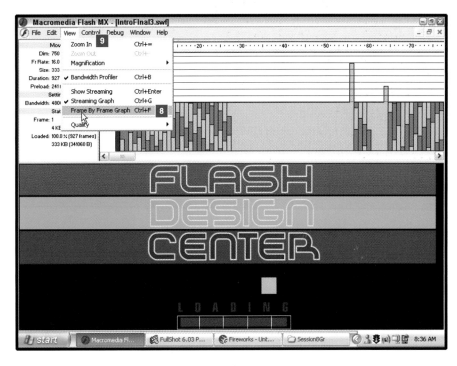

7. **Drag the playhead to the first frame of the Preloader scene.**

8. **Select View→Frame by Frame graph from the menu bar.**
   Frame-by-frame gives you a different view of the bandwidth profile. It's much easier to identify individual frames.

9. **Select Control→Rewind from the menu bar.**
   You can see the very first setting of the preloader graph. As soon as it starts running, you should be able to see a percentage of loaded materials.

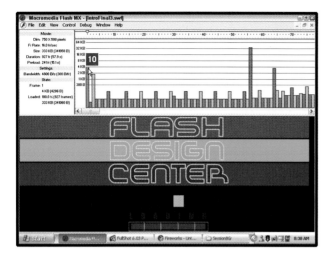

10. **Select the bar in the first frame of the Preloader scene.**

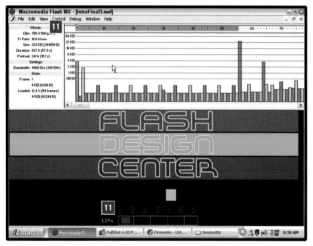

11. **Select View→Show Streaming.**

    As soon you release the mouse button, your movie is off and running. However, it's taking a long time to load and you can see the preloader bar inching forward and the long count as each percent of the movie loads. That is what someone with a 56K modem is seeing, and she may not want to sit through this kind of long load more than once or twice. However, you will see that as soon as the movie has loaded, the rest of the movie runs at a normal speed. That's because once all of the movie is in the computer's memory, the connection to the server with your Web site on it is broken, and it's running on your computer fully. (You can now see why a preloader is so important if you have a big movie.)

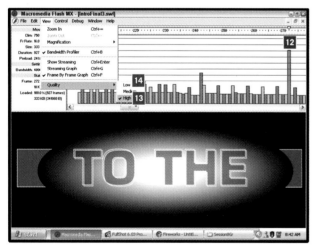

12. **Select the tall bar in Frame 272.**

13. **Choose View→Quality→High.**

    Watch the segment run; you see several graphics being moved.

14. **Choose View→Quality→Low.**

    You can now see the ragged edges in the oval and even the text graphics. For computers with slower processors, changing the Quality to Low would help them move the movie along but at a sacrifice of quality.

Tutorial
» Using the Publish Formats

Flash MX provides eight different settings in the Publish Settings window. Of these eight settings, you generally only use two — Flash and HTML. The Flash setting publishes the SWF file and the HTML setting publishes an HTML file with all of the code to embed your SWF file into the HTML page generated. If you select the HTML option, it automatically selects the SWF option because it needs the SWF file to embed. Three graphic image files options, GIF Image (.gif), JPEG Image (.jpg), and PNG Image (.png), are available as well. The value of publishing a single graphic image may not be immediately obvious, but the option does allow you to publish any single frame in the movie — including objects in the middle of a tween operation. The third set of options in the Publish Formats window are three stand-alone players: Windows Projector (.exe), Macintosh Projector, and QuickTime (.mov). The Macintosh Projector is published as a compressed .hqx file when published on a Windows platform and a Projector file on a Macintosh. That makes it handy for Windows users to attach the compressed file and e-mail it as an attachment to friends and colleagues with a Macintosh computer. (Mac users can reciprocate by publishing .exe files for Windows viewing.) The QuickTime option generates a .mov file that can be viewed on either a Macintosh or Windows platform.

1. **Open IntroFinal3.fla.**

2. **Select File➔Publish Preview➔Flash from the menu bar.**
   Your Movie plays in the Flash player. This option is very similar to testing the movie from the editor when you select Test Movie from the Control menu in the menu bar.

3. **Select File➔Publish Preview➔HTML from the menu bar.**
   Your movie plays in the browser. This gives you an opportunity to see what your movie looks like in your default browser. You can also test it in any other browsers by simply loading the SWF file directly into the browser.

<NOTE>
While talking about all of the publish formats and the ability of Macintosh and Windows users to publish projector files for those with the opposite operating systems, keep in mind that all SWF files and FLA files can be used interchangeably on Mac and Windows platforms with no conversions at all. So before you do anything fancy to create movies for your colleagues with opposite platforms, remember that sometimes the simplest solution is the best!

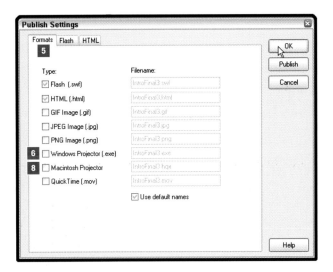

4. **Select File→Publish Settings from the menu bar.**
   You see the Publish Settings window.

5. **Click the Formats tab (if not already selected).**
   The default settings for the Format Type are Flash (.swf) and HTML (.html). At the beginning of this session, you published your movie, and both an SWF and HTML file were generated. That was because the Flash and HTML options were selected in this window.

6. **[Windows users only] Click the Windows Projector (.exe) options and click OK.**

7. **Select File→Publish Preview Projector from the menu bar.**
   You see your movie play like it would if you had tested it any other way. However, when you look on your disk, you will find a file named IntroFinal3.exe. This file is a run-time file that you can send to anyone with a Windows computer, and it runs. If you create professional software for distribution, this format is often selected for Windows computers. You will find the file to be relatively large compared with your SWF file. The SWF file should be about 333KB (depending on which sound file you put in), but your .exe file will be around 1.1MB (again depending on which sound file you used). Nevertheless, many developers prefer .EXE files for distribution because no player at all is required and there is no need to be concerned about whether the user has the right version of player.

8. **[Macintosh users only] Click the Macintosh Projector options and click OK.**

9. **Select File→Publish Preview Projector from the menu bar.**
   You see your movie play like it would if you had tested it with any other way. However, when you look on your disk, you will find a file named IntroFinal3 Projector. This file is a run-time file that you can send to anyone with a Macintosh computer, and it runs. The SWF file should be between 300–400KB depending on which sound file you used, but your projector file will be about 1.2MB or three times as large. When sharing your movies with friends, using SWF files is probably a better idea because they can view them on a player they can download from www.macromedia.com and they don't take up as much room as a projector file.

Tutorial

» Selecting Output Options

This tutorial covers setting your movie so that it can be played back in the way you want. Generally, you use Flash Player 6, and if you use some of the new features of Flash MX, you have to use Flash Player 6 for the movie to run correctly. However, if you want your movies to run on older players or on certain platforms (Cell Phone or Pocket Computer, for example), you may have to use a certain version other than Flash Player 6.

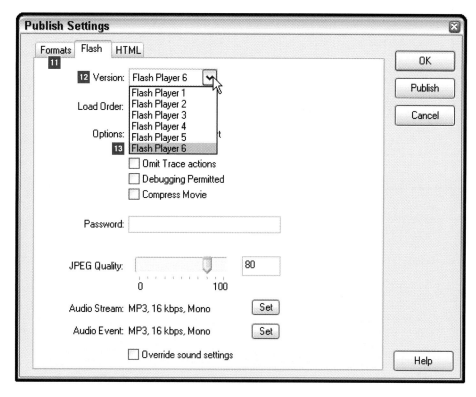

10. **Select File→Publish Settings from the menu bar.**

11. **Make sure that Flash and HTML are selected in the Formats tab and click the Flash tab in the Publish Settings window.**

12. **Click the Version popup menu at the top of the window.**
    You see several versions of the Flash Player.

13. **Select the version of player you want.**
    Generally, you select Flash Player 6 or sometimes Flash Player 5. However, if you want your movies to be viewed on much older players, you have those options as well. If you publish your movie for a Flash 6 player for general Web use, if the viewer does not have a Flash 6 plug-in for her browser, she is automatically sent to the Macromedia site where she can download a free plugin for any of the common browsers currently available. However, for some devices, such as the Pocket PC, only Flash 5 works at the time of this writing.

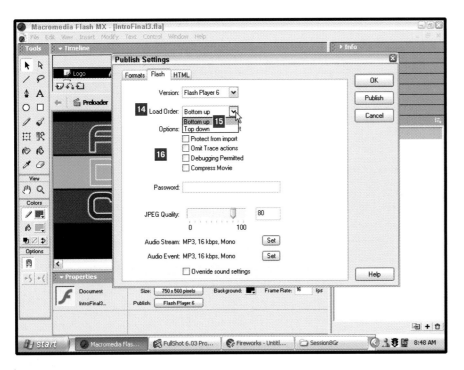

14. Click the Load Order popup menu.

Two Options appear.

15. Select Bottom up or Top down.

By and large this option is for a slow modem and determines which layers of your movie it draws first. Out of convention and practical exigency, the lower layers (bottom) are used for background items and so they are generally loaded first so that the movie has a background or setting prior to the more animated elements being placed on top. However, you can use the opposite tact and load the higher layers first if you want to get across a message, for example, before the background materials settle in.

16. Click any of the following options:

» Generate Size Report: This option provides a report on the amount of data frame by frame your movie creates. The file is saved as a text file to your folder with the FLA. (This option is hidden beneath the Load Order popup menu when the menu is open.)

» Protect from Import: This is a security feature to keep the file from being converted back into an FLA file.

» Omit Trace Actions: The trace ActionScript statement is ignored. Once debugging has reached a certain stage, you may not want to be bothered by the trace information in the Output window, especially if the trace indicates that everything is working well.

» Debugging Permitted: For collaborative work, this option lets someone else work on your file. By selecting this option, you activate the password protection by typing a password in the Password text window beneath the options list.

» Compress Movie: You can compress a Flash Player 6 movie to reduce the file size. The SWF file is smaller when published. This is the only default option in the set.

17. **Click the HTML tab in the Publish Settings window.**

18. **Click the Template popup menu.**
    Twelve templates appear. These are not the same templates that you select from the File menu, but rather, they are publishing templates for movie output. For example, to publish only for a Pocket PC 20, you would select Flash Only For Pocket PC 20. (At the same time you set up the template for the Pocket PC, you would have to be sure that the Flash 5 is the selected player version in the Flash tab of the Publish Setting.) The default Template is Flash Only and is the one you publish to for the great bulk of your work unless you specialize in applications for other than general Web pages.

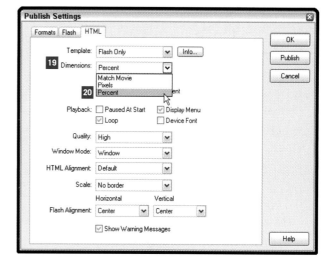

19. **Click the Dimensions popup menu.**

20. **Select Percent from the menu selections.**
    As soon as you select Percent, the Width and Height text windows become active. By default, their values are 100 percent. What this means is that your Flash movie takes up 100 percent of the HTML page. This option is helpful when you do not know what size the viewer will have set his browser, the size of the screen, or the resolution used.

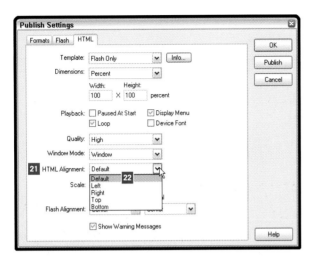

21. **Click the HTML Alignment popup menu.**

22. **Select Default.**
As long as you have selected 100 percent for your dimensions, the HTML alignment won't affect your movie very much because it is taking up 100 percent of the browser window. However, if you change the Dimensions to Match Movie, those movies with a small stage size can be positioned at different locations on the browser window.

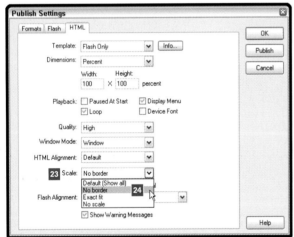

23. **Click the Scale popup menu.**

24. **Select No Border.**
By selecting No Border, you scale the movie to fill an area and maintain its aspect ratio. If required, the movie is cropped.

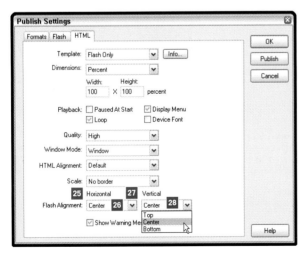

25. **Click the Horizontal Flash Alignment popup menu.**

26. **Select Center.**

27. **Click the Vertical Flash Alignment popup menu.**

28. **Select Center.**
Now your Flash movie is aligned to the Center. Depending on the nature of your movie and the content in the HTML page, you should make the necessary adjustments here. With a movie as large as the project movie, you see very little effect of placement options in HTML.

Tutorial
» Using Flash Templates

Flash templates give you a running start on projects. Many of the little settings that have to be done in the Publish Settings window have already been done. Likewise, special settings for the stage size, inserting layers, and other mundane but important chores are all complete when you open the template. Some of the more complex templates that use ActionScript and UI Components give you a very big head start. For example, the Quiz template has six layers, several movie clips, ActionScript, UI components, and a full set of instructions on how to use the template to create your own quizzes. This tutorial takes you through a simple template used to create a banner ad.

1. **Open Flash.**

2. **Select File→New From Template.**
   The New Document Window opens. You see eight categories of templates.

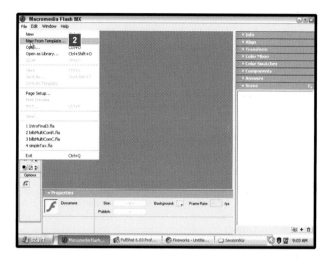

3. **Select Ads from the Category column.**

4. **Select banner_468x60 from the Category Item column.**
   The selection represents a banner ad with the dimensions 468 pixels wide and 60 pixels high.

5. **Click Create.**
   When the banner template appears, you see two layers. The top layer is a special one that does not appear when you publish your movie. It's the layer that contains a three-screen (three keyframes) set of instructions for the voluntary guidelines for rich media ad formats. If you are at all interested in marketing, you should take a look at the guidelines. They provide some useful insights about how customers respond to banner ads on the Web. Because Flash is so good at creating animated banners, developers who create banners often use Flash. However, technical expertise is only part of the equation in making a successful banner. The other part is knowing how to do so in such a way that viewers will be attracted instead of repelled.

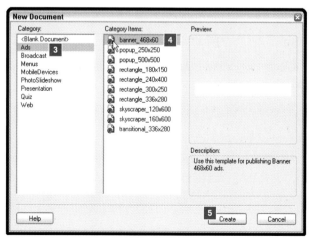

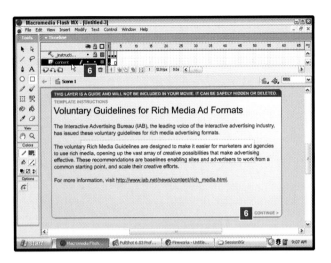

6. **Click the Continue button on the lower-right side of the stage to read the guidelines.**

   You can use the button to functionally click through the set of instructions because the template set the Control menu options to Enable Simple Frame Actions, Enable Simple Buttons, and Enable Live Preview.

7. **Click the content layer.**

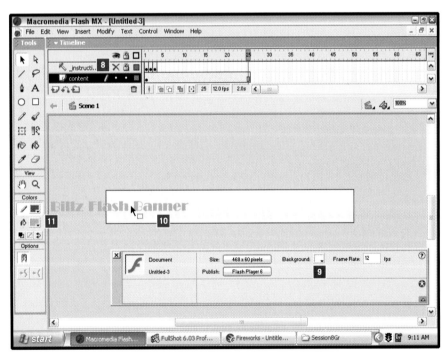

8. **Click the Eye column of the instructions layer.**

   The instructions disappear.

9. **Select a light yellow for the background color.**

10. **Choose the Text tool and, using an Art Deco font such as BroadwayBT (or any other font you want), type** <Your Name's> Flash Banner **in 24-point green.**

11. **Position the text on the left side of the banner stage.**

12. **Click Frame 25 and press the F5 key to insert a frame.**

13. **Click Frame 25 and press the F6 key to insert a keyframe.**

14. **With the keyframe in Frame 25 selected, move the text to the far right end of the stage.**

< T I P >

To make sure that a banner will flow smoothly, set up the beginning of the banner centered vertically on the left side of the stage. Then, select the last keyframe for the banner's horizontal scroll, select the text, and press Shift + Right Arrow to move it horizontally without changing its vertical position.

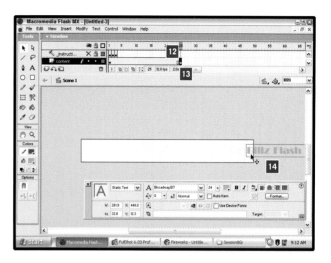

15. **Click the first frame.**

16. **In the Properties panel, select Motion from the Tween popup menu.**

That's it. You're all finished with your banner ad. Save it under any name you want. Because it's a template page, it comes up as Untitled, and when you save it, you won't have to use Save As or overwrite an existing file.

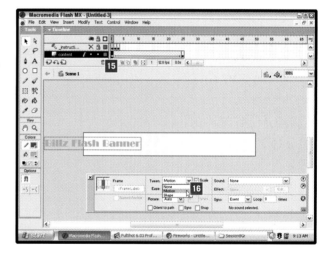

Tutorial

» Creating Templates for Special Devices

Suppose you were offered a contract to create Flash pages for Nokia phones or MS Pocket PCs? Would you know what to do? Those kinds of opportunities and challenges are easily met using Flash templates. As more and more people are using the Internet over mobile phones and Personal Digital Assistants (PDAs) such as the Pocket PC, the need for Flash pages that can be used effectively in such small spaces is increasing. (And you thought your 15-inch screen was too small!) Flash MX has templates for these small, portable personal devices. This next tutorial shows you how easy it is to create a Flash movie that looks good on a Pocket PC.

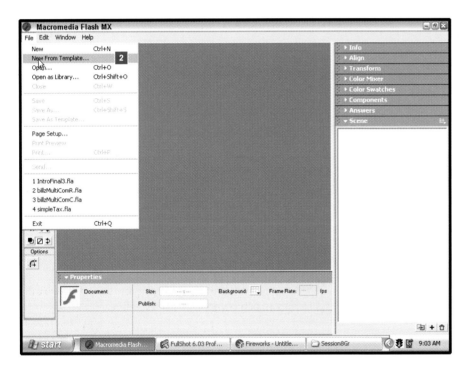

1. **Open Flash.**

2. **Select File→New From Template.**
   The New Document Window opens. You see eight categories of templates.

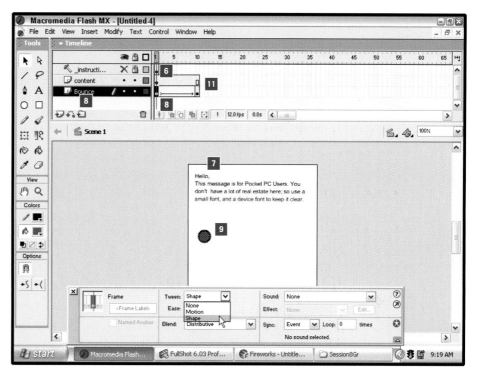

3. **Select MobileDevices from the Category column.**

4. **Select PocketPC2002 from the Category Item column.**

5. **Click Create.**
   A small stage and timeline with two layers appears.

6. **Click the first frame of the _instructions layer.**
   You see a short set of instructions for developing materials for PDAs, but more importantly you see a URL for more information on developing Flash for PDAs:
   `http://www.macromedia.com/software/`
   `flashplayer/pocketpc/`.

7. **Select the Text tool and a 10-point Verdana black type, select the Use Device Fonts option, and type a message.**
   When you get to smaller type sizes, Flash doesn't do too well. However, by selecting the Use Device Fonts option, you allow the font in the device to be displayed. Because a good deal of testing went into the fonts selected for the mobile devices, take advantage of the special qualities they possess for those devices.

8. **Add a layer, name it Bounce, and select Frame 10 of the content and Bounce layers and press F5 to add keyframes.**

9. **Select the Bounce layer, use the Oval tool to draw a ball, and then select Frame 10 and press the F6 key to insert a keyframe.**

10. **Select the first frame of the Bounce layer and in the Tween popup menu of the Properties panel choose Shape.**

11. **Select Frame 10 in the Shape layer and move the ball from its original position.**
    The movie is ready to publish. But first you better check the publishing options.

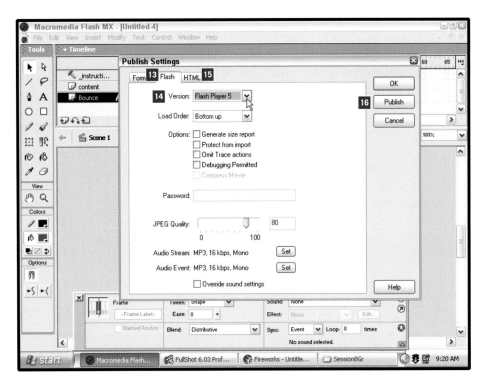

12. **Select File→Publish Settings form the menu bar.**

13. **Click the Flash tab in the Publish Settings window.**

14. **Look at the Version popup menu.**

    Because Pocket PCs can only use Flash 5 right now, the template was smart enough to know that. So had you done a lot of work getting your Flash movie ready and forgot to change the player from Flash 6 to Flash 5, using the template, you can rest assured that that chore has already been completed.

15. **Click the HTML tab and select Exact fit from the Scale popup menu.**

16. **Click Publish.**

    Your movie is published. When you run it, you see a relatively small screen that provides a good approximation of what the viewer will see on his Pocket PC.

» Session Review

This session covers publishing Flash MX movies and preparing them for publication. The preparation includes debugging the movie, testing its speed, and setting publication options. In addition, it includes working with templates.

1. What are the default files Flash MX generates when you publish a movie? (See "Tutorial: Publishing a Movie.")

2. Where are the debugging controls found in the Flash MX player? (See "Tutorial: Debugging Controls.")

3. What is the Bandwidth Profiler and what different options do you have in the Profiler? (See "Tutorial: Viewing a Movie with the Bandwidth Profiler.")

4. How do you select a modem speed for reviewing a Flash movie and then watch the movie in the real time of the modem? (See "Tutorial: Testing the Speed of Your Movie.")

5. In the Bandwidth Profiler, how do you create a graph to examine individual frames? What information about the efficiency of your movie do the graphs provide? (See "Tutorial: Testing the Speed of Your Movie.")

6. What are some ways you can reduce the weight of your movie? (See "Tutorial: Testing the Speed of Your Movie.")

7. How can you test a preloader using the Streaming in the View menu and any modem in the Debug menu in the movie test player? (See "Tutorial: Testing the Speed of Your Movie.")

8. What are the default publishing Formats in the Publish Settings window? (See "Tutorial: Using the Publish Formats.")

9. What happens when a Flash MX movie is published as a static graphic file such as GIF or JPG? (See "Tutorial: Using the Publish Formats.")

10. How many versions of the Flash player can you select from in the Flash tab of the Publish Settings? Which of these players must be used with Pocket PCs? (See "Tutorial: Using the Publish Formats.")

11. What option must be selected for the Password window to become active? (See "Tutorial: Using the Publish Formats.")

12. What are the different templates Flash MX provides? What publication parameters can templates set? (See "Tutorial: Using Flash Templates" and "Creating Templates for Special Devices.")

» Additional Projects

The following is a list of projects that relate to this session and can help you refine your expertise in working with text in Flash MX.

» To see how different players affect your project movie, publish the project movie with as many different players as you can. Run the movies to see what difference the different players make.

» Research has found that a movie that won't load in about 10 seconds is likely to be skipped by impatient Web surfers. Using a 28.8K modem in the Debugger and Streaming in the View menu, see how many different 30-frame layers of object tweening you can put into a movie before it exceeds the 10-second load rule.

» Find a mobile device that uses the Internet and create a movie for it that works well in the device. Once you have created the movie, save it as a template. (To create a template, all you have to do is choose Save as Template from the File menu.) Then, using your own template, create a different movie for the same device to see if it works as well.

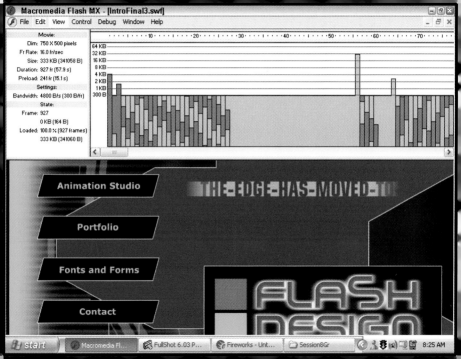

Part IV:
Dynamic Controls

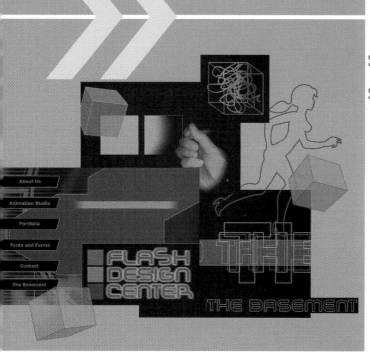

Editing and Navigation

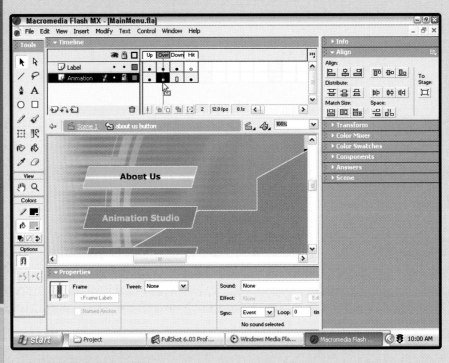

Session Introduction

In the real world of publishing, you spend a good deal of time making changes to your movie. A dynamic Web site is one that not only provides the viewer with an experience of dynamic elements, but also one that you update and keep new, fresh, and improved. You may also find that once you complete certain aspects of a movie, you want to make changes. Part of this chapter is dedicated to editing layers.

It also looks at another aspect of creating a Flash MX site — that of navigating a site. You navigate a single movie by going from one frame to another. While internal movie navigation is important and is covered in this session, when dealing with complex movies, you need to understand how to move from one movie to another. Ideally, if you have a single movie with different scenes, you can contain all navigation to moving from one frame to another. However, as you have seen with the introduction to the project, the more you add to a movie, the more bandwidth and time to load it takes. Navigation can help with that problem in two ways. First, it allows you to link smaller movies so that the viewer does not have to wait too long for any movie to load. Second, as you see in this session, you can rescue a long introduction by providing the viewer with the option to jump directly to the home page or main menu. So even with a Skip Introduction button, the introduction still takes too long to load for a typical system with a modem. By providing the option of jumping over the long introduction altogether, you give the user with a slow Internet connection fast access to the site.

You also learn a good deal more ActionScript. Most of it is short and simple, but some scripts are a bit longer. However, the longer scripts are really only a series of shorter scripts combined in one place. Not only does this allow you to keep all your scripts in one place, it also allows you to cut and paste your navigation from one module to another. Thus, while it may take a little longer to write the first script, you more than make up for it with the ability to duplicate it.

TOOLS YOU'LL USE
Properties panel, Actions panel, Text tool, Test Movie window

MATERIALS NEEDED
From the accompanying CD-ROM, you'll need the Banner.fla, MainMenu.fla, InitialOpener.fla, PortfolioPortal.fla, AboutUs.fla, and PaintBrush.fla files.

TIME REQUIRED
90 minutes

SESSION OUTCOME
How to move to different places in a Flash MX movie

PROJECT PORTION
Portal buttons

Tutorial
» Simple Layer Editing

Changing the length of a layer is generally pretty easy in Flash MX. For the most part, all you generally have to do is to Ctrl+drag/Cmd+drag the end keyframe or frame, indicated by a frame with a little vertical rectangle. This first tutorial shows you how to fine-tune the speed of a banner. Often when you test a movie, you find that the speed is wrong, and by adjusting the length of a key layer you can get just the speed you want. However, you do not have to make the adjustments by adding and deleting individual frames, but can do it by dragging whole groups of frames as this next tutorial shows.

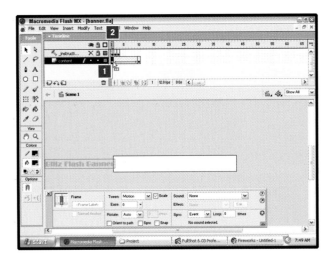

1. **Open banner.fla and click the first frame.**

   This is the movie created using the template in Session 8 that you will also find on the CD-ROM.

2. **Select Control→Test Movie.**

   You will see that the banner looks more like it's blinking instead of scrolling. Ten frames isn't much room for a banner. Instead of starting over from the beginning, you want to increase the length of the layer so that your banner has a slower, smoother scroll.

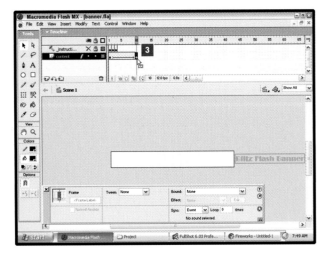

3. **Click the last frame.**

   The banner should appear off the right side of the screen.

4. **Hold down the mouse button and press the Ctrl/Cmd key.**

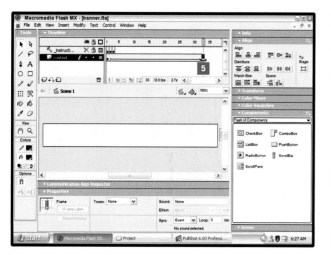

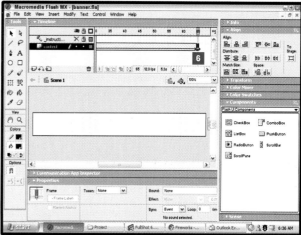

5. **Begin dragging the layer's end to the right, keeping the Ctrl/Cmd key pressed while doing so.**

   You can tell if you're doing it correctly by the appearance of a two-headed horizontal arrow. If you do not see the arrow, start over and try again.

6. **Continue dragging the layer and keyframe to Frame 65.**

7. **Release the mouse.**

   You should see your movie now.

8. **If you separate the end of the layer from the keyframe and tween, drag just the layer to Frame 65.**

   Sometimes you might only drag the end of the frame with a little dot on the end to the desired frame. This can occur if you drag the layer without first pressing the Ctrl/Cmd key.

9. **Now drag the keyframe to Frame 65.**

   This two-step method can work just as well but takes two steps instead of one.

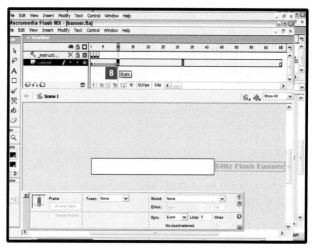

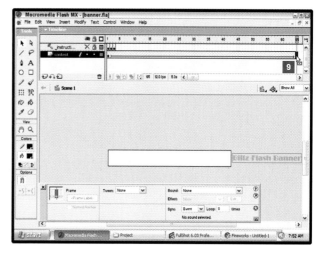

Tutorial
» Changing Multiple Layers

In developing a Web site, you're bound to find things you want to change that involve more than a single layer. In developing the buttons for the main menu, not only might you find the layers in different lengths, but they may also contain masks and other types of special layers. However, you need not make changes frame by frame. You can make changes by selecting several frames at the same time and then by making wholesale changes. This tutorial shows how a lengthy movie clip that made up part of a button was scaled down without losing the button's look and feel. What's more, when you edit a single button, all of the instances of the same button are changed as well.

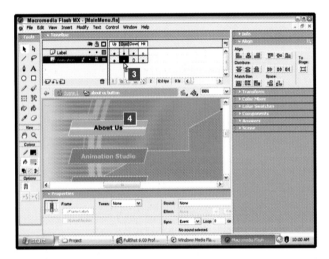

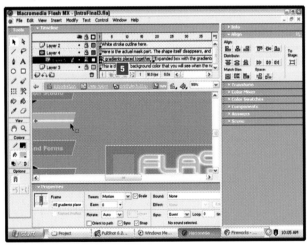

1. **Open MainMenu.fla.**
   You see a reconstruction of how the buttons were changed from a long set of multiple layers to just the amount of space needed for the desired effect.

2. **Double-click the top button.**
   You are in the Symbol Editing Mode with two layers employed. The top one is used to label the button and the bottom is for animation.

3. **Click the Over keyframe in the Animation layer.**

4. **Double-click the button.**
   You see several new layers that make up the animation portion of the button. After looking at the button, it was decided to scale back the length of the layers. Otherwise the buttons would blink every so often if the mouse pointer were over the button.

5. **Locate the motion tween, and click in the frame after the end of the tween.**
   This is where you want the revised layers to end.

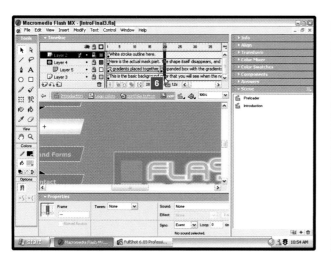

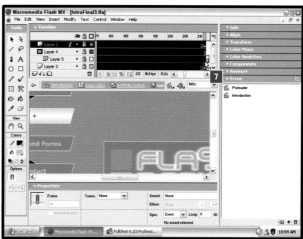

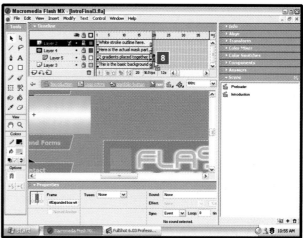

6. **Hold down the Shift key and select all of the frames in that column.**
   You want to remove all of the superfluous frames.

7. **Hold down the Shift key and drag the horizontal scroll bar to the last frame and click the timeline where the selection area will terminate.**
   One extra frame may stick out but that's okay. All of the selected frames should turn black. Do not try and drag the playhead.

8. **With the Shift key still held down, press the F5 key.**
   All of the frames are cleared except for the one that stuck out an extra frame. Because the extra frame is on a masked layer, the masked object "flares" out.

9. **Click the extra frame and hold down the Shift key and press F5 once more.**
   Now you can see that the flare is gone because it is covered by the mask layer.

10. **Select the last Layer 5 key and press F9 to open the Actions panel.**

11. **Select Actions→Movie Control→Stop and press the plus (+) button.**
    A stop() action is added to the last frame so that the button doesn't sit there and madly blink. Each time a user presses the button, it plays the tween for just the right effect.

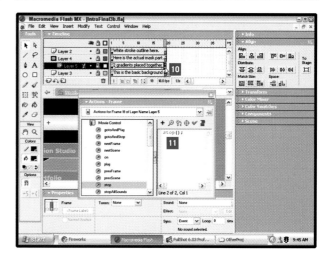

Tutorial

» Creating Masked Animated Navigation Buttons

The deceptively simple buttons in the main menu not only serve as navigation tools, but they have an interesting internal movie of their own. Part of the introduction uses the technique of masking a changing object on a masked layer. If you change one aspect of a mask or masked layer, you must change the other. If a mask layer is shorter than a masked layer, the frames beyond the end of the mask layer show everything of the mask layer — generally something you want to avoid.

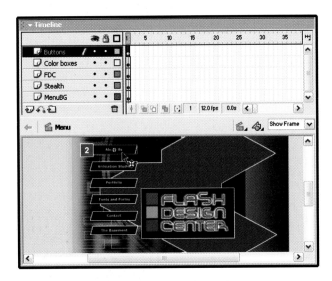

1. **Open MainMenu.fla.**
   This is the Home Page or Main Menu of the Flash site.

2. **Select the About Us button.**

3. **Right-click the mouse (Control+click the Macintosh) to open the context menu.**

4. **Choose Edit In Place.**
   You are now in the Symbol Edit Mode.

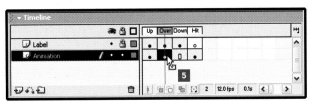

5. **Move the playhead to the Over frames.**

6. **Right-click the mouse (Control+click the Macintosh) to open the context menu.**

7. **Choose Edit In Place.**
   You're inside the next level of the button where the animation occurs.

8. **Lock all layers if they are not already locked.**
   When the layers are locked you can see the mask working with the masked layer.

9. **Move the playhead to the first frame.**
   You will see a narrow blurred line.

10. **Move the playhead to the last frame.**

Notice how the size of the glow increases. This is caused by the actions on the masked layer. The parallelogram-shaped "glow bar" is actually caused by changes beneath the mask layer.

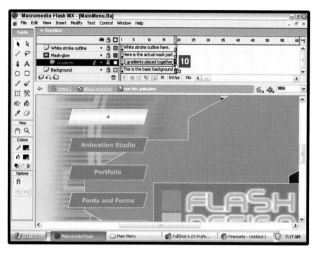

11. **Move the playhead to the first frame.**

12. **Unlock all layers.**

You can clearly see the parallelogram that makes up the mask in the Mask-glow layer. Beneath the layer, you can now see the narrow glow made up of a double rectangle with a bottom and top gradient.

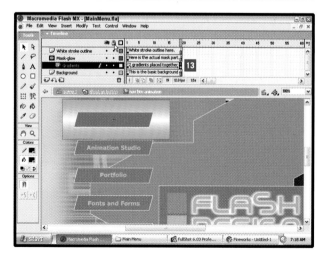

13. **Move the playhead to the last frame.**

Now you can see the background glow box. It is simply tweened from a narrow to wide size. The simple process to create this effect requires a few tricks shown in the next tutorial. But before that, you'll need to finish up the button.

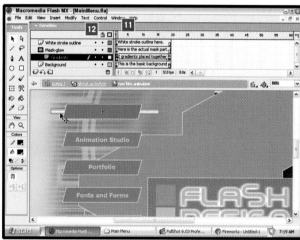

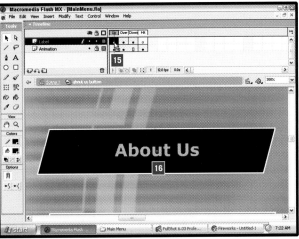

14. **Click the About Us button icon above the stage to move up a level.**
    You will see the special button timeline.

15. **Click the first frame in the top layer.**

16. **Use the text tool to type** About Us **in green over the parallelogram.**

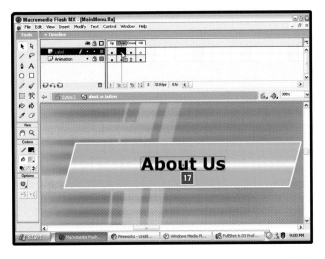

17. **Repeat steps 14–16 using a black font and with the Over frame selected in the Label layer.**

18. **Repeat steps 14–16 using a dark pink font and with the Down frame selected in the Label layer.**

Tutorial
» Making a Glow Bar

Sometimes little things make a huge difference in a Flash MX movie. Creating the glow bar used in the menu buttons (and elsewhere in the movie) is very easy to do. But, you have to know a few tricks. This little tutorial shows how it's done. When reproducing the button in the menu, you will need a glow bar!

1. **Open a new movie.**

2. **Create a green to white gradient in the Color mixer.**

3. **Use the Rectangle tool and draw a vertical rectangle with no stroke and the gradient fill.**

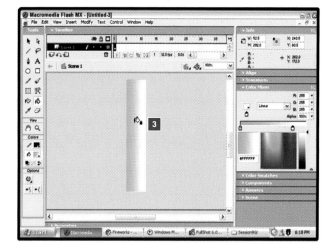

4. **Rotate the rectangle so that the white side is on the bottom.**
   When you use a gradient fill, the fill is from left to right. Therefore, you have to begin with the rectangle standing upright and then rotate it so that the gradient flows in the desired direction.

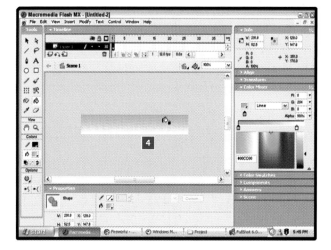

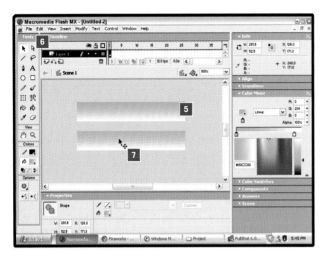

5. **Select the entire rectangle.**

6. **Choose Edit→Copy.**

7. **Choose Edit→Paste.**
   Now you have two gradient rectangles.

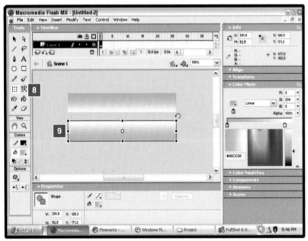

8. **Using the Free Rotate tool, flip the bottom rectangle so that the white is facing upward.**

9. **Open the Align panel and left-align the two rectangles.**
   The white part of the gradient on the bottom faces upward, and the white on the top gradient faces downward.

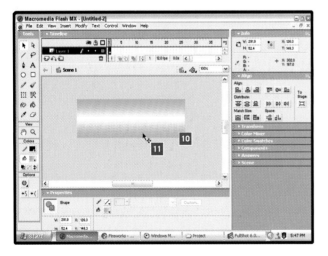

10. **Select the bottom rectangle by clicking it.**

11. **Use the up arrow key to move the bottom rectangle upward so that it touches the top one.**
    Because you have aligned the two rectangles, using the arrow keys ensures that the vertical alignment is maintained.

12. **Select both rectangles and press the F8 key to open the Convert to Symbol dialog box.**

13. **Choose the Graphic behavior and click OK.**
    Now you have a graphic symbol of the glow bar that you can use in the buttons.

Tutorial

» Navigating Around Introductions

If you have a modem connection as your primary Internet access, you will appreciate this tutorial. Users with high-speed cable modems or DSL lines literally live in a different Internet reality than those using phone modems. At the time of this writing, most people who look at your Web site generally use a phone modem, most likely a 56K or even 28K version. So, if you want the user to visit your Web site more than once, you better have a shortcut to your main navigation page. For this movie, the shortcut takes the user around the introduction and right into the main menu. The user doesn't even have to watch the pre-loader because the identical menu, which the user sees if he goes through the introduction, is now a separate movie. So the jump is directly from the opening page to the menu. To provide a choice, two buttons, both with associated ActionScript, are included.

1. **Open InitialOpener.fla.**
   The top button is labeled Go to Home Page and the bottom one is Play Intro.

2. **Select the top button.**

3. **Open the Actions panel.**

4. **In the upper-right corner of the Actions panel, open the popup menu and select Expert Mode.**
   The Expert Mode of entering ActionScript does not imply you're an expert code-writer. It allows you to write ActionScript like you would in a text-editor. In many cases it can be easier than using the Normal Mode. Either of the two popup menus can be used to switch to the expert mode.

5. **Enter the following script in the right pane of the Actions window:**

```
on (release) {
    getURL("MainMenu.html");
}
```

6. **Select the bottom button, Play Intro.**

7. **Enter the following script in the right pane of the Actions panel:**

```
on (release) {
    getURL("IntroFinal3.html");
}
```

This option lets the viewer choose to watch the Introduction.

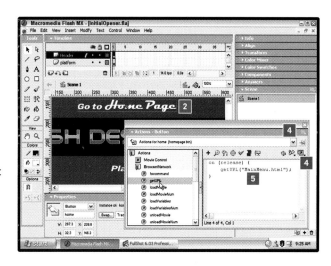

Tutorial
» Writing ActionScript for the Main Menu Navigation

The main menu works just like the main menu in any Web site. If the site were smaller, you could have a single movie and navigate by going from frame to frame, but given the size and complexity of this Flash MX site, you need a menu that opens different HTML pages containing elements of your Flash site. One of the first tasks you will be required to perform is to publish all of the pages. Using the getURL() action requires an HTML or SWF file. Often you can use SWF, but you have more flexibility by using HTML because you can have both the Flash page and any HTML components you may want to add.

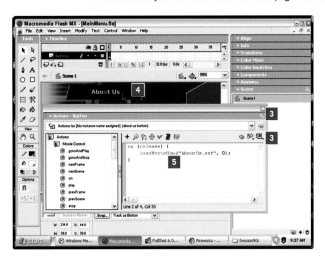

1. **Open the MainMenu.fla.**

2. **Open the Actions panel.**

3. **Select the Actions panel popup menu and choose Expert Mode.**

4. **Click the About Us button to select it.**

5. **Click the right pane and type the following script:**

```
on (release) {
    getURL("AboutUs.html");
}
```

This script opens the AboutUs file and removes the current file from memory.

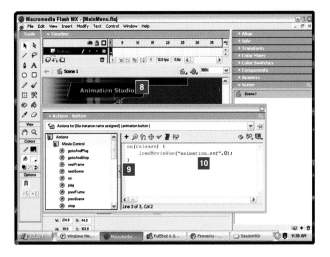

6. **Click in the right pane and press Ctrl+A/Cmd+A to select the entire script.**

7. **Press Ctrl+C/Cmd+C to copy the script.**

8. **Select the Animation Studio button.**

9. **Click in the right pane and press Ctrl+V/Cmd+V to paste the script into the pane.**

10. **Edit the script so that it reads:**

```
on (release) {
    getURL("animation.html");
}
```

11. **Repeat steps 6–10 with the Portfolio button selected and the following script:**

```
on(release) {
    getURL("PortfolioPortal.html");
}
```

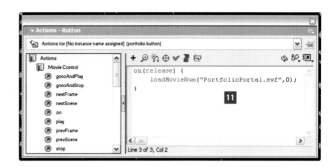

12. **Repeat steps 6–10 with the Fonts and Forms button selected and the following script:**

```
on(release) {
    getURL("TypeTrix.html");
}
```

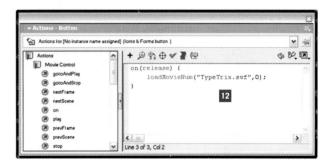

13. **Repeat steps 6–10 with the Contact button selected and the following script:**

```
on(release) {
    getURL("contact.html");
}
```

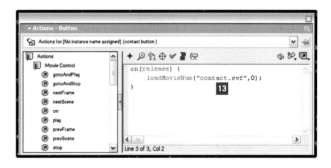

14. **Repeat steps 6–10 with the Basement button selected and the following script:**

```
on(release) {
    getURL("basement.html");
}
```

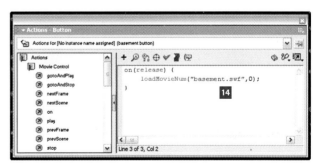

< N O T E >
You may have noticed that the code in the steps calls for HTML files, but the code in the screen shots calls for SWF files. Either can be correct depending on your project, but it's best to call for HTML files in this tutorial.

Tutorial

» Creating ActionScript-Controlled Buttons in Submenus

Once away from the main menu, you still need good navigation. In this site, some of the elements are single movies, such as the TypeTrix.swf movie. Its submenu is within the movie itself using navigation to different frames and the movie clips in the frames. Other parts of the site are made up of multiple movies, such as the Portfolio selection. This tutorial shows how one portal submenu takes the user to where she wants to go.

1. **Open PortfolioPortal.fla.**
   This menu is like the main menu except the links are to different movies.

2. **Open the Actions panel.**

3. **In the upper-right corner of the Actions panel, open the panel's menu and select Normal Mode if not already selected.**
   You will find that the Actions panel has two different menus, the View Options popup menu and the unnamed popup menu in the upper-right corner of the panel. You can select the mode from either menu.

4. **Select the Logo button by clicking it.**

5. **In the Actions toolbox select Actions→Browser/Network→getURL.**

6. **Press the plus (+) button.**
   The button's official title is "Add a new item to the script button," or at least that's the message that comes up when you pass the mouse over the button.

7. **Type** logo.html **in the URL window in the upper portion of the right pane in the Actions panel.**
   You have completed the ActionScript for opening the logo. You can either repeat steps 1–7 for the other links or use a shortcut as the rest of the tutorial demonstrates.

8. **Open the Options View popup menu on the upper-right side of the Actions panel.**

9. **Select Expert Mode.**
   You will see the following script:

```
on(release) {
      getURL("logo.html");
}
```

10. **Select the script by dragging the mouse pointer over it.**

11. **Select Edit→Copy from the menu bar.**

12. **Select the Logo Toon button.**

13. **Click in the right pane of the Actions panel.**

14. **Select→Edit→Paste from the menu bar.**

15. **Select logo.html in the script and change it to** logoToon.html.
    Your script should now read:

```
on(release) {
      getURL("logoToon.html");
}
```

16. **Repeat steps 12–15 for each of the other buttons using the following scripts:**

```
Button: Paintbrush
on(release) {
      getURL("paintBrush.html");
}

Button: Sound Ideas
on(release) {
      getURL("SoundIdeas.html");
}

Button: Shape Tween
on(release) {
      getURL("shapeTween.html");
}
```

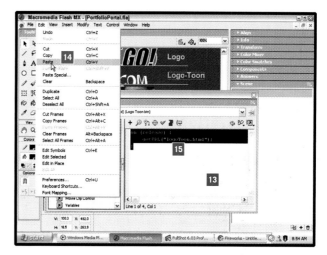

Tutorial
» Using ActionScript for Common Submenus

Throughout this course, the examples have been based on real-world examples. However, to provide the variety of the real-world options in navigation, some different approaches to the same challenge have been included. Several of the movies and portals have virtually identical navigation systems. A horizontal set of buttons directs the user to the same set of options as the main menu, so you don't have to keep going back to the main menu to visit a different portion of the site.

In this tutorial you also see a shortcut using a bit more sophisticated ActionScript. Typically, ActionScript programs are short and are associated with buttons, frames, or movie clips. However, using button instance names, Flash MX allows you to write scripts that you can place with frames to give instructions to different buttons. This is possible because of the use of function literals. A function literal is a delayed value assigned to an event. When the event occurs, the function triggers and the script fires. This may seem like a convoluted way of doing something simple, but it actually saves a good deal of time because you can copy and paste the entire script from one navigation to another. So while it may take a little more time to create the first script, the rest go pretty quickly.

1. Open AboutUs.fla.

2. Use the Arrow tool to select the group object below FLASH DESIGN CENTER.

3. **Drag the group label bar downwards so that the underlying button objects are revealed.**

4. **Select the first button and enter the instance named "home" in the Properties panel in the window beneath the Button selection on the popup menu.**

5. **Repeat step 4 for the other buttons except About Us from left to right after the button above the About Us label using the following instance names: animation, fonts, contact, and portfolio.**
   These instance names can be used in a script to activate the buttons.

6. **Open the Actions panel and select Expert Mode.**

7. **Click the first frame of the top layer and type the following script:**

   ```
   _root.home.onPress=function() {
       getURL("MainMenu.html");
   }
   _root.animation.onPress=function() {
       getURL("animation.html");
   }
   _root.fonts.onPress=function() {
       getURL("typeTrix.html");
   }
   _root.contact.onPress=function() {
       getURL("contact.html");
   }
   _root.portfolio.onPress=function() {
       getURL("PortfolioPortal.html");
   }
   ```

   Each of the script segments is identical except for the instance name and the URL. The instance name is the script word `between` _root and onPress. The onPress action is the event (pressing the mouse button) that triggers the function. The advantage of associating the script with a frame is that all of the script can go together in the same place.

8. **Click the group that makes up the labels.**

9. **Use the arrow keys to place the labels back over the buttons.**

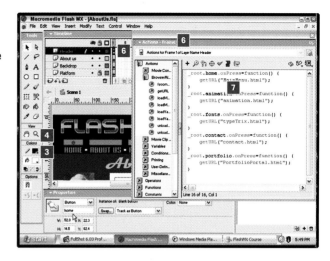

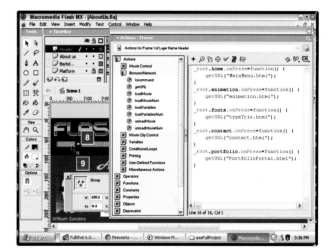

Tutorial
» Copying Navigation Scripts

The previous tutorial showed you how to create scripts in a single frame that would assign actions to all of the buttons. This tutorial is a continuation of the previous one and shows you how to cut and paste from one menu to another. It saves you lots of time and gives your menu systems greater consistency.

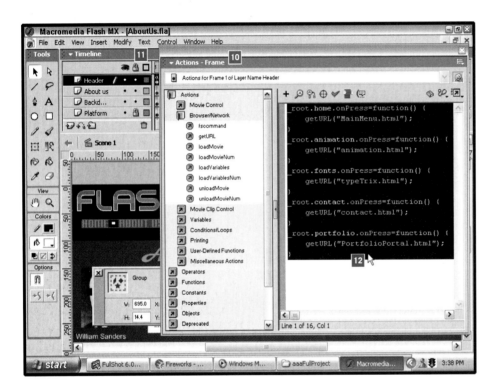

10. Open the Actions panel in AboutUs.fla.

11. Select the first frame of the top layer.
You will see the ActionScript for the menu.

12. Click inside the right pane of the Actions panel and press Ctrl+A/Cmd+A to select all of the script.

13. **Open PortfolioPanel.fla.**

14. **Drag the grouped overlay covering the buttons down and away from the buttons.**

15. **Provide an instance name for all of the buttons as was done in steps 4 and 5 and add the name aboutUs. (The Animation button is shown selected and named.)**
    You will notice that no button is provided for the Portfolio panel.

16. **Click the first frame of the top layer.**

17. **Click in the right pane of the Actions panel and press Ctrl+V/Cmd+V to paste the script from the AboutUs movie.**
    The script is now pasted in the right pane of the Actions panel. The same script is used in both, which not only adds consistency to the navigation system, it also saves time.

18. **Change the last line**

```
_root.portfolio.onPress=function() {
     getURL("PortfolioPortal.html");
}
```

    to

```
_root.aboutUs.onPress=function() {
     getURL("AboutUs.html");
}
```

    With a simple copy and paste, naming the buttons, and making a few changes, you have been able to duplicate the navigation.

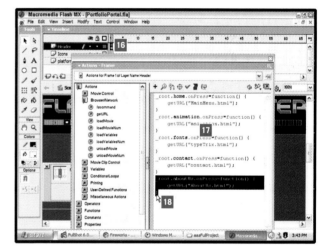

Tutorial
» Navigation within a Movie

This tutorial represents the most fundamental kind of movie navigation, navigating within a single movie. You may recall that the PaintBrush.fla movie is made up of several different pages linked by buttons. As the user sees each page, he is provided with a button to go to the next page. Because the PaintBrush.fla movie shows the most typical kind of navigation found in Flash, it is used as an example.

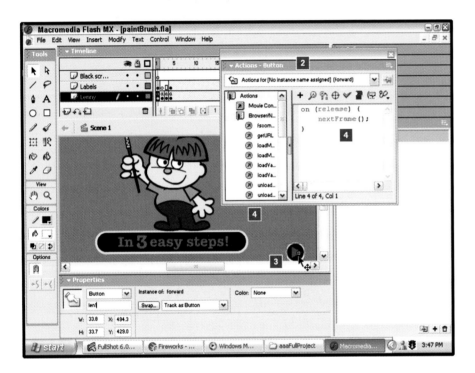

1. **Open PaintBrush.fla.**

   Notice in the Lenny layer a series of keyframes with an "a" marker indicating that ActionScript is associated with the frame. Each frame represents a different page in the movie. Because navigation within movies is handled by going to different frames, you organize your movies around frames.

2. **Open the Actions panel.**

3. **Click the button in the lower-right corner.**

4. **Enter the following script:**

   ```
   on (release) {
       nextFrame();
   }
   ```

5. **Click the second frame of the Lenny layer.**

6. **Click the button in the lower-right corner.**

7. **Enter the following script in the Actions panel:**

```
on (release) {
    nextFrame();
}
```

The same script is used again. You could have cut and pasted it from the first page.

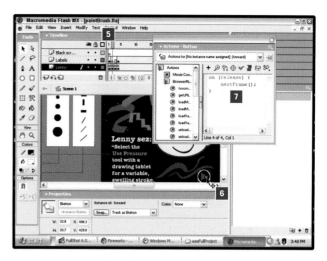

8. **Click the third frame of the Lenny layer.**

9. **Click the button in the lower-right corner.**

10. **Enter the following script in the Actions panel:**

```
on (release) {
    gotoAndPlay(4);
}
```

Instead of using the next frame action, this one does the same thing using a specific target frame number.

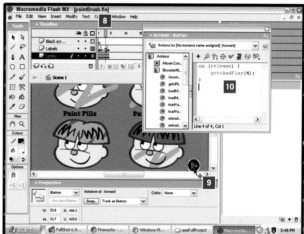

11. **Select Control→Go To End.**

12. **Click the button in the lower-right corner.**

13. **Enter the following script in the Actions panel:**

```
on (release) {
    gotoAndStop(1);
}
```

This last button completes the loop. The movie returns to the first frame.

» Session Review

This session covers editing Flash MX movie layers and setting up navigation systems within and among movies. Layer editing involves both single and multiple layers. Single layer editing involves dragging layer ends to lengthen and shorten them while multiple layer editing requires selecting blocks of frames for cutting and pasting them. The navigation system of any Flash MX site relies on ActionScript to detect events, like button clicking, to navigate among different movies and within a single movie. Different strategies for using ActionScript show how to accomplish navigation in different ways.

1. What are some of the common uses for changing the length of layers in movies? (See "Tutorial: Changing Multiple Layers.")

2. When you want to cut multiple frames from different layers of different lengths, what must be done to accomplish this task? (See "Tutorial: Changing Multiple Layers.")

3. What happens when the masked layer is shorter than the masking layer? How would you edit the mask or masked layer to fix this problem? (See "Tutorial: Creating Masked Animated Navigation Buttons.")

4. In creating complex navigation buttons, how do you make special effects such as masking a part of a single button state (for instance, Up, Over, or Down)? (See "Tutorial: Creating Masked Animated Navigation Buttons.")

5. If you have a big introduction, what can be done to avoid it so that the user is quickly sent to the main menu? Under what circumstances is such as tactic advisable? (See "Tutorial: Navigating Around Introductions.")

6. What kind of ActionScript instructions are written for navigation buttons for loading external files that differ from the kinds of scripts written for navigation within a movie? (See "Tutorial: Writing ActionScript for the Main Menu Navigation.")

7. How can ActionScript programs be written for buttons that are associated with frames? How are the buttons given instance names? (See "Tutorial: Creating ActionScript-Controlled Buttons in Submenus.")

8. How can ActionScript written for one submenu be used for another submenu by using cut and paste techniques and minimal editing? (See "Tutorial: Using ActionScript for Common Submenus.")

9. What role does a function literal play in ActionScript associated with a frame that is used for launching an action? (See "Tutorial: Using ActionScript for Common Submenus.")

» Additional Projects

The following projects relate to this session and can help you refine your expertise in working with text in Flash MX.

» Take some aspect of the project and change the speed that a movement will play first to a slower speed and then to a faster one by changing the length of the layers. Use either a movie clip or part of the main timeline.

» Create a "minimal" navigation system for the project that loads quickly but can be used to navigate to any place in the site. Make it so that it is re-usable for any submenu as well.

» Take the code that was used for defining functions for the buttons but was associated with a frame and see if you can create a navigation system for another project. Remember, all that you will have to change is the URL and the instance name for the buttons.

» Create a movie that begins with a navigation menu but only navigates to different frames in the movie, but has as many different elements as in the project movie.

Controls with ActionScript

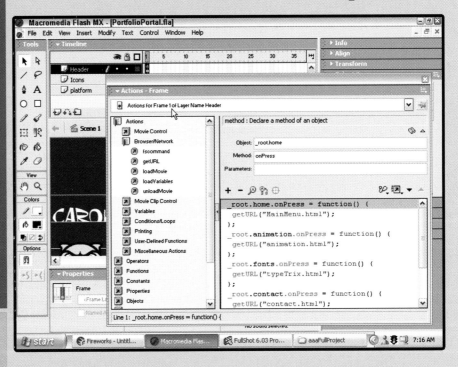

Discussion: **Understanding ActionScript**

Tutorial: **Using the Actions Panel**

Tutorial: **Scripting with the Normal Mode**

Tutorial: **Scripting with the Expert Mode**

Tutorial: **Creating the Preloader**

Session Introduction

This session introduces the basic rudiments of Flash MX's new ActionScript. You'll learn the basic elements of ActionScript and how to get started using this powerful scripting language. If you're interested in going beyond the basics, you should read *Flash MX For Dummies* or *Flash MX ActionScript Bible* (Wiley, 2002), both of which explain the language more fully. This session's purpose is to explain some basic ActionScript concepts, and then show you how it has been used in the course project. If you completed the tutorials up to this point, you have seen several examples of ActionScript at work.

If you are new to Flash and ActionScript, fear not. You'll find that the Flash MX tools available for entering scripts into frames, buttons, and movie clips will greatly ease the learning process. In previous sessions, especially Session 9, you have seen how to enter ActionScript in both frames and buttons. This session simply builds on what you already know.

TOOLS YOU'LL USE
Text tool, Arrow tool, and the Properties and Actions panels

MATERIALS NEEDED
From the accompanying CD-ROM, you'll need IntroFinal3.html and PortfolioPortal.fla.

TIME REQUIRED
60 minutes

SESSION OUTCOME
Completing the Preloader scene and working with both the Normal and Expert Mode of the Actions panel to create ActionScript programs

Discussion

Understanding ActionScript

You have already seen that ActionScript can be used to stop and start movies, go to different places in a movie, load movies, and go from one URL to another. Those simple yet essential functions are required for a dynamic Flash movie with which the viewer is involved by responding to something happening on the screen. With ActionScript, the designer can allow the user to make choices, such as where he wants to go and what effect he'd like to see.

Scripting languages were developed to be as close to natural language as possible, and although ActionScript is a hybrid between scripting and traditional programming languages, it is an easy language to learn. What makes ActionScript easier than some other computer-related languages is the ActionScript Editor, which automates much of the programming work. For example, in the Normal mode, event handler scripts are automatically inserted for buttons and movie clips when the user selects an action from the Action menu. In Session 9, for example, you saw that by selecting a term in the ActionScript toolbox and clicking the add button (+), in ActionScript associated with a button, not only are the button's event handlers added, so too is the correctly formatted code. In the Expert Mode, you can type code like you would in a text editor. Usually all you need to do is to double-click an action and it appears correctly in the ActionScript program pane of the Actions panel.

Addressing Objects in Expressions with the Dot Syntax

<NOTE>
If you haven't learned the old slash syntax, don't bother with it unless you have to deal with Flash 4 players or updating Flash 4 movies. (Most Flash 4 movies are automatically updated when loaded into Flash MX.)

The dot syntax is based on the period (.) character referenced as a "dot." The top or root level is helpfully called _root. All objects are part of the root level, and although you can use relative addressing for objects, I generally prefer to use absolute addresses that all begin with _root. For example, if I want to address an MC within an MC using the dot syntax, I would write the following:

```
_root.bigMC.littleMC
```

To set a variable in an embedded MC, I'd just add another dot and the name of the variable.

Variables

One of the fundamental components of any kind of programming is the variable. As the name implies, variables change — they vary. Probably the best way to think of a variable is as a box of different things. In programming, variables store data of different sorts with different values. For example, a house can be considered a variable because its contents may change. Initially, the house (variable) may contain only a husband and wife. As the couple have children they may move to a bigger house and then a completely different family moves in. The house (variable) is the same building with the same location, but it has a different mix of inhabitants. Therefore, its contents have changed.

For programmers, an important characteristic of Flash ActionScript is the contextual nature of variables. Languages such as C++ have strongly typed characteristics that require the programmer to declare not only a variable, but also the type of variable. Is the variable going to store text, integers, or floating point numbers? ActionScript, like virtually all scripted languages, does not require such declarations. ActionScript automatically deals with different types of data stored in variables.

The name that you select for a variable should give a clue as to what the variable does. Names such as VariableA or VariableB tell you very little. However, names such as ItemCost and Tax tell you what the variable contains and make them easy to find, remember, and use accordingly. If you use shortcuts when naming variables in longer scripts or complex movies and call them a, b, and c, always go back and provide descriptive names before you start working on other parts of your action script. In Flash, clear variable naming is even more important because the scripts are short (generally) and scattered all over the place. For example, if you have a button that uses a variable named B and you use the name B in a script associated with a frame, the likelihood of conflict is high. Both the button and the frame respond to the value of B unless both use the variable as a local one. So not only is a name like B vague, it's likely to be duplicated.

Variable names must consist of a single string of connected characters, with no spaces between the words. Variable names such as Dog House or John Smith are not acceptable; however, doghouse, Dog_House, or DogHouse are. Moreover,

ActionScript is not case sensitive. If a variable is named `DogHouse`, you can use `DOGHOUSE` or `doghouse` to call the variable's current value. However, `Dog_House` will not be recognized as the same variable as `DogHouse` because it contains an extra character — the underscore. This lack of case sensitivity makes it easier when you want to call a variable by name, but make sure that you don't use names such as `BIGSTORE` and `bigstore` for your variables in the same button or frame. You may think they are different, but ActionScript won't.

Data Types in ActionScript

ActionScript is typical as a scripting language in the types of data it recognizes and uses. The basic data types include strings, numbers (both integer and real, or floating point), expressions, functions, and Boolean expressions.

Strings

The easiest way to think of strings, initially, is just as words or text. In programming, you will often see strings used as messages. Any variable that contains a string is a string variable. For example, the following can be a string in a variable:

```
Automobile = "PT Cruiser"
```

The variable is `Automobile` and the string literal is `"PT Cruiser"`. A literal is the raw data that goes into a variable. The type of car can change in a variable, but the string literal `PT Cruiser` is always going to be a PT Cruiser. Sometimes a string can be a numeral, such as the following:

```
LotNumber = "521"
```

The variable `LotNumber` is just another string literal that consists of numeric characters. In fact, just about any alphanumeric string of characters is a string. A string of characters can contain most punctuation marks and spaces as well as alphabetic characters and numbers. (Note that `"PT Cruiser"` includes a space.) Characters and numbers can be used in any combination. Strings, such as the following, have to make sense only to the designer and Flash; the user doesn't have to see them or understand them:

```
MixUp = "UR4me"
```

An important fact to keep in mind about strings is that they are not numbers. You can spot a string because it has quotation marks around it. In the preceding `LotNumber` example, the number `"521"` is in quotation marks. If `"521"` were added to "521" the result would be "521521", not "1042". Quotation marks around a literal usually mean that it's a string literal.

Expressions

Expressions are considered compound because they contain more than a single element. In ActionScript, a simple logical expression looks like the following:

```
Total = 7 + 5;
```

The value of `Total` is 12. The expression is compound (the 7 and 5 make it compound), but the value of `Total` is 12 because it is not broken down into its component properties. However, why type **7 + 5** when you know it's 12? Programmers generally do not enter such a simple expression. However, the concept of expressions begins to make more sense if you look at the following:

```
Total = ItemCost + Tax;
```

The variable `Total` is the total value of two other variables. You may not know the value of the variables because they are variables. Variables change. You don't keep track of what's in the variable; ActionScript does it for you and calculates the total. For example, consider the following script using variables and expressions:

```
ItemCost = 23.45;
Tax = ItemCost * .07;
sum = ItemCost + Tax;
```

The first variable — `ItemCost` — is defined with a literal having the value 23.45. The second variable — `Tax` — is an expression using the value of the first variable multiplied by .07. (The .07 represents a 7-percent sales tax rate.) The third variable — sum — uses another expression that is the total of the first two variables.

String Concatenation

When two or more strings are joined together, the process is known as concatenation. All concatenations are treated as expressions. In ActionScript, the add operator — plus sign (+) — joins strings. The expression

```
Both = "Big" + "John";
```

results in "BigJohn". The value of the variable `Both` becomes " BigJohn ". Concatenation is very useful when you're putting together strings that go together, such as first and last names. You've probably filled out forms in which you enter your first name in one field and your last name in another. Using concatenation, the names can be joined. Because a space is needed between the first and last names, the concatenation has to add a space, as shown here:

```
WholeName = "John" + " " + "Davis";
```

Two plus (+) signs are needed. The first one joins `"John"` and the space (two quotation marks with a space between them), and the second joins `"Davis"` with `"John"` and the space. The output is then `John Davis` instead of `JohnDavis`.

Boolean Expressions

A Boolean expression is one that is true or false (1 or 0, yes or no). For example, if I say that 10 is greater than 15, the statement would be false, but if I say that 15 is greater than 10, the statement would be true. Thus, the following statement would return a value of false:

```
Bigger = 10 > 15;
```

The literal is the expression `10 > 15`, which can result in a true or false outcome. Boolean expressions can be used in a type of conditional math as well. Because `"true"` equals `"1"` and `"false"` equals `"0"`, the script,

```
More=5 > 4
Total=More + 19
```

would result in the value of `Total` equaling 20. That's because 5 is greater than 4, making the variable `More` equal 1. When `More` is added to 19, the sum is 20. Obviously, Boolean expressions are special cases when it comes to different interpretations of the outcome of the expressions. If a Boolean expression's outcome is placed into a text field, it will show either true or false, but if the same variable associated with the text field is used in a math expression, the Boolean value will be interpreted as a 0 or 1.

Numbers: Integers and Real Numbers

Numbers are pretty straightforward. Unlike strings, numbers must be written only as such. Any nonnumeric characters can cause problems unless they have been defined as a variable. A variable defined as a number is a number and has all the properties of a number.

Numbers can have positive or negative values. You can create a variable that includes both positive and negative numbers, such as

```
Nuts = -5 + 15;
```

or

```
ReallyNuts = -5 + -15 + 3;
```

Integers are simply real numbers with decimals lobbed off. The numbers can be rounded up or down, but only whole numbers without decimals are integers. In creating variables, you do not have to declare what type of variable you are using (integer or floating point). You must, however, tell the variable that the numbers are to be treated as integers. An integer is declared as such by using the integer function. For example, to create an integer, you may write the following:

```
whole =parseInt(71/24);
```

The expression `71/24` results in `2.958333`, but the `parseInt()` function lobs off the decimal leaving the value of the variable at `2`. You can use other `Math` functions such as `Math.round()` to round up or down to create an integer as well.

In a Flash movie, you frequently use integers when your script loops (see "Loops" later in this session). Because loops are generally incremented or decremented in single units, some designers make sure that all of the steps are integers. Likewise, frame numbers are integers (there's no Frame 7.5). If you use calculated values with frame numbers, you should make sure the outcomes are integers to ensure that you are referencing the correct frame.

To avoid losing or adding decimals and to have greater accuracy, use real (or floating point) numbers. The default character of numbers in ActionScript is floating point. Also, unless an integer function is used, integers return to floating point values when further calculations are made. The following shows an example:

```
roundOff = Math.round(88/9);
keepDecs = roundOff / 7;
```

If the result of dividing the variable `roundOff` by 7 is a fraction, the variable `keepDecs` would include the decimal values even though `roundOff` and 7 are integer values. (Whole became an integer because it was rounded by the `Math.round()` function, and 7 is a literal with no decimal points.)

Variable Scope

A variable has a scope that encompasses either the whole movie or just segments of it. Before Flash MX, the ActionScript variables were global. As long as the addressing was done correctly, you could access any variable on any level and in any scene. The same is true in Flash MX, but Flash MX has both global and local variables. Global variables are defined using the new _global identifier. For example, the following defines "myCar" as a global variable:

```
_global.myCar = 200;
```

All timelines can share global variables if the proper paths to them are referenced. A global variable set by a button script three levels down in a hierarchy of movie clips has the same global scope as one in the first frame on the main timeline. Every object can affect and be affected by the changes in a global variable. When you need to coordinate several objects with information from a single variable, global variables can be very helpful. However, when you use the same variable name in different places, you can get confused about which value has been assigned the same variable. For example, a common loop variable is "i" because it has conventionally been shorthand for "increment". If the same loop variable is used in two different scripts inside the same timeline, the value of the variable may have been changed in one loop, yet it affects another loop. So, although global variables have important uses, they can also be a problem.

Local variables are ones declared using the var statement inside of a script. When a variable is declared using var between the curly braces { } of a script, only changes within that script affect the variable's value. For example, whenever a button is used to launch a script, it creates a block of code contained within curly braces. It is possible to localize the variables in the buttons by making all of the variables in the button local. The following shows an example of a script with local variables:

```
on(release) {
var helium=300;
var baloonLift=helium-weight;
var flight= 400-baloonLift
output=flight;
}
```

By having local variables in your buttons, you can use similar scripts to do different things. Several different buttons' scripts can use the same variable names in their scripts, as can scripts in movie clips and frames. However, other than the variable output, which is a global variable, none of the local variables' values can be changed or accessed by other scripts.

Conditional Branches

A computer program can only have one of three basic structures. It can go from one statement to the next in a sequential structure, it can branch to a program segment, or it can loop. All of the structures in the examples so far have been sequential. In this section, we'll examine ActionScript's conditional branching statements and structures.

Computer and scripting languages all have some kind of structure that allows for comparisons and alternative courses of actions. With the IF... structure, the program (or code or script) waits until a single condition occurs and then takes one or more courses of action. For example, in making a Preloader, you use the if statement to wait until all of the frames are loaded before proceeding to the Introduction scene. The script looks like the following:

```
if (nowLoaded == totalLoaded) {
    gotoAndPlay("Introduction",1);
}
```

Associated with a frame, the script is fired each time the playhead passes over the frame. Fortunately, the entire movie and not just the preloader scene are being loaded together so that it can count all of the movie that is loaded.

Flash MX ActionScript uses the curly braces { } to enclose an action in response to a true condition. You will also find the curly brace used with functions, loops, and event handlers. Flash MX has other conditional statements, but for this course, only the simple if statement is used.

For a quick overview of the kinds of different characters you will encounter in Flash MX, the following table lists all of the operators you will find in ActionScript.

Table 10-1: ActionScript Operators and Uses

Type	Symbol	Use
Numeric		
	+	add (and concatenate)
	−	subtract
	*	multiply
	/	divide
	%	modulus
	++	increment
	− −	decrement
Comparison		
	<	less than
	>	greater than
	<=	less than or equal to
	>=	greater than or equal to
Logical		
	&&	logical AND
	||	logical OR
	!	logical NOT
Equality and Assignment		
	==	equal
	===	strict equality
	!=	unequal
	!==	strict inequality
	=	assignment
	+=	add and assign
	−=	subtract and assign
	*=	multiply and assign
	%=	modulus and assign
	/=	divide and assign
Function, Dot, and Array Access		
	( )	function arguments
	.	structure member (called a Dot)
	[ ]	array access

In using conditional statements in your scripts, you need to be careful not to use the wrong type of operator, especially with equal (assignment) (=) and double-equal (==). To make matters more interesting, Flash MX has a triple-equal (===) know as "strict equality." Strict equality occurs only if both the value and the type of data are the same. However, the most common mistake occurs when a single equal (=) is used instead of a double (==) in a conditional statement. The following shows an example:

Wrong:

```
if (total=all) {....
```

Correct:

```
if (amount==11) {....
```

Getting used to using the right format is not too difficult, and with practice you can use conditional statements wherever you want.

Loops

To keep from having to re-write a script that repeated itself, programmers developed the loop. The loop simply repeats a process the number of times required to meet a given condition. In ActionScript and Flash, the looping process is achieved using either conditional statements or a loop statement. Flash MX ActionScript has four different types of loop actions:

while

In the while loop, a condition at the beginning of the loop specifies the conditions under which the loop terminates. All loop actions take place between the curly brackets and typically include an incremental or decremental counter variable. Here is an example:

```
count=20;
while (count >10) {
score = score + 7;
count = count - 1;
}
```

do...while

The `do...while` loop works like the while loop except the counter is at the bottom of the loop, allowing at least one pass through the loop before the termination conditions are met, as shown in the following example:

```
do {
          score = score + 7;
          count = count - 1;
}
while (count >10)
```

for

The `for` loop specifies a beginning value, a termination condition, and the counter (index) for the loop in a single line:

```
for (count=100; count >10; count--) {
      score = score + 7;
}
```

for...in

This type applies only to properties of objects. Using a variable name to search the object (feature in the following example), the loop examines all of the object elements:

```
auto = {make:'Ford', model:'Explorer', condition:'New'};
for (feature in auto) {
 rollem+=("auto."+feature+"="+auto[feature])+newline;
}
```

The output from the preceding example, where `rollem` is the name associated with a text field, would be as follows:

>> `auto.make=Ford`

>> `auto.model=Explorer`

>> `auto.condition=New`

Properties

Properties refer to certain characteristics of an object. Some properties in MCs can be changed, and all properties can be read. The following table shows the full list of properties. Those with an asterisk after them can be changed, but the others can only be read by action scripts.

Table 10-2: Flash Object Properties

Code	Description
_alpha*	The percent of opaqueness in an object (Alpha). A value of 100 percent is totally opaque; 0 percent is totally transparent.
_currentframe	Frame number of an MC's current frame.
_droptarget	The value of the path of the MC on which another MC is dropped.
_framesloaded	Current number of frames loaded thus far in an MC.
_height*	Height of an MC measured in pixels.
_name*	The instance name of an MC.
_rotation*	Rotation angle (0 to 360).
_target	Full target path of an MC.
_totalframes	Number of frames in an MC.
_url	URL of SWF file containing an MC.
_visible*	Boolean of visibility (true/false, 1/0).
_width*	Width of an MC measured in pixels.
_x*	The number of pixels from left boundary of the stage to the center point of an MC.
_xmouse	The current x position of the mouse pointer.
_xscale*	Percent scale of an object's horizontal (x-) axis.
_y*	The number of pixels from top boundary of the stage to the center point of an MC. If the clips are nested, the _x and _y are relative to the clips in which they're nested.
_ymouse	The current y position of the mouse pointer.
_yscale*	Percent scale of an object's vertical (y-) axis.

Functions

Flash MX ActionScript has two types of functions. First, ActionScript contains built-in functions. These functions can be envisioned as "little programs" that do something. For example, the `random()` function generates random numbers. Second, and new to Flash MX, are user functions. User functions are so called because the user (you — not the viewer) builds the function. For example, you might want to build a function that keeps score in a game for different objects. You build one function and use it for all the game's objects. So instead of having to rewrite the code every time you need a score-keeping script, you just invoke the function.

How you use a function in a movie depends on the function. Functions generally require that some kind of value or parameter is entered. For example, the `random()` function requires a value used as a range minus 1 because the function includes 0 as a possible value. So if you want random numbers between 1 and 10, you would enter the following script:

```
sum = 17/3;
newSum=parseInt(sum);
```

The variable `haphazard` will contain a different value each time the script is encountered in the movie. The `random()` function generates values between 0 and 9, and by adding 1, the `haphazard` variable can have values from 1 to 10. To find all the functions used by Flash MX, see the Functions folder in the Actions menu in the Actions panel.

The do-it-yourself function (user function) is at the core of functions in Flash MX. With a user function, you can create any code you want and execute it with different scripts in the movie. Essentially, you code once and execute many times. Use the following format the create a custom function:

```
function FunctionName (arguments) {
script
script
}
```

The arguments can be any variable used in the script within the function. The arguments can be passed from external sources if need be. You can even use other functions within your custom function, which gives you a good deal of flexibility.

The project for this course did not use a great deal of ActionScript, and much of what was used was incorporated in the navigation elements in the previous session. In the next two sessions, you will see more that will refer back to this session.

Tutorial

» Using the Actions Panel

The Actions panel is context sensitive, which means it changes depending on whether you have a frame or object selected. The panel contains the Actions toolbox where the script terms are listed and the ActionScript pane where you enter your code. You can open the Actions panel by selecting Window→Actions or by pressing the F9 key. For the actions to be alive (working), a movie clip, button, or frame must be selected first. This tutorial shows you the different options you have for entering ActionScript. Use the one you most prefer. As you become more experienced, you can change both the mode of entering code and the Mode (Normal or Expert) to use while writing ActionScript.

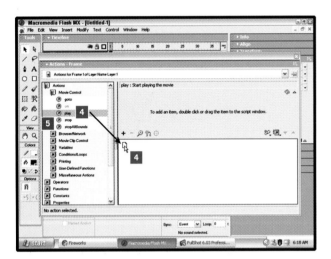

1. Open a new movie file and select Window→Actions or press the F9 key to open the Actions panel.

2. Click the first frame.

3. Select Actions→Movie Control in the Actions toolbox.

4. Drag the play action icon to the right pane of the Actions panel.
   Select the script you want and drag it from the Actions toolbox on the left to the ActionScript pane on the right. As soon as you release the button, your ActionScript appears, and the play action will show play();

5. Double-click Stop in the Actions toolbox.
   As soon as you double-click stop, the action stop(); appears in the Actions pane.

6. Click Stop in the Actions toolbox.

7. Click the plus (+) button.
   A menu appears.

8. Select Actions→Movie Control→Stop.
   Basically, you re-trace what you've already done. This method is a left-over from much earlier versions of Flash for those who get used to a way of entering Flash and don't want to change. If you're new to Flash, any of the other methods is easier than this one!

9. **Open the View Options popup menu and select Expert Mode.**

10. **Type the code as you would text in a word processor or text editor.**
As you become more adept at writing code, you will find the Normal Mode awkward and restrictive. When that occurs, try the Expert Mode. You don't have to be an expert in Flash. Also, if you've coded in languages like Visual Basic or even HTML, you may find it easier to begin with the Expert Mode.

11. **While in the Expert Mode, click the Show Code Hint button.**
A new feature in Flash MX, the code hints show you what you need to complete a line. Usually, these hints are very helpful and, once you get used to them, you'll be able to enter ActionScript much faster.

12. **Type** on(**in the ActionScript pane.**
With Code Hint turned on, as soon as you type the open parenthesis after the word "on" you will be presented with a dropdown menu containing all of the events handled by the on action.

13. **Click release and press Enter/Return.**
As soon as you press the Enter or Return key, the word release tucks itself right next to the open parenthesis.

14. **Select the script and press Backspace/delete to remove the script.**

15. **Select Actions➔Browser/Network and double-click getURL.**
The getURL function appears in the ActionScript pane with the parameters url, window, method shown as parameters within the parentheses. The parameter hints help you learn what needs to be included in the function's arguments and what options are available. As you type each parameter and place a comma after the parameter, the next parameter appears in bold to let you know which to type next.

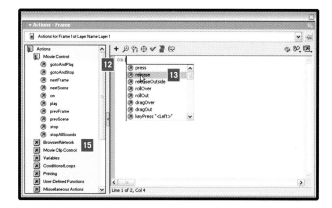

Tutorial
» Scripting with the Normal Mode

Entering script in the Normal mode is recommended for getting started. When you enter script in the Normal mode, the parameters are clearly laid out for each script element, whether it's an action, function, operator, property, or object. You create ActionScript programs by clicking and adding actions and scripts in small modules. If you select a frame, the Frame Actions panel comes up, but if a button or movie clip (MC) is selected, the Object Actions panel appears. Double-clicking a frame will bring up the Frame Actions panel, but with a button or MC, you have to open it by clicking the Show Actions icon on the Launcher bar or by selecting Window➔Actions from the menu bar.

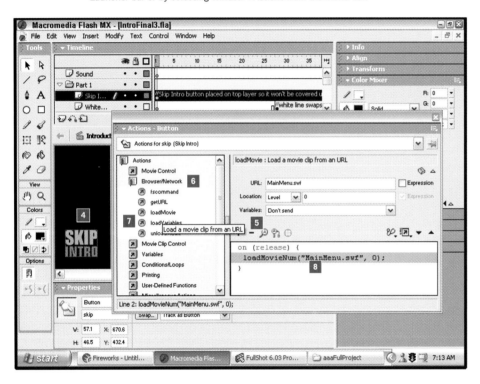

1. **Open IntroFinal3.fla.**

2. **Select the first frame of the Introduction scene.**

3. **Press F9 to open the Actions panel and switch to the Normal Mode if it's not already in that mode.**

4. **Find and select the Skip Intro button.**

5. **Select any script it currently contains and press the minus (–) button in the ActionScript pane.**
   You're removing the script so that you can see how to enter it using the Normal Mode. You'll simply be re-entering it to see how the Normal Mode automatically inserts event handlers.

6. **Select Actions➔Browser/Network➔loadMovie in the Actions toolbox.**

7. **Double-click loadMovie.**
   You will see the following:

   ```
   on (release) {
       loadMovieNum("",0);
   }
   ```

8. **In the URL box, type MainMenu.swf.**
   The rest should default to Level and 0. Leave it as it is. The nice aspect of the Normal Mode is that it automatically includes the event handlers when you select buttons and movie clips.

9. **Open PortfolioPortal.fla.**

10. **Click the first frame.**
You will see the script that handles all of the buttons in the top menu.

11. **Click the Pin current script button in the right corner of the Actions panel.**
This action will keep the Actions panel pinned to the frame no matter what other frames or objects you select.

12. **Click the About Us button in the top menu.**
Now you can see the instance name of the button in the Properties panel. However, you can still see the script that uses that instance name in its script. Because the script requires you to use several different instance names, by pinning the script, you can click the different buttons to check their instance names and make sure you're using the correct ones in your script. If you did not pin the Actions panel, each time you clicked a different object, the script associated with that object would appear, which in this case would be blank. Once you're finished with a script segment, remember to unpin the Actions Panel.

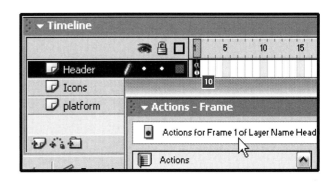

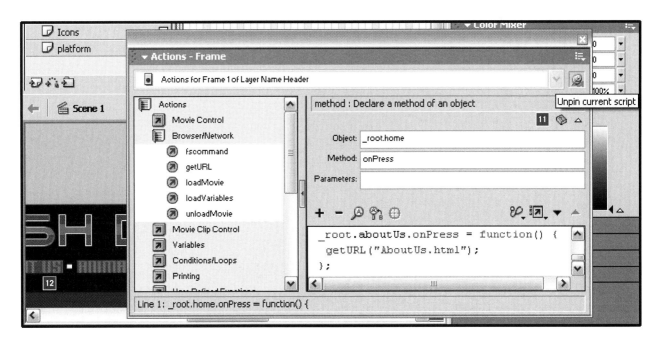

Tutorial

» Scripting with the Expert Mode

Many times you will want several actions and functions in a single button or MC event, and you may find it awkward to remove the many on (release) segments that you must pull out of the script. Each time you add a new action in the Normal mode with a button or MC selected, you get the accompanying default event handlers — even if one is already in the ActionScript Editor. When you select the Expert mode, you give up the guidance you get with the Normal mode, but you are not hampered by unnecessary help either. Flash MX provides a number of different features to help you in editing your scripts. This tutorial shows you how to use three of the key features not yet discussed.

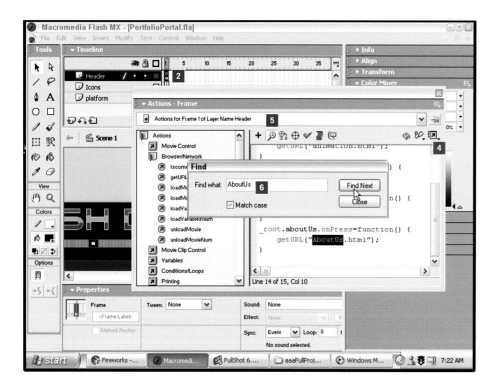

1. **Open PortfolioPortal.fla.**

2. **Click the first frame in the top layers.**

3. **Press the F9 key to open the Actions panel.**

4. **Select Expert Mode from the Actions from the View Options popup menu.**
   You will see the script listing for all of the buttons in the top menu.

5. **Click the Find button (a magnifying glass icon containing the letter A — right above the pane where you enter the ActionScript).**
   The Find dialog box appears.

6. **Type** AboutUs **in the Find What text window and press the Find Next button.**
   At the very bottom of the script is the AboutUs term as part of a getURL action. When you have longer scripts, the Find feature comes in handy for debugging.

7. Click the Check Syntax button.

A message box telling you no errors are in the script should appear. If it does not, you will be informed that the script has errors that are listed in the Output window.

8. Select one of the getURL actions in the script.

9. Click the Reference button.

The Reference panel opens at the position in the Reference that tells you about the term you had selected. When learning ActionScript, knowing about this handy little source will help when you're not sure if you have the format correct.

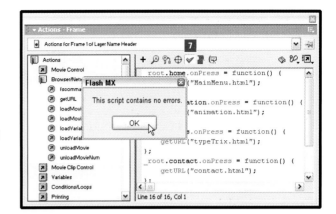

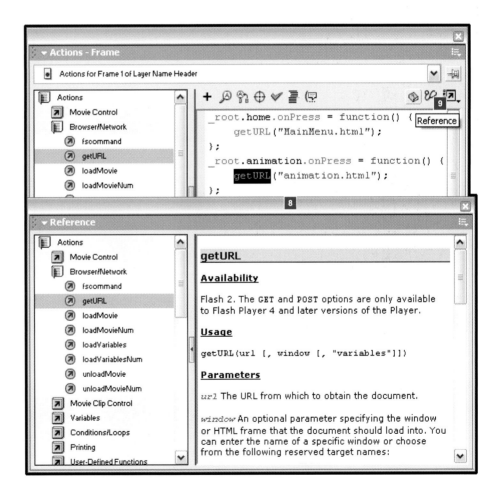

Tutorial
» Creating the Preloader

The Preloader scene at the beginning of the introductory movie is simple ActionScript. Once you understand it, it is less complex and offers many lessons. This next tutorial shows how to build the Preloader and the ActionScript associated with it. However, before beginning, you need to know what a preloader does and a little about some special Flash MX ActionScript properties.

The Preloader operates to hold the movie in the first scene until all of the movie has been loaded. As the movie travels across the Internet, the Preloader keeps track of the number of frames, and optionally, bytes loaded in the movie. Once all of the frames have been loaded, it begins playing the movie. By using a preloader, the viewer is able to see the progress of the loading while waiting to see the movie. Sometimes when a movie is partially loaded, its performance is degraded because it will stop in the middle of the movie while more information loads. So in addition to letting the viewer know the loading progress, a preloader keeps the movie in one piece in the viewer's computer.

In the "Conditional Branches" section of the ActionScript discussion, you saw how conditional statements work. It asks if a condition has been met, and if it has, it takes an action. The preloader asks if all of the frames have been loaded, and if they have, it takes the action of going to the next scene where the main movie is played.

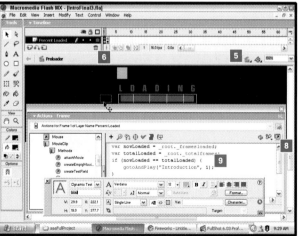

1. **Open IntroFinal3.fla.**

2. **Select Control→Test Movie from the menu bar.**

3. **While the movie runs, select Debug→56K (4.7 KB/s) from the Player's menu bar.**

4. **Select View→Show Streaming from the Player's menu bar.**
   Before looking at the code, you want to see clearly what the ActionScript will do in the movie. It does three things. First, it keeps track of the number of frames that are loaded and will not let the movie proceed until all of the frames are loaded. Second, the preloader gives the viewer an accurate reading of what percent of the movie is loaded through a dynamic text field. Finally, a graphic chart shows the same percent as a moving bar.

5. **Select the Preloader scene from the Edit Scene popup menu.**

6. **Click the first frame of the Percent Loaded layer.**

7. **Press the F9 key to open the Actions panel.**

8. **Select the Expert Mode from the View Options popup menu.**

9. **Click in the right pane and type the following:**

   ```
   var nowLoaded = _root._framesloaded;
   var totalLoaded = _root._totalframes;
   if (nowLoaded == totalLoaded) {
   gotoAndPlay("Introduction", 1);
   }
   ```

   Double-check your typing. It has to be exactly as you see it. The first line assigns the number of frames loaded to a variable, nowLoaded. The variable name is descriptive so that you'll know what it does. The second line places the total

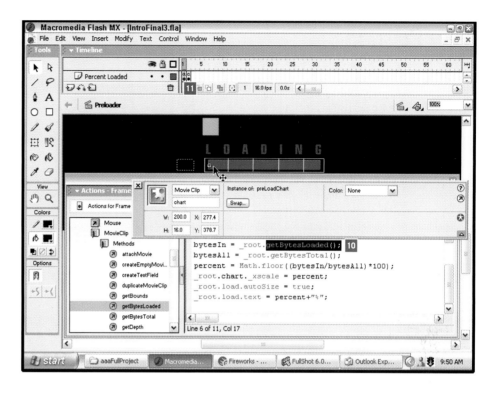

number of frames into another variable. The third line is a conditional statement. It sees whether the number of frames loaded equals the total number of frames. If it does, it jumps out of the first scene and begins playing the movie. Otherwise, it does nothing.

10. **Type the following lines right after the first block of ActionScript:**

```
bytesIn = _root.getBytesLoaded();
bytesAll = _root.getBytesTotal();
percent = Math.floor((bytesIn/bytesAll)*100);
_root.chart._xscale = percent;
_root.load.autoSize = true;
_root.load.text = percent+"%";
```

The first two lines place the number of bytes loaded and the total bytes in the movie into variables. Next, the percentage of bytes is placed into a variable named `percent`. The variables in this second portion of the script are all global variables because they were not defined as local by using the precedent `var` as was done with the part of the script. (This was done simply to demonstrate scope in variables.) The percent variable finds the percent by using the `Math` object's method `floor()` to create an integer rounded down. The number of bytes loaded are divided by the total bytes to arrive at a decimal fraction that is converted into a percent by multiplying it by 100. Because it is an integer, all results will be a whole number. Next, using the instance name of the rectangle bar (`chart`), the horizontal scale (`_xscale`) is changed to the percent value. Because the center point of the bar chart object is placed on the left side of the object, when it scales horizontally, it "grows" to the right. Next, the dynamic text field with the instance name "load" is made to auto size so that its size will change from single to double to triple digits. Finally, the dynamic text field is loaded with the value of the percent and concatenated with a % sign.

11. **Click the second frame of the Percent Loaded layer.**

12. **In the ActionScript pane of the Actions panel, type the following script:**

```
gotoAndPlay(1);
```

The playhead is sent back to the first frame to refresh and update the information being sent to the screen. As soon as the first script determines that the movie is fully loaded, this frame will be skipped and the main movie played. When you test the movie, select View→Show Streaming in the player menu to see the preloader working.

» Session Review

1. What is the dot syntax in Flash and how is it used to address different objects? (See "Discussion: Understanding ActionScript.")

2. What are variables and what are they used for in ActionScript? (See "Discussion: Understanding ActionScript.")

3. What are the different data types that can be used in ActionScript? (See "Discussion: Understanding ActionScript.")

4. How do you concatenate strings? (See "Discussion: Understanding ActionScript.")

5. What are Boolean expressions? (See "Discussion: Understanding ActionScript.")

6. Flash MX ActionScript recognizes different types of numbers? What are the number types in Flash MX? (See "Discussion: Understanding ActionScript.")

7. What are the two variable scopes in ActionScript? (See "Discussion: Understanding ActionScript.")

8. Which conditional branches are used creating the Preloader? (See "Tutorial: Creating the Preloader.")

9. What role do operators play in a script in Flash MX? (See "Discussion: Understanding ActionScript.")

10. How are loops used in ActionScript? (See "Discussion: Understanding ActionScript.")

11. What are properties and which ones are used in creating the Preloader? (See "Discussion: Understanding ActionScript" and "Tutorial: Creating the Preloader.")

12. Compare using the Normal and Expert Modes of entering ActionScript. What are the advantages and disadvantages of each? (See "Tutorial: Scripting with the Normal Mode" and "Tutorial: Scripting with the Expert Mode.")

» Additional Projects

» Take the preloader and apply it to an entirely different application. One suggestion would be to apply it to the SoundIdeas.fla file because it has several sound files in it and is fairly heavy.

» Using one of the course elements in the project, change one of the tweened movements and see if you can create an ActionScript program that will accomplish the same task. (When you do this project, keep in mind that it is an exercise and that usually the most efficient way to change an object's state is to use a tween.)

Part V:
Working with
External Elements

Working with QuickTime Movies and UI Components

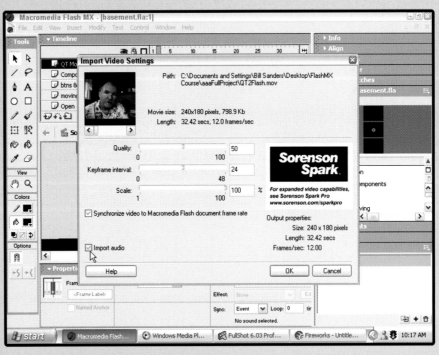

Session Introduction

Movies can be converted into QuickTime movies on both Windows and Macintosh computers. The process generally involves an Export command. When you're queried in a dialog box or menu as to which movie format you want to export, simply select QuickTime. For example, Adobe Premiere is a popular editing program for digital movies for both platforms. If you have an AVI-formatted movie you want to convert to QuickTime, all you need to do is to load the movie into Premiere.

Another inexpensive option is to purchase QuickTime Pro. QuickTime Pro lets you edit movies and convert other file types into QuickTime Pro. If you have a Macintosh computer, you can transfer your digital video to iMovie, edit the movie, and then export the movie in QuickTime format.

The most interesting projects with Flash and a filmed movie include adding special effects and exporting it as an SWF file. You can incorporate all of the tricks you've learned on an underlying QuickTime movie. You can create movies that used to take multi-million-dollar studios to make.

The other major part of this session is devoted to the new Flash MX UI Components. UI stands for *user interface*, and the different components all rely on ActionScript to trigger some aspect of the Flash movie. Like buttons that need ActionScript to make something happen, components require functions for an action to take place. So you may want to brush up on Session 10, in which the main features of ActionScript were introduced.

TOOLS YOU'LL USE
All of the tools in the Toolbox that create vector graphics, and the following panels: Actions, Align, Color Mixer, Components, Library, Properties, and Transform

MATERIALS NEEDED
From the accompanying CD-ROM you'll need the basement.fla file.

TIME REQUIRED
120 minutes

SESSION OUTCOME
The reader learns how to import a QuickTime Movie, add Flash animation, and employ key UI Components.

Tutorial
» Preparing for QuickTime Movies in Flash MX

The very first step in getting a QuickTime movie to import into Flash MX is to make a movie or get your hands on a pre-existing QuickTime movie. Most digital video (DV) cameras come with an IEEE 1394 port (sometimes called a Firewire port). By connecting the IEEE 1394 in the DV camera with one in your computer, you can easily import the digital video to your computer. All new Macintosh computers come with a Firewire port, and you can find any number of IEEE 1394 cards for computers running Windows.

Once you have your DV camera all hooked up, you need a way to convert the movie into a QuickTime or .MOV file. If you have a Macintosh, you're in luck because you can import the digital video into iMovie and then export the movie in QuickTime format. (All Macs come with iMovie.) Other movie editing software such as Adobe Premier and Apple Computer's Final Cut Pro can also do nice jobs editing and exporting movies in QuickTime format. One package for PC users is the Dazzle DV-Editor VideoStudio 4.0 that comes with the Dazzle IEEE 1394 port. The Dazzle package comes with all you need to get up and running with digital video. Also, check the freeware and shareware sources for software that will convert from one digital video format to QuickTime.

Once you save your .MOV file in a safe place, you're all set. Be sure to edit out any unnecessary frames or any other materials you do not want in your movie. Editing DV movies in Flash is possible but generally awkward. However, making filmed digital images a part of your Flash MX movie is very easy. Finally, install QuickTime 4. Just go to http://www.apple.com and download it for either Microsoft Windows or Macintosh OS.

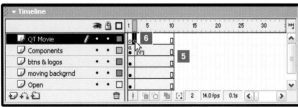
QT2Flash.mov

1. **Using digital video or video that can be re-formatted as digital, create a short movie.**
   Your movie should not be much over 30 seconds. Even a 30-second digital file will be quite large, and you may try the patience of the viewer with a video that size.

2. **Convert the movie into a QT format.**

3. **Save the movie.**
   Ideally, save your QT movie in the folder where you have your Flash MX movie. The Desktop is another good place to save it, and then you can put it where you want after you've loaded it into Flash.

4. **Open the Basement.fla file.**
   Normally, you would be opening a new movie, and so you will be taken through the steps in the Basement as though it only has the background elements and components.

5. **Add 10 frames to all of the layers.**
   When you add a QuickTime movie to your Flash MX movie, it will want to add more frames to your Flash MX movie anyway. Generally, you do not want to begin your QT movie in the first frame, and so the additional frames are a reminder.

6. **Click the second frame of the QT layer.**

7. **Press the F6 key to add a keyframe.**
   In the first frame you will be setting up a title and a trigger using the Push Button component.

Tutorial
» Importing QuickTime Movies into Flash MX

Importing QuickTime movies into Flash MX is quite easy, but if you're used to earlier versions of Flash, you may find Flash MX a very difference experience. The main difference between earlier versions of Flash and Flash MX is that you can make a QuickTime movie a part of your Flash movie without resorting to turning the movie into a sequence of single JPG, GIF, or PNG files. Moreover, you can preserve both the audio and video in a Flash SWF file.

The import process goes through a Sorenson Spark compression system. This system is extremely efficient, but you need to experiment using it to ensure getting the file size and quality. However, the process is all automated and is not much different than loading a file into memory.

1. **Click the second frame of the QT Movie layer.**
   This is the frame your QuickTime movie begins in.

2. **Select File→Import from the menu bar.**

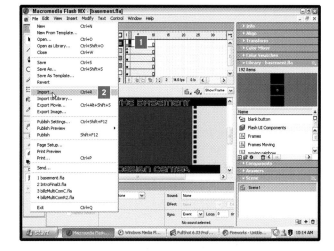

3. **Click the QuickTime movie in the directory where you saved it.**
   Usually you can distinguish a QuickTime movie by the icon and the popup message that appears when you select it.

4. **Click Open.**

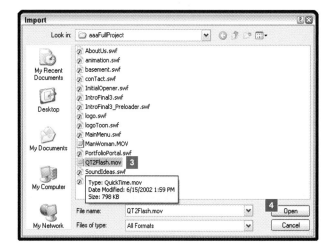

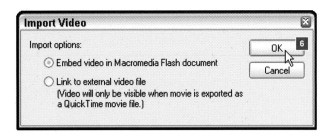

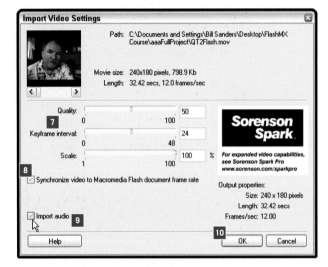

5. **When the Import Video dialog box appears, select Embed video in Macromedia Flash document.**
The other option should be selected only if you plan to export the movie as a QuickTime movie and link to it.

6. **Click OK.**

7. **Select Quality, Keyframe interval, and Scale.**
The higher the quality, the larger the file. The default quality of 50 provides a very small comparative file size, and while the appearance is not as good, you can have a workable size. The Keyframe interval refers to the number of frames between elements of the movie that are to be treated as keyframes with the other frames to be part of a tween. A lower keyframe interval will result in a larger file while a higher interval results in a smaller file. The default is 24, and is used in this example as a benchmark.

If a movie is set to run at 12 fps, every two seconds a new keyframe is set. So a 30-second movie would have 15 keyframes. You can re-import the movie and experiment with different interval sizes. Finally, set the scale. The scale has more effect of appearance than file size. A smaller scale gives both a smaller size viewing area and better appearing resolution. This movie is left at the 100 percent scale because the movie was set at a smaller size in the process of creating the QuickTime movie.

8. **Select Synchronize video to Macromedia Flash document frame rate.**

9. **Select Import Audio.**
The sample movie includes audio, so you do have an option to include the audio track. If you have a QuickTime movie with an audio track you do not want to use, leave the selection unchecked. For example, you may want to add your own sound track in Flash MX.

10. **Click OK.**

11. Check to see if the Importing dialog box appears.

As soon as you click OK to the settings, you should see the Importing dialog box. The longer the box stays on the screen the larger the file.

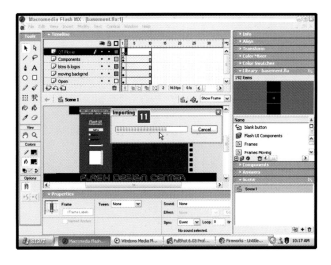

12. Find the number of frames that will have to be added to your movie in the Information box that appears.

If the number of frames is greater than you care to place in your movie, you can select No. With 454 frames to be added after the frame currently selected, the movie is going to be fairly long and possibly heavy, bandwidth-wise. Given the settings of 24-frame keyframe intervals, this movie will generate only 18 keyframes. The rest will be tweened.

13. Click Yes.

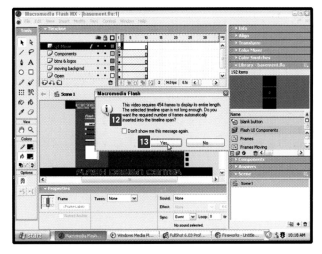

Tutorial
» Arranging the QuickTime Movie on the Stage

Once you import the QuickTime movie into Flash, it essentially becomes a series of frames and audio that you cannot edit without exporting the movie as a series of picture files (JPEG, GIF, or PNG) and re-importing them as a sequence. Doing so removes the audio from the movie. Sometimes that is exactly what you want to do, but for now assume that your QuickTime movie is a single object that includes both movie and audio. You can move it where you want in the context of the other objects on the Flash stage. You can transform the size of the object and even put it into a movie clip and tween the clip to move around the stage. In this movie, the QuickTime movie is placed on the main timeline on top of a movie clip that puts on an animated show behind the movie and frames it. This little tutorial shows you how to put the movie where you want it on the stage.

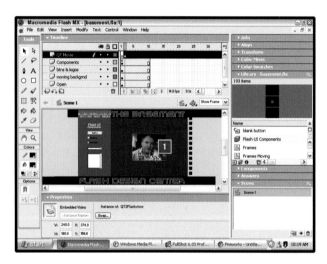

1. **Position the QuickTime movie where you want it on the stage.**
   In this Flash MX movie, a movie clip beneath the movie plays, so center the QuickTime movie with the underlying movie clip by centering it using the Align panel. Alternatively, you can move it by dragging it and using the arrow keys to position it at X=375, Y=159.

2. **Move the horizontal scroll bar so that you can see the last frame of the QT Movie Layer.**
   Initially, you will see only a single layer that has frames to Frame 455.

3. **Hold the Shift key down and click Frame 455 for all of the other layers.**
   Optionally, you can drag the cursor over the 455th column to select the frame for all the columns.

4. **Press the F5 key to add frames for all of the layers to Frame 455.**

Tutorial
» Building the Flash Environment Around the QuickTime Movie

Once you place your movie in Flash MX, you can build around the movie to add special effects, an opening frame that precedes the movie, a closing for the movie after it completes, or anything else you want. The whole purpose of placing the movie into Flash MX is to add a richer environment than you can with QuickTime alone. Also, once you position your QuickTime movie, you can use it as a template for other objects you want to build into the environment. In the case of this Flash MX movie, instead of starting with a blank screen and having the movie pop up in the second frame, it starts with a title in the first frame. This tutorial shows how to create the materials in Flash MX that precede the movie.

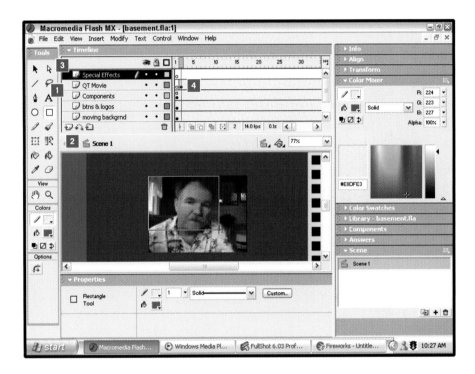

1. **Click the QT Movie layer.**

2. **Click the Insert Layer button.**
   A new layer appears above the QT Movie layer.

3. **Rename the new layer** Special Effects**, and add a keyframe to the second frame and to the last frame of the layer.**
   You won't need this layer right way, but now is a good time to put it in so that it will be there when you need it.

4. **Click the second frame of the QT Movie layer.**

5. **Select the Rectangle tool and a medium blue (#EODFE3) fill color and white stroke color.**

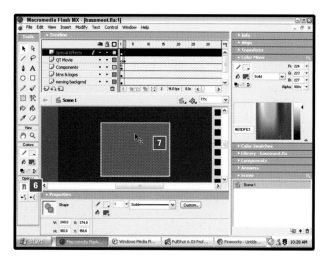

6. **Click the Snap to Objects magnet at the bottom of the toolbar.**

7. **Draw a rectangle directly over the QuickTime movie on the stage.**
   The Snap to Objects selection should allow you to draw the rectangle to the exact size of the movie.

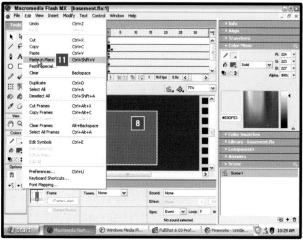

8. **Select the rectangle.**

9. **Select Edit→Cut from the menu bar.**

10. **Click the first frame of the QT Movie layer.**

11. **Select Edit→Paste in Place from the menu bar.**

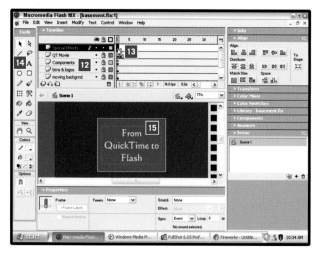

12. **Lock all of the layers except the Special Effects layer.**
    By locking these other layers, you will find adding text on top of the rectangle easier.

13. **Click the first frame of the Special Effects layer.**

14. **Select the Text tool and choose white from the color well of the Properties panel.**

15. **Type in the middle of the rectangle,** From QuickTime to Flash, **using a 32-point font.**
    Calligraph421BT is used in the example, but if that font is not in your system, Palatino is another good font for the same effect.

Tutorial
» Adding Special Effects over a QuickTime Movie

Adding animation to films is nothing new, and a good deal of special effects in movies today are created by first making a film and then adding all of the special effects once the film is complete. This tutorial shows how to add special effects to your Flash MX movie, and while the effect is simple, it introduces you to the possibilities of what you can do. With a bit of imagination, you can create the digital video to anticipate animation from Flash MX and create your original film so that when you add the special effects, it appears as though the filmed image and the Flash animation are interacting.

1. **Click the Special Effects layer.**
   It's not important where you click the layer as long as it's selected.

2. **Click the Add Motion Guide button.**
   A Guide Special Effects layer appears above the Special Effects layer.

3. **Lock all of the layers except the Guide Special Effects layer.**

4. **Select the Pencil tool and white in the color well in the Properties panel.**

5. **Beginning near the bottom left of the QT movie, draw a crooked line ending near the starting point.**
   You can make it as crooked as you want, but be sure not to let any part of the line touch any other part of the line. This line will be your guide for an object that will appear over the movie.

6. **Click the Special Effects layer.**

7. **Select Insert➔New Symbol from the menu bar.**
   The Create New Symbol dialog box appears.

8. **Type** Bug **in the Name text box.**
   You will be making a little bug to fly over the movie.

9. **Select Graphic for Behavior and click OK.**
   You will enter the Symbol Edit Mode.

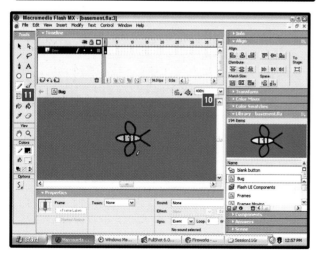

10. **Set the magnification to 400%.**
    With a large magnification, you will find it easier to draw a small bug.

11. **Use the Line tool, the Oval tool, and Pencil tools to create a bug with a yellow body with black stripes.**

12. **Click the second frame of the Special Effects layer.**

13. **Click the Snap to Objects magnet button.**

14. **Drag an instance of the Bug symbol to the stage.**

15. **Use the Magnify tool to enlarge the area near the beginning and end of the line in the Guide layer.**

16. **Drag the bug so that it snaps to the beginning of the top part of the line.**

    The bug begins its path on the higher of the two line tips.

17. **Select Motion from the Tween popup menu in the Properties panel.**

18. **Click the Orient to path option.**

    The bugs "flight" will appear more natural if it is oriented to the path it flies along.

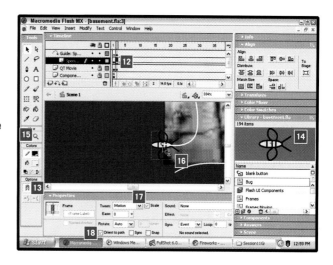

19. **Move the playhead to the last frame.**

    You'll probably have to move the horizontal scroll bar as well unless you have a very, very wide monitor.

20. **Drag the instance of the Bug object to the bottom end-point of the line.**

    The bug will now fly around during the movie. Because it is on top of the QT Movie layer, it will be visible on the screen.

21. **Select File→Publish.**

22. **Open the movie (basement.html) in your browser or simply double-click the basement.swf file to watch the movie.**

    You will be able to see and hear the movie with the bug flying over the face of the narrator. If the file is too big (it should be about 264KB), you can reduce the quality of the movie or increase the number of spaces between keyframes. However, the quality of the movie is about as low as you want to go right now.

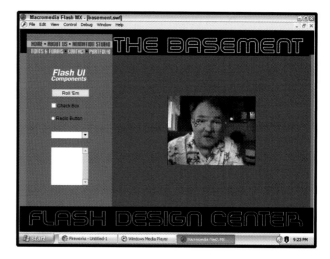

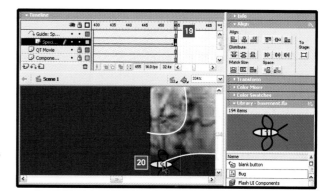

Tutorial
» Using the PushButton UI Component

The QuickTime movie in basement.fla begins when the viewer presses a button to start the movie. So at the very beginning, the movie needs a `stop()`; action to keep the Flash movie and the embedded QuickTime movie from beginning at all. You can use any kind of button to start the movie, but for this movie you learn how to use the first of the new Flash MX UI Components. The "UI" stands for "User Interface," and by using the UI Components, you can begin to build consistent user interfaces.

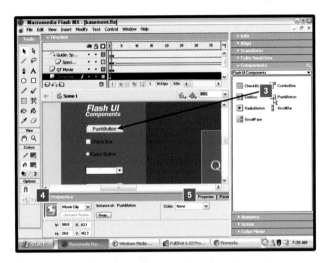

1. Open the basement.fla file.

2. **Select Window→Components to open the Flash UI Components panel.**
   Your system may have more than one set of components, and if it does, select the Flash UI Components.

3. **Drag an instance of the PushButton object from the Components panel to the stage.**

4. Open the Properties panel.

5. **Locate the Properties and Parameters tabs in the Properties panel, and click the Properties tab.**
   You will see the PushButton component is treated as a Movie clip.

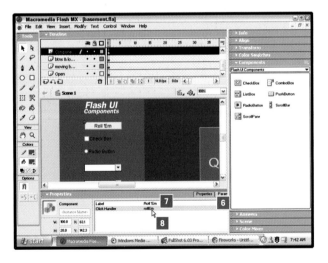

6. **Click the Parameters tab.**
   You will see two elements, Label and Click Handler. The default label is PushButton. Also notice that the object type is now listed as Component in the Properties panel.

7. **Change the name in the label row from PushButton to** Roll 'Em.
   The label is a property of the PushButton component object.

8. **Type the handler name,** rollEm, **in the Click Handler row.**
   The Click Handler is a function you will write in the Actions Panel.

9. **Press the F9 key to open the Actions panel.**

10. **Click the first frame of the Components layer.**

11. **Open the View Options menu and select Expert Mode.**

12. **Type the following script in the right pane of the Actions panel:**

```
//Push button handler
function rollEm() {
play();
_root.openUp.play();
}
stop();
```

The way click handlers work with PushButton components is to fire a function whenever they're clicked. The rollEm() function plays the main movie and it also starts a movie clip with the instance name openUp. The stop() action stops the playhead, and so the movie will not go beyond the first frame until a play() action is issued. Thus, when the button is clicked, the movie and movie clip both play.

13. **Select the Roll 'Em push button.**

14. **Click the Properties tab in the Properties panel.**

15. **Select Advanced from the Color popup menu.**

16. **Click the Settings button.**

17. **Set all of the values in the left column to 100% and the following values for the right column: R=102, G=51, B=255, A=255.**
    With the push button, these settings change only the color of the label. It is possible to use the same color as the background to the push button component because it resides in a white frame.

18. **Click OK.**

19. **Select Control→Test Movie.**
    The movie begins by presenting only the first frame. Click the Roll 'Em button and the movie begins playing. When it is finished it should stop at the beginning.

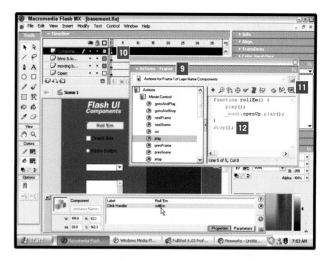

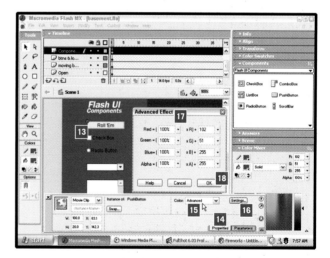

Tutorial
» Using the CheckBox UI Component

The CheckBox UI Component has two states — checked and unchecked. With those two states you can create a function to do different things depending on the checked state. At the very beginning of the movie, the state will be unchecked, but the default state does not affect the Change Handler because no change has yet occurred. In this movie, a little text field with a scroll bar UI Component attached will act as a "marquee" that announces different movies.

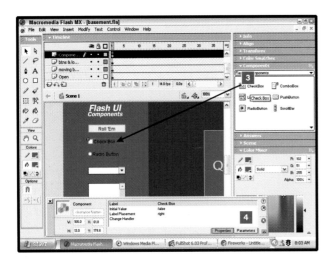

1. **Open the basement.fla file.**

2. **Select Window→Components to open the Flash UI Components panel.**
   Your system may have more than one set of components, and if it does, select the Flash UI Components.

3. **Drag an instance of the CheckBox object from the Components panel to the stage.**

4. **Open the Properties panel and click the Parameters tab.**
   The CheckBox component has four different parameters, Label, Initial Value, Label Placement, and Change Handler. The Label is the name that appears next to the check box. The Initial Value is false by default. That means that the check box initially appears unchecked. The Label Placement is either to the left or right of the check box with the default to the right. Finally, the Change Handler is an ActionScript function that will be fired when the check box changes from checked to unchecked.

5. **Change the Label in the Parameters tab to Preview A.**
   As soon as you have changed the label in the Parameters tab, the label on the right side of the check box changes to the new label.

6. **Leave the Initial Value and Label Placement parameters with the default value.**

7. **Type** checkIt **for the Change Handler.**

8. **Type the instance name** prevA **in the Properties panel.**
   This component needs an instance name for the ActionScript function that will be written for it.

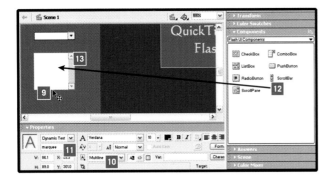

9. **Select the Text tool and create a Dynamic text field.**
   This text field will be used to test the check box and radio buttons.

10. **Select Multiline for line type and click the Show Borders option.**

11. **In the Properties panel, type** marquee **for the instance name.**

12. **Drag a ScrollBar component from the Component panel to the stage and place it so that it touches the Dynamic text field.**
   The ScrollBar object automatically conforms to the size of the text field.

13. **With the ScrollBar component selected, examine the values in the Properties panel.**

The instance name of the text field has been incorporated as the Target TextField.

14. **Press the F9 key to open the Actions panel.**

15. **Click the first frame of the Components layer.**

16. **Open the View Options menu and select Expert Mode.**

17. **Type the following script in the right pane of the Actions panel:**

```
//Check box handler
function checkIt() {
    var copyA = "This exciting movie shows a man
talking while a bug flies around the stage.";
    var sniffer = prevA.getValue();
    if (sniffer) {
            _root.marquee.text = copyA;
    } else {
            _root.marquee.text = " ";
    }
}
```

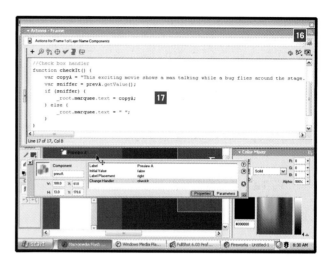

In Session 10, you learned about conditional statements that include a second option when an `if` statement results in a false condition. The script begins by creating a variable assigned a string message. Then, it assigns a variable named `sniffer` the value of the check box with the instance name `prevA`. If the check box is checked, it will return a Boolean true, and if not, it returns a false value. The `if` statement looks for a true or false, and since the variable `sniffer` is one or the other, all you need to put in the condition is the variable name. If the box is checked, it places the string stored in the `copyA` variable into the dynamic text field with the instance name `marquee`. If `sniffer` is false, which occurs as soon as the box is unchecked, the marquee is cleared.

< N O T E >
You can close the left pane of the Actions panel by clicking the border between the left and right panes. By doing so, you have more horizontal room to see your script.

18. **Select Control→Test Movie from the menu bar.**

19. **Click the check box named Preview A.**

A message appears in the text field.

20. **Click the check box a second time to remove the check.**

The message disappears. A check box can be programmed with ActionScript to perform all sorts of tasks, and this example is used primarily to show you one application, but you can have the check box trigger any function you want.

Tutorial

» Using the RadioButton UI Component

The RadioButton UI Component works very much like the CheckBox UI Component. However, while the radio buttons have two states — on and off — you can set them up to be mutually exclusive. As soon as one is selected, the other is de-selected. When working with radio buttons in groupings, as you would for a questionnaire, a quiz, or any other application where you want the user to select only one option from a set, using a radio button instead of the check box is advised. This tutorial shows not only how to use the radio buttons, but includes a general lesson about UI Components as unique objects. As you will see, once you add a UI Component to the stage, you cannot draw another component of the same type from the Components panel.

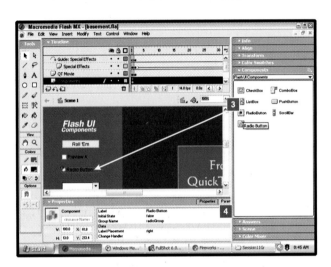

1. **Open the basement.fla file.**

2. **Select Window→Components to open the Flash UI Components panel.**
   Your system may have more than one set of components, and if it does, select the Flash UI Components.

3. **Drag an instance of the RadioButton object from the Components panel to the stage.**

4. **Open the Properties panel and click the Parameters tab.**
   You will see six parameters. You will only be changing the Label, Group Name, and Change Handler. Everything else you will leave at the default.

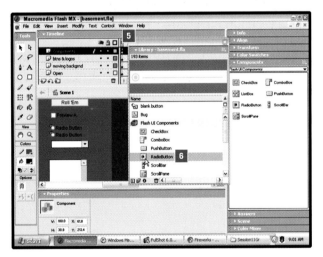

5. **Select Window→Library to open the Library panel.**

6. **Drag an instance of the RadioButton from the Library to the stage.**

7. **Place the second radio button object directly under the first and use the Align panel to align them on the left.**

8. **Select the top radio button.**

9. **Select the Parameters tab of the Properties panel.**

10. **Type** Preview B **as a label,** radioPrev **as the Group Name, and** radioDaze **as the Change Handler.**

11. **Type the Instance name window in the Properties panel,** prevB.

12. **Select the bottom radio button.**

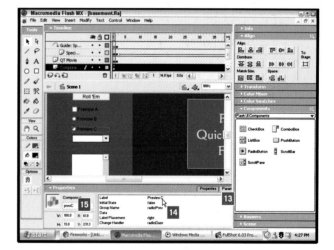

13. **Select the Parameters tab of the Properties panel.**

14. **Type** Preview C **as a label,** radioPrev **as the Group Name, and** radioDaze **as the Change Handler.**
    Both buttons use the same Group Name and Change Handler. Radio buttons in the same group represent mutually exclusive choices. That means if you select one, the other is automatically de-selected. To keep them mutually exclusive, they must be in the same group. When creating movies with several groups of radio buttons, such as a multiple choice questionnaire, each group must have a unique Group Name identifier.

15. **Type the Instance name window in the Properties panel,** prevC.

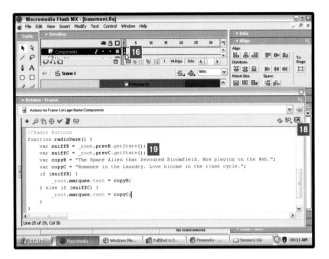

16. **Select the first frame of the Components layer.**

17. **Press F9 to open the Actions panel.**

18. **Select Expert Mode from the View Options popup menu on the Actions panel.**

19. **Add the following script to the right pane of the Actions panel:**

```
//Radio Buttons
function radioDaze() {
    var sniffB = _root.prevB.getState();
    var sniffC = _root.prevC.getState();
    var copyB = "The Space Alien that Devoured
Bloomfield. Now playing on the Web.";
    var copyC = "Romance in the Laundry. Love
blooms in the rinse cycle.";
    if (sniffB) {
        _root.marquee.text = copyB;
    } else if (sniffC) {
        _root.marquee.text = copyC;
    }
}
```

The script begins by creating two variables and assigning them the values of the two buttons. The getState() method returns a Boolean true or false depending on whether the radio button has been selected or not. (The check box object used the getValue() method.) Next, two variables are assigned a string message. The conditional statement then looks to see if one or the other statements is true. Because the sniffB and sniffC variables are Booleans, they can be placed in the if and else if statements as variables instead of expressions.

20. **Use the Text Tool to create a Dynamic text field and give it the instance name marquee in the Properties panel.**
If you completed the previous Tutorial, "Using the Check Box UI Component," this step is already completed.

21. **Select Control→Test Movie from the menu bar.**

22. **Click the Preview B radio button.**
You should see the text field filled with the first message (string variable) you created in the ActionScript program.

23. **Click the Preview C radio button.**
The first radio button becomes deselected automatically as the second button is selected and a different message appears in the dynamic text field. Where you want mutually exclusive choices in a Flash site, you can use the RadioButton UI Component to allow only a single choice.

» Session Review

1. What are some ways digital video movies are formatted as QuickTime movies? (See "Tutorial: Importing QuickTime Movies into Flash MX.")

2. Which steps are used to import a QuickTime movie into a Flash MX movie? What are the different decisions that must be made during import? (See "Tutorial: Importing QuickTime Movies into Flash MX.")

3. How do you position a QuickTime movie on the stage? How is it different from and similar to a regular movie clip? (See "Tutorial: Arranging the QuickTime Movie on the Stage.")

4. Compared to a movie clip, what can you do with the environment around a QuickTime Movie? (See "Tutorial: Building the Flash Environment Around the QuickTime Movie.")

5. How are special effects added to a Flash MX movie containing a QuickTime movie? (See "Tutorial: Adding Special Effects over a QuickTime Movie.")

6. What must be done to add a Guide Layer and movement along a path as part of the special effects overlying a QuickTime movie? (See "Tutorial: Adding Special Effects over a QuickTime Movie.")

7. Flash MX ActionScript recognizes different types of numbers. What are the number types in Flash MX? (See "Tutorial: Building the Flash Environment Around the QuickTime Movie.")

8. What information about a Push Button UI component do the Properties and Parameters tabs in the Properties panel provide? (See "Tutorial: Using the Push Button UI Component.")

9. What role does the Click Handler play in triggering actions with a Push Button? (See "Tutorial: Using the Push Button UI Component.")

10. What method is used in ActionScript to see whether a CheckBox UI Component has been checked or not? (See "Tutorial: Using the Check Box UI Component.")

11. What happens when you attempt to drag more than one instance of a Radio Button UI Component from the Component panel? How do you drag more than a single instance of a UI Component to the stage? (See "Tutorial: Using the Radio Button UI Component.")

12. What ActionScript method is used to determine whether a Radio Button UI Component is selected or not? (See "Tutorial: Using the Radio Button UI Component.")

13. How can Radio Buttons be made mutually exclusive? What Radio Button parameter must you use to create mutual exclusivity in Radio Buttons? (See "Tutorial: Using the Push Button UI Component.")

14. When using mutually exclusive Radio Buttons in a movie, what happens to the other buttons in a Radio Button group when you click any of the buttons? (See "Tutorial: Using the Push Button UI Component.")

» Additional Projects

» Borrow the Preloader from the previous session and attach it to the beginning of the basement.fla file. By adding a QuickTime movie with sound, the basement.fla file went from a few kilobytes of bandwidth to a few hundred kilobytes. That means a longer load, so to keep the viewer informed, you can use the Preloader.

» Redo the entire navigation system using UI Components. A lot of fancy buttons are great for learning different tricks and effects, but often you need clear consistency and that is one thing that the UI Components provide. See how much lighter or heavier your files will be using the UI Components.

Session 12

Using External Files and Finishing Up

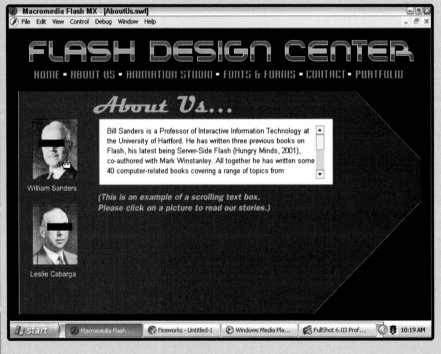

Session Introduction

This session covers how to get started using external files in Flash MX. Besides being an excellent animation tool, Flash MX is a good *front end*. When dealing with external data, the front end is what the viewer sees on her screen and serves as an interface with the user. A *back end* is some kind of middleware and database that sends information to the front end. However, instead of getting into the advanced materials required to learn how to use back ends such as ASP, PHP, ColdFusion, Perl, or one of the .NET technologies along with SQL databases, we use the humble text file instead. So, even as a beginner, you can call up all of the back end text fields you want.

In addition to getting you started on back ends, this session also finishes up elements of the project that represent a mix of so many different techniques that they are best placed at the end so that you are familiar with all of the techniques. In particular, you will see how a 3-D technique in Flash MX is possible, how to use a scanner to create bitmapped graphics of objects, and a trick that makes the movie appear as though the timeline slipped down from the top of the movie and onto the stage.

TOOLS YOU'LL USE
All of the tools in the Toolbox that create vector graphics, and the following panels:
Actions, Align, Color Mixer, Components, Library, Properties, Transform

MATERIALS NEEDED
From the accompanying CD-ROM, you'll need the FinalIntro3.fla and AboutUs.fla files.

TIME REQUIRED
120 minutes

SESSION OUTCOME
The reader will understand how to load external data files and how to recreate the special effects at the end of the Introduction.

Tutorial
» Preparing Text Fields for External Files

In previous versions of Flash, the primary connection between variables and text fields was the association text fields had with variables by virtue of the fact that you can give a variable Input and Dynamic text fields. That is still possible, but like a good deal of ActionScript in Flash MX, you can now treat text fields as objects that have a text value, just as you can assign a variable a string literal. All the designer needs to do is provide an instance name for the text field. You can assign values to the text field using the format:

```
textFieldInstanceName.text = variableOrLiteral;
```

When preparing a text field for an external value, instead of assigning a variable name to the text field, then, the focus is on the instance name. When data are pulled from external sources, you can place any number of different variables sequentially into a single text field without having to use a single variable name. This tutorial shows you how to prepare the text field so that any number of different variables from external sources can be brought to the screen.

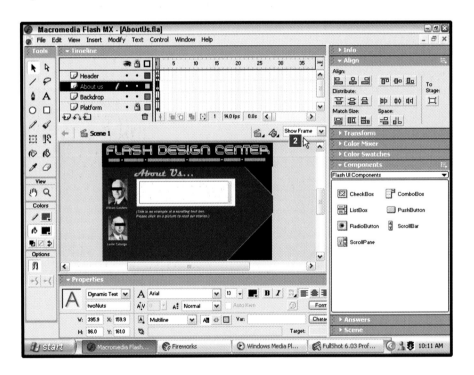

1. **Open the AboutUs.fla file.**

2. **Select Show Frame in the popup menu in the upper-right corner of the stage.**
   You will see two images and a large white area that will be used for the dynamic text field.

3. **Click the About Us layer.**

   This will be the layer where you will put your text field. The text field will be used to load data about the gentlemen represented by the pictures on the left.

4. **Use the Text tool to place a Dynamic text field in the middle of the white rectangle.**

   You might want to lock the backdrop layer so you don't accidentally move it.

5. **Select the text field.**

6. **Type the name** twoNuts **for the instance name of the text field in the Properties panel.**

   This instance name identifies the target for a later ActionScript program that will load an external file.

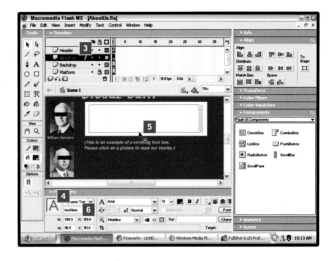

7. **Drag a ScrollBar UI Component from the Components panel to the stage.**

8. **Drag the scroll bar so that it locks to the right side of the dynamic text field.**

   It should both lock and resize itself to fit the vertical side of the text field.

9. **With the scroll bar selected, click the Parameters tab of the Properties panel.**

   You should see the Target TextField listed as twoNuts.

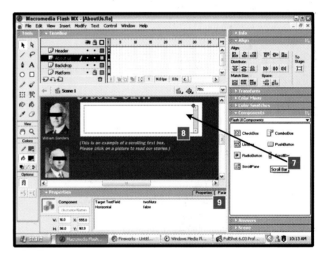

Tutorial
» Passing Variables from External Sources to Flash

Flash has a unique and curious way of defining variables for external data. In this application, two text fields are used to provide information. Each field has a single variable in the format:

```
variableName=Data
```

The data are treated as text or a string, and you can enter text and numbers. Be careful with punctuation because some of it is used to demarcate variable names. The ampersand (&) is the division between variables, and you must put no space between ampersands, variable names, and equal signs. For example, the following represents two different variables formatted for Flash:

```
variableAlpha=A fine had was timed by all.&variableBeta=I would rather be flying.
```

The first variable, `variableAlpha` has a value of "A fine had was timed by all." and `variableBeta` has a value of "I would rather be flying." When the file is loaded into Flash, it has the same effect as writing,

```
var variableAlpha = "A fine had was timed by all."
var variableBeta = "I would rather be flying."
```

So the next step involves writing two text files and then a script that loads them into Flash. You can begin with the assumption that both of the images on the left side of the stage are buttons.

1. **Open a text editor such as Notepad (Windows) or SimpleText (Macintosh).**
   You can use any text editor that can save a file as a text file or even a word processor.

2. **Type** bill=Bill Sanders . . . **and the rest of the copy.**
   Do not place quotation marks anywhere in the copy.

3. **Save the file as bill.txt in the same folder where your Flash movie is saved.**
   For this example, you will be using the same folder, but you can draw text in from any source as long as you have the correct URL.

4. **Open a new file in text editor.**

5. **Type** les=Leslie Cabarga . . . **and the rest of the copy.**
   Do not place quotation marks anywhere in the copy.

6. **Save the file as les.txt in the same folder where your Flash movie is saved.**

7. **Press F9 to open the Actions panel.**

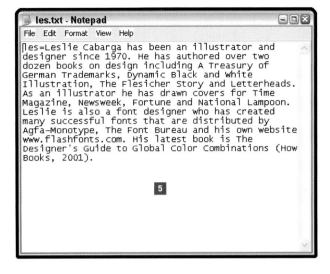

8. **Select the View Options popup menu and choose Expert Mode.**

9. **Select the top image (a button) on the left side of the stage with the caption William Sanders beneath it.**

10. **In the right pane of the Actions panel, type the following script.**

```
on (release) {
    willieLoad = new LoadVars();
    willieLoad.onLoad = function() {
        _root.twoNuts.text = this.bill;
    };
    willieLoad.load("bill.txt");
}
```

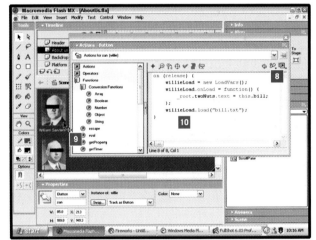

A new object willieLoad is defined as a LoadVars() object. Next, the onLoad method is used with the next object in creating a function. The dynamic text field is identified by _root.twoNuts.text and the variable bill is in the willieLoad object, and so it is this.bill. (It could be willieLoad.bill.) This keyword can be used when it references the object that calls it. Just like you need to reference the level a variable may be on (such as, _root.variableName), you must reference the object associated with a variable. After the function literal, the object uses the load() method with the URL of the text file. Because the text file is in the same directory as the calling file, the path is simply the name of the file.

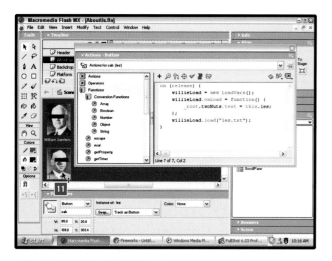

11. Repeat steps 9 and 10 but select the bottom button (Leslie Cabarga) and enter the following script:

```
on (release) {
    leslieLoad = new LoadVars();
    leslieLoad.onLoad = function() {
            _root.twoNuts.text = this.les;
    };
    leslieLoad.load("les.txt");
}
```

You might wonder what the advantage of using this method may be. First, you can update material easily simply by changing the contents of the text file. Second, there's no need to add additional text weight to the Flash movie. It's only used when it is needed. Finally, you can use multiple messages in the same screen space. By adding the scroll bar, you can use messages of different lengths.

12. **Select Control→Test movie from the menu bar.**

13. **Click the top button.**
You can see the text flows beyond the bottom of the screen and it references the named individual in the top button.

14. **Click the bottom button.**
The text now switches to describe the bottom individual. Thus, beginning with a blank screen, Flash MX was able to effectively bring in more data from an external source and place it so that the user can view and use it.

Tutorial
» Creating an Iris Effect

One of the more interesting transitions in the opening movie is part of one of the movie clips. It takes just a second, and you may have forgotten it. The transition between one set of events and another occurs when an iris, similar in appearance to those in a typical camera, closes around the object. You see a hand holding a pencil, an iris closes around the hand creating a transition to black, and then a hand drawing boxes appears. You can possibly use the iris, contained in a movie clip, for any other project you have where you want an "Iris Transition." This tutorial shows how to do it.

1. **Open InfoFinal3.fla and select the Introduction scene.**

2. **Drag the playhead to Frame 363.**
   You will see a hand object beneath a sign that says CENTER.

3. **Click the sequential Multiple clips layer in Frame 363.**

4. **Click the hand object.**
   The Properties panel should identify the object as hand and pencil.

5. **Double-click the hand object.**
   You are now in the Symbol Editing Mode for the hand and pencil Graphic instance.

<NOTE>
You see six angles in the iris corners. Each one is 60°. To recreate the iris, you need only two panels plus the irregular one. Make the first panel horizontal. Make a copy of it, and those two panels can be placed at the top and bottom of the iris. Then make a second panel and use the Transform panel to angle it to 60°. Make three copies of the angled panel, and flip two vertically. Arrange them into an iris using the figures in this tutorial as a guide.

6. **Move the playhead to Frame 130.**

7. **Select 15% from the Magnification popup menu.**
   You can now see the open "Iris" surrounding the stage.

8. **Click part of the iris Graphic instance.**
   The Properties panel should identify it as "lens Iris down."

9. **Double-click part of the lens iris down object.**

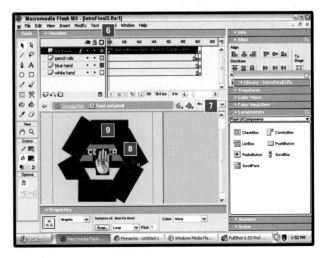

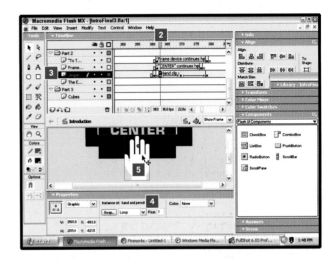

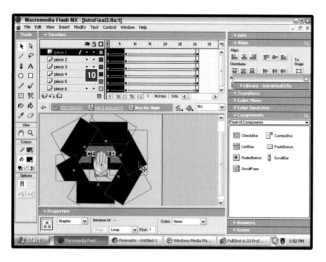

10. Hold down the Shift key and click all of the first frames.

You can see that each piece of the iris is a graphic with an angled black rectangle inside it set at different angles. One of the iris panels has an odd shape so that closing the iris ring will still look like the panels are sliding on top of one another.

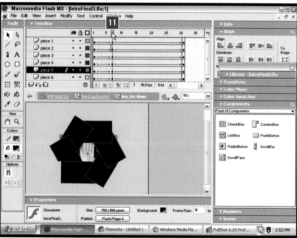

11. Drag the playhead to Frame 7.

You can see the iris begin closing around the hand.

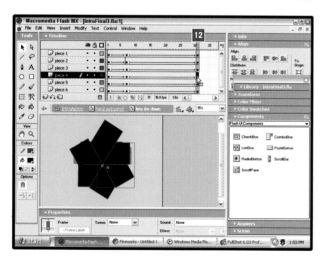

12. Drag the playhead to Frame 31.

The iris closes and you are left seeing only the blue outlines of the six panels that make up the iris. That is exactly the effect you want.

Tutorial

» Making a Pseudo-Timeline

When viewers first see the timeline at the end of the introduction drop down, the reaction is generally one of incredulity. "How'd he do that?!" summarizes my reaction to Leslie Cabarga's cool trick of letting the timeline "drop" down into the running movie. This tutorial shows how the pseudo-timeline, complete with moving playhead, is created. At the end of the session, you will see how the pseudo-timeline comes crashing down at the end of the introduction.

1. **Open IntroFinal3.fla and select the Introduction scene.**

2. **Select Window→Library to open the Library panel.**

3. **Find the timeline symbol movie clip and double-click it.**
   You are now in the symbol-editing mode. On the stage are two objects. One is the timeline.gif, made up of a screen shot of the timeline and a "needle" object that serves as the movable playhead.

4. **To re-create the timeline image, position the playhead and time-line so that you cannot see the playhead and make a screen shot.**
   You can make a screen shot on Windows computers by pressing the Print Screen key. The image goes into a copy buffer, and then you can paste it into a graphics program like Macromedia Fireworks or Adobe Photoshop. If you have a Macintosh, pressing Shift+Command+3 places a copy of the screen in your copy buffer.

5. **Crop the screen shot image so that all that shows is the timeline.**

6. **Save or export the timeline image as a GIF file.**

7. **Import the timeline GIF into Flash by selecting File→Import to Library from the menu bar.**

8. **Drag the timeline GIF to the stage, select it, and then press the F8 key to convert it into a movie clip.**

9. **In the Symbol Editing Mode create a playhead "needle" so that it is the same size as the playhead needle on the actual timeline and convert it into a graphic symbol.**
   When you create the needle, make the head transparent using 63% alpha. In that way when the needle moves along the timeline, you can see the frame numbers beneath it just like the actual one.

10. **Click the layer and click the Insert Layer button.**
    You now have two layers in the timeline symbol's Symbol Editing mode.

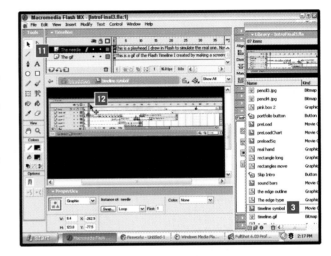

11. **Rename the top layer** The needle **and the bottom layer** The gif.

12. **Click The needle layer and place the needle object on top of the timeline object on the stage.**
    Position it where the fourth frame would go.

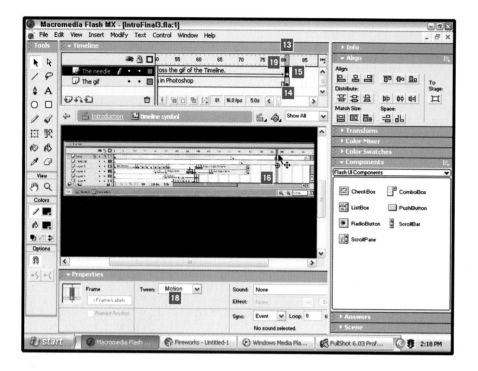

13. Click Frame 80 in the real timeline.

14. Press the F5 key to add frames from the beginning to Frame 80 for both layers.

15. Click the last frame and press F6 to add a keyframe to the last frame.

16. With the last frame selected, drag the needle on the stage to a position near the end of the graphic timeline.

Depending on the size and resolution of your screen, the actual frame position on the graphic will vary, but on the project, it will be around Frame 77.

17. Click the first frame of The needle layer.

18. Select Motion from the Tween popup menu in the Properties panel and select both the Sync and Snap options at the bottom of the Properties panel.

19. Drag the actual playhead left and right.

Now the needle-playhead on the graphic image timeline should move left and right, just like the playhead on the actual timeline.

< T I P >

If you want to test movie clips in the player, the easiest way to do that is to open a new file and drag an instance of the movie clip into the new file. Then select Control→Test movie and the movie clip plays in the player without having to go through the entire movie.

Tutorial
» Creating 3-D Effects in Flash

One of the complaints you sometimes hear about Flash MX is that it lacks tools for rendering three-dimensional objects. The truth of the matter is that the Internet simply lacks the bandwidth to handle rendered 3-D objects, but with Flash you can certainly create 3-D objects. This next tutorial shows the process artist Leslie Cabarga went through to create the 3-D cubes in the introduction.

1. **Find some household item that approximates a cube.**
   The artist found a tea box that was pretty close to a cube.

2. **Using a digital camera, create photographs showing the different angles you want the Flash MX cube to follow.**
   The artist wanted a rolling effect to one side or the other.

3. **With the photos as a guide, sketch the cube sequence.**
   By having sketches available, you can better see what you will
   need to create using the Flash drawing tools.

4. **Open IntroFinal3.fla and select the Introduction scene.**

5. **Press Ctrl+L/Cmd+L to open the Library panel.**

6. **Locate the Graphic symbol, boxes twirl blue, in the Library panel.**

7. **Double-click the boxes twirl blue symbol.**
   You are now in the Symbol Editing Mode.

8. **Insert keyframes in the following frames: 1, 4, 7, 10, 12, 14, 16,
   18, 20, 22, 24, 26, 27, 29, 31, 33, 36, and 37.**

9. **Place the following drawings in the indicated keyframes:**

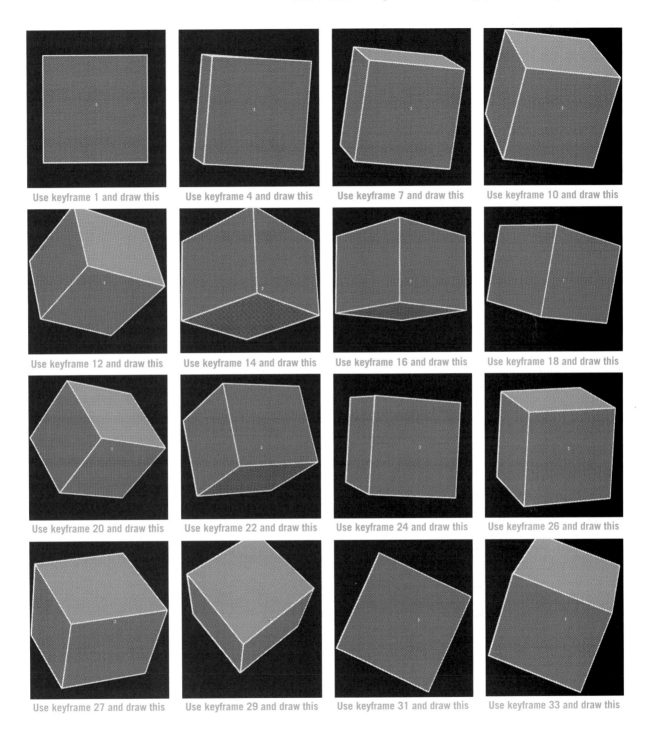

Use keyframe 1 and draw this

Use keyframe 4 and draw this

Use keyframe 7 and draw this

Use keyframe 10 and draw this

Use keyframe 12 and draw this

Use keyframe 14 and draw this

Use keyframe 16 and draw this

Use keyframe 18 and draw this

Use keyframe 20 and draw this

Use keyframe 22 and draw this

Use keyframe 24 and draw this

Use keyframe 26 and draw this

Use keyframe 27 and draw this

Use keyframe 29 and draw this

Use keyframe 31 and draw this

Use keyframe 33 and draw this

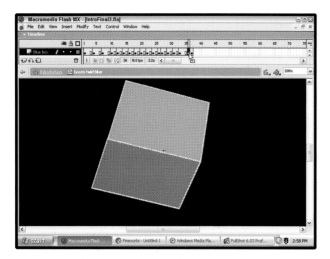

10. **Select keyframe 36 and draw this image.**

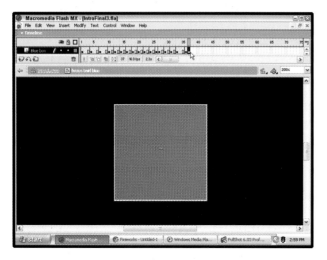

11. **Select keyframe 37 and draw this image.**

12. **Press the Enter/Return key to test the movie in the Symbol Editing mode.**

The cube should spin around showing a realistic three-dimensional spin. Who says that you can't do 3-D in Flash?

Tutorial
» Making the Hand and Drawing Images

Another interesting effect in the Introduction is the hand with the pencil spinning on it that turns into a hand that begins drawing boxes. In all, you see three different views of a hand — a flat hand and two different angles holding a pencil. All of the hands are digital images, but instead of creating them using a digital camera, the artist simply placed his hand into a flatbed scanner and scanned it. This tutorial looks at these hands and discusses how to create them.

1. **Open IntroFinal3.fla.**

2. **Press Ctrl+L/Cmd+L to open the Library panel.**

3. **Locate the Graphic symbol, blue-hand.jpg, in the Library panel.**

4. **Select File→New from the menu bar.**

5. **Open the IntroFinal3.fla Library panel in the new movie.**

6. **Drag the image blue-hand.jpg to the stage.**
   This hand was created by the artist placing his hand in a flatbed scanner and scanning his hand.

7. **Repeat steps 4–6 with blue-hand2.jpg.**
   In this JPEG image the artist placed a pencil in his had with a downward position.

8. **Repeat steps 4–6 with blue-hand3.jpg.**
   In this JPEG, the pencil angle was increased.

9. **Select each of the JPEG images and press F8 to convert them into symbols.**
   Once the JPEG images are imported to Flash MX, they are converted to symbol files. In this way, the designer can use more than a single instance of the image, but use only the weight of a single image. As you will see in the next tutorial, the hands with the pencils are used repeatedly.

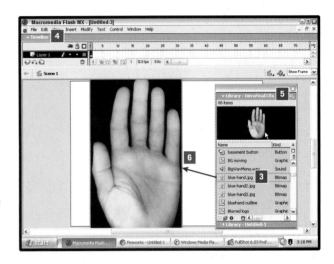

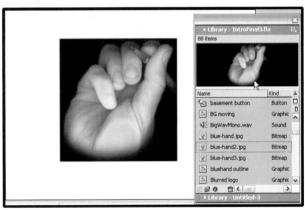

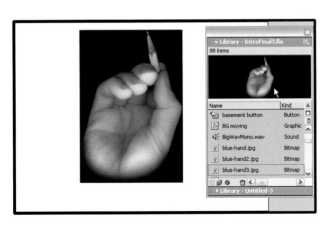

Tutorial
» Animating the Drawing Hand

Once the two drawing hands have been placed in symbols, you can now animate them.

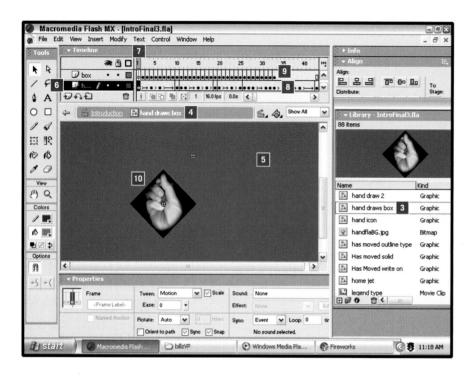

1. **Open IntroFinal3.fla.**

2. **Press Ctrl+L/Cmd+L to open the Library panel.**

3. **Locate the Graphic symbol hand draws box in the Library panel.**

4. **Double-click the image to open it in the Symbol Editing Mode.**

5. **Click the stage, and change the background color from black to a charcoal gray.**
   Changing the color to a gray better shows you the different angles of the hand objects. Two different graphic symbols are used for the drawing hand.

6. **Name the top layer** box **and the bottom layer** hand drawing.

7. **Add a keyframe to the second frame of the box layer.**

8. **Click the second frame in the box layer and use the Rectangle tool to draw a blue square with a two-point stroke and no fill, with each side 172.5.**
   To make a perfect square, hold down the Shift key while drawing.

9. **In the box layer, add keyframes in every frame out to Frame 33.**
   The top layer is where the box appears. In an earlier tutorial, you learned that it can be easier to draw the complete image on the last frame and then erase what you don't need as you go along.

10. **Click the first frame of the hand drawing layer and drag an instance of the hand draw 1 symbol from the library and place it so that the pencil is positioned where the lower-left corner of the box will be beginning in the second frame.**

11. **Place keyframes in Frames 4, 6, and 10 of the hand drawing layer and add motion tweens in Frames 1, 4, and 6.**
    A few keyframes are skipped, but at each one change the angle of the hand slightly.

12. **Change the angle of the hand in Frame10 so that it is parallel with the stage.**

13. **Erase all of the rectangle except for the left side.**

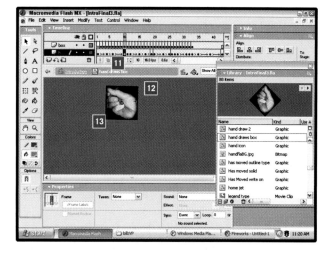

14. **Move the playhead to Frame 15.**

15. **Swap in the hand draw 2 Graphic.**
    The drawing seems all the more realistic because the picture of the hand changes as it would in an actual hand drawing. Moreover, it only takes two drawing angles to create this realism.

16. **Erase all of the rectangle except the upper-left corner.**

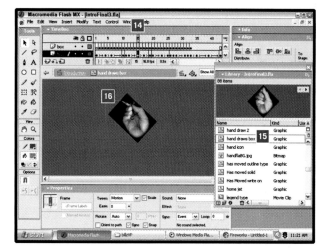

17. Move the playhead to Frame 20.

18. Swap back to the hand draw 1 Graphic.

19. Erase all of the rectangle except the left and top sides.

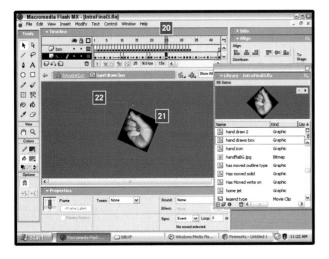

20. Move the playhead to Frame 25.

21. Change the angle of the hand drawing 1 Graphic.

22. Erase the bottom and part of the right side of the rectangle.

23. **Move the playhead to Frame 31.**

24. **Change the angle of the hand draw 1 Graphic.**

25. **Erase the left part of the bottom line of the rectangle.**

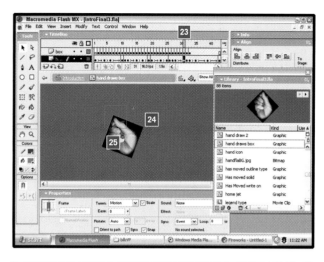

26. **Move the playhead to Frame 35.**

27. **Change the angle of the hand draw 1 Graphic.**
    The box is complete, so you need not erase any more of it.

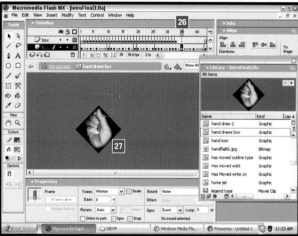

28. **Move the playhead to the last frame.**

29. **Drag the hand object to the right of the rectangle.**

30. **Change the background color back to black.**
    As you can see, little tweens were used throughout the hand drawing layer. The whole thing could have been done with four tweens and four keyframes on both layers, but it would lose its realism in animation.

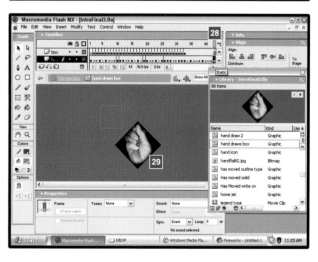

Tutorial

» Setting Up the Last Graphic Movie

A good size movie has been placed in a Graphic instance. This instance works the same as a Movie Clip, but ActionScript cannot address it. (You can create the movie as a Movie Clip if you want, and it has no adverse effect on the outcome.) So, to get ready for the Grand Finale, this tutorial shows how to prepare the movie inside the Graphic symbol instance.

1. **Open IntroFinal3.fla and open the Introduction scene.**

2. **Drag the playhead to Frame 755.**

3. **Double-click the object (logo colors) to open it in the Symbol Editing Mode.**
   You will find seven layers in the Logo colors Graphic instance. The only image is a thin white line.

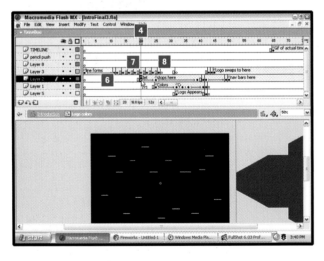

4. **Drag the playhead to Frame 20.**
   You will see the single solid line first expand using a Shape tween in Layer 3, and then break up into smaller lines.

5. **Place a single line in the middle of the stage in Frame 1, Layer 3.**

6. **Place a keyframe in Frame 11 and add a line that goes from one side of the stage to the other.**

7. **Beginning in Frame 12 of Layer 3, place keyframes in Frames 12, 14, 16, 18, 20, 22, and 24 of Layer 3.**
   In each of the keyframes, move the small lines farther to the top or bottom.

8. **Place a blank keyframe in Frame 26 of Layer 3.**
   At this stage the big purple Jet is entering the stage.

9. **Drag the playhead to Frame 25.**

10. **Place the Color Blocks upright Graphic on the nose of the Jet.**

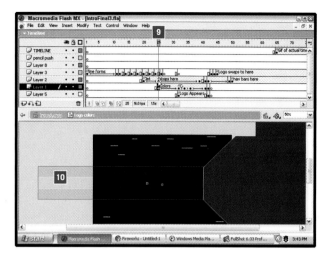

11. **Move the playhead to Frame 32 and click Layer 5.**

12. **Place an instance of the movie clip logo blur 1 on top of the Color Blocks upright.**

    The movie clip is a simple blurring one.

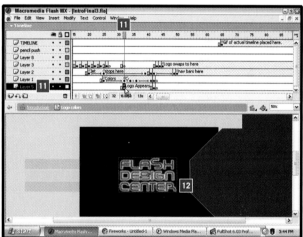

13. **Move the playhead to Frame 42.**

14. **Move the Jet closer to the logo.**

15. **Draw three boxes, colored pink, green, and blue, select them all, and select Modify→Group.**

16. **Place the three color boxes next to the Flash Design Center logo.**

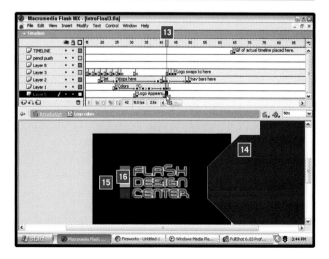

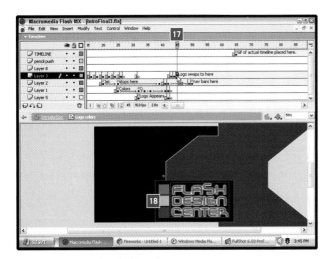

17. **Move the playhead to Frame 45.**

18. **Select the Flash Design Center and color block group and select Modify→Group from the menu bar.**

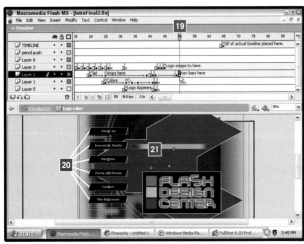

19. **Move the playhead to Frame 50.**
    The "Jet" is now fully in place.

20. **Add the six navigation buttons.**

21. **Position the "Jet" so that it is beneath the logo and navigation buttons.**

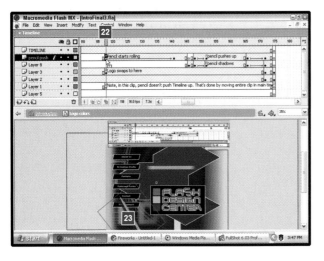

22. **Move the playhead to Frame 118.**
    The timeline symbol was put in place in Frame 65, but you can put it in here instead.

23. **Place the pencil rolling Graphic beneath the Jet in the pencil push layer.**
    The pencil rolling Graphic will eventually work its way to just beneath the timeline symbol. However, the effect of it pushing the timeline back into place is accomplished on the main timeline.

Tutorial
» Wrapping Up the Introduction

This tutorial represents the last in the course, and it shows how the end of the Introduction creates the effect of the timeline crashing down on the movie only to be saved at the last second by the intervention of the pencil, which nudges it back into place. In an earlier tutorial in this session you saw how to create a pseudo-timeline (Tutorial: Making a Pseudo-Timeline). This final tutorial shows how it works in conjunction with a movie clip and the main timeline.

24. **Click the Introduction scene icon to return to the main timeline.**

25. **Move the playhead to Frame 822.**

26. **Set the magnification so that you can see the entire stage and all of the elements around it.**
    In the viewing area the user will only see the main menu part at this stage.

27. **Place a keyframe in the Cubes layer.**

28. **With the keyframe selected, choose Motion from the Tween menu in the Properties panel.**

29. **Move the playhead to Frame 829.**

30. **Place a keyframe in Frame 829 in the Cubes layer.**

31. **Drag the big Graphic instance to an angle using the Free Transform tool.**
    With the tween in place, this should appear to be slipping down.

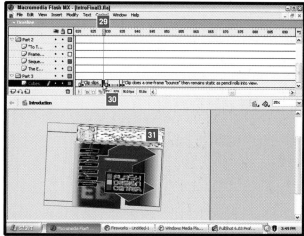

32. **Move the playhead to Frame 831.**

33. **Place a keyframe in Frame 831 in the Cubes layer.**

34. **Use the Free Transform tool to level the Graphic instance and the Arrow tool to drag it downward so that the pseudo-timeline can be viewed on the stage.**

35. **With the keyframe selected, choose Motion from the Tween menu in the Properties panel.**

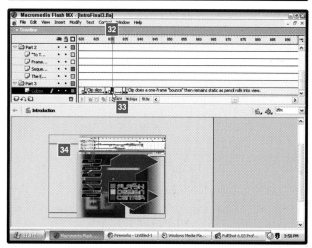

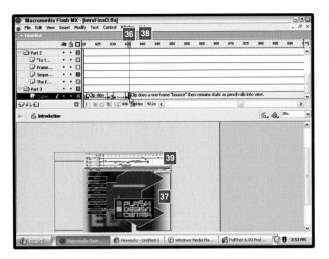

36. **Move the playhead to Frame 830 and add a keyframe to the Cubes layer.**

37. **Drag the Graphic down farther so that the bottom part of the image is off the stage.**

38. **Move the playhead to Frame 831 and add a keyframe to the Cubes layer.**

39. **Select the Graphic image and press the Shift+up arrow to "bounce" the Graphic up eight pixels.**
    This one-frame "bounce" effect makes it look like the menu fell down bringing the timeline with it and then bounced when it hit the bottom.

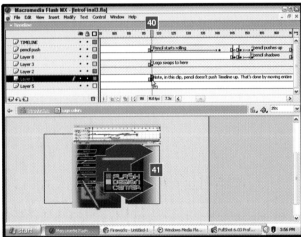

40. **Double-click the Graphic instance on the main timeline to return to the Symbol-Editing Mode.**

41. **Move the playhead to Frame 118.**
    This is where the movie was before looking at the main timeline.

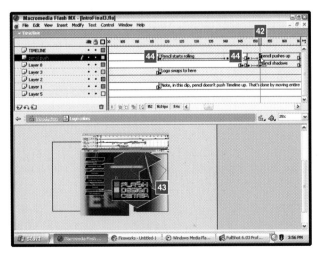

42. **Move the playhead to Frame 148 and place a keyframe in the pencil push layer and add a Motion tween.**

43. **Drag the playhead to Frame 152 and drag the instance of the 1pencil object so that it is just under the pseudo-timeline.**
    The effect of the pencil pushing the timeline back into place is accomplished by coordinating the upward movement of the pseudo-timeline on the main timeline with the positioning of the pencil under the timeline within this Graphic instance.

44. **Place keyframes and motion tweens in the pencil push layer at Frames 118 and 140 with an instance of pencil rolling, with the movement from the lower left to upper right, well below the pseudo-timeline.**

45. **Drag the playhead to Frame 906 on the main timeline.**
    You can see that at this point, the pencil in the underlying Graphic instance movie is moved beneath the pseudo-timeline.

46. **Insert a keyframe in Frame 906 of the Cubes layer.**

47. **Select Motion from the Tween popup menu in the Properties panel to add a motion tween.**

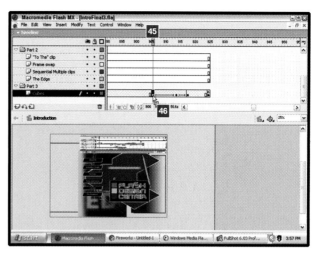

48. **Drag the playhead to Frame 914 on the main timeline.**

49. **Insert a keyframe.**

50. **Use the Free Transform tool to angle the Graphic instance upward.**

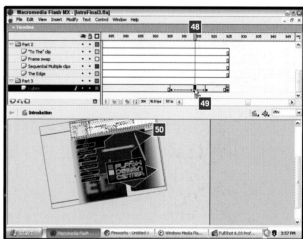

51. **Drag the playhead to Frame 918 on the main timeline.**

52. **Insert a keyframe in the Cubes layer.**

53. **Drag the Graphics instance back into place.**

54. **Open the Actions panel, and add the following script:**

```
loadMovieNm("MainMenu.swf",0;)
```

    The main menu now loads and removes the IntroFinal3.html from memory.

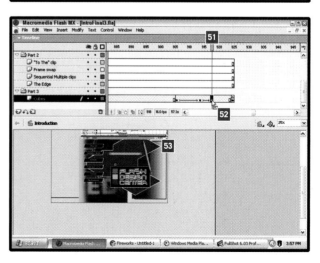

» Session Review

1. How are instance names associated with dynamic text fields used with external files? (See "Tutorial: Preparing Text Fields for External Files.")

2. How do you set up variable names in text files? (See "Tutorial: Passing Variables from External Sources to Flash.")

3. How many panels does it take to create an "iris" in Flash MX? What common angle value (in degrees) do all of the panels have? (See "Tutorial: Creating an Iris Effect.")

4. What techniques are used to create a pseudo-timeline? How do you make a screen shot using Windows and Macintosh computers? (See "Tutorial: Making a Pseudo-Timeline.")

5. What is a practical strategy for creating 3-D images in Flash using vector graphics? (See "Tutorial: Creating 3-D Effects in Flash.")

6. How were the images of the "drawing hands" created? What hardware was employed that is usually employed with flat objects such as photographs? (See "Tutorial: Making the Hand and Drawing Images.")

7. How many different bitmapped "hands" shots had to be made to get a realistic sequence of images for the hand drawing the boxes? (See "Tutorial: Animating the Drawing Hand.")

8. When working with the hand drawing the boxes, what technique was used to get a perfectly square box even though the box had to be made in short sequences? (See "Tutorial: Animating the Drawing Hand.")

9. What was used to create the animation for the last part of the movie? How did the animation object interact with the main timeline? (See "Tutorial: Setting Up the Last Graphic Movie.")

10. What was moved when the timeline appears to come crashing down into the movie? How did the pencil "push" the timeline back into place? (See "Tutorial: Wrapping Up the Introduction.")

» Additional Projects

» Create a movie with several dynamic text fields, each with a UI Component scroll bar. Each text field should represent a different information source that must be updated on a regular basis such as Weather, Breaking News, and other types of information that changes regularly. For each of the text fields have a text file that can be easily changed simply by typing new information. Each text file should begin with `variableName="` that is followed by any information you want to present on your Web site.

» Imagine a 3-D effect you want to create in Flash MX. Then, using real objects that come close to the object you want to make, create a series of digital photos of the object's movement, and then create the 3-D object using Flash's different drawing tools. Finally, animate the 3-D object (or objects) in Flash.

» Create a new introduction that uses all of the tricks and techniques you learned in this course. Make it as light as possible (use vector graphics instead of bitmapped graphics, and use instances of Graphic and Movie Clip symbols wherever you have to use the same image more than once). Be sure to include a "skip to the menu" page at the beginning.

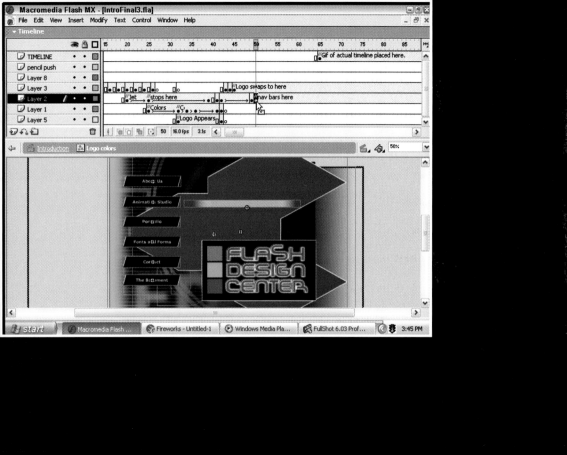

What's on the CD-ROM

This appendix provides you with information on the contents of the CD-ROM that accompanies this book. For the latest and greatest information, please refer to the ReadMe file located at the root of the CD-ROM. Here is what you will find:

» System Requirements

» Using the CD-ROM with Windows and Macintosh

» What's on the CD-ROM

» Troubleshooting

System Requirements

Make sure that your computer meets the minimum system requirements listed in this section. If your computer does not match up to most of these requirements, you may have a problem using the contents of the CD-ROM.

For Windows 98, Windows 2000, Windows NT, Windows Me, or Windows XP:

» PC with a Pentium class III or 4 processor

» At least 128MB of total RAM installed on your computer

» At least 280MB of free hard drive space

» A color monitor with at least 800 x 600 resolution and a 16-bit video card

» A CD-ROM drive

For Macintosh:

» Macintosh OS computer with a G3 or G4 PowerPC processor running OS 9.1, OS 9.2, or OS X

» At least 128MB of total RAM installed on your computer

» At least 320MB of free hard drive space

» A color monitor with at least 800 x 600 resolution and a 16-bit video card

» A CD-ROM drive

Using the CD-ROM with Windows

To install the items from the CD-ROM to your hard drive, follow these steps:

1. Insert the CD-ROM into your computer's CD-ROM drive.

2. The interface will launch. If you have autorun disabled, click Start→Run. In the dialog box that appears, type **D:\setup.exe**. Replace *D* with the proper letter if your CD-ROM drive uses a different letter. (If you do not know the letter, see how your CD-ROM drive is listed under My Computer.) Click OK.

3. A license agreement appears. Read through the license agreement, and then click the Accept button if you want to use the CD — after you click Accept, you will never be bothered by the License Agreement window again.

4. The CD interface Welcome screen appears. The interface coordinates installing the programs and running the demos. The interface basically enables you to click a button or two to make things happen.

5. Click anywhere on the Welcome screen to enter the interface. This next screen lists categories for the software on the CD.

6. For more information about a program, click the program's name. Be sure to read the information that appears. Sometimes a program has its own system requirements or requires you to do a few tricks on your computer before you can install or run the program, and this screen tells you what you might need to do, if necessary.

7. If you do not want to install the program, click the Back button to return to the previous screen. You can always return to the previous screen by clicking the Back button. This feature allows you to browse the different categories and products and decide what you want to install.

8. To install a program, click the appropriate Install button. The CD interface drops to the background while the CD installs the program you chose.

9. To install other items, repeat steps 7-10.

10. When you have finished installing programs, click the Quit button to close the interface. You can eject the CD now. Carefully place it back in the plastic jacket of the book for safekeeping.

If you are using a Windows operating system other than Windows XP, you will have to change the read-only status of the copied tutorial files. Otherwise, you will not be able to write over the files as you work through the tutorials. To do so, select all the files in a folder that you have copied to your computer. Right-click one of the files and choose Properties. In the Properties dialog box, uncheck Read-only.

Also, you can instruct Windows to display the filename extensions of the copied tutorial files, if it is not already set up to show them, so that you can see the file formats (.psd, .tif, .jpg, and so on). Find your Folder Options dialog box. It is located in a slightly different place in different versions of Windows; in Windows XP, it is in the Appearance and Themes Control Panel; in Windows 2000 and Me, in the My Computer→Tools folder; in Windows 98, in the My Computer→View folder. Click the View tab. Uncheck Hide File Extensions for Known File Types, which is checked by default.

Using the CD-ROM with the Macintosh OS

To install the items from the CD-ROM to your hard drive, follow these steps:

1. Insert the CD-ROM into your CD-ROM drive.

2. Double-click the icon for the CD-ROM after it appears on the desktop.

3. Double-click the License Agreement icon. This is the license that you are agreeing to by using the CD. You can close this window after you have looked over the agreement.

4. Most programs come with installers; for those, simply open the program's folder on the CD-ROM and double-click the Install or Installer icon. *Note:* To install some programs, just drag the program's folder from the CD-ROM window and drop it on your hard drive icon.

What's on the CD-ROM

The following sections provide a summary of the software and other materials that you will find on the CD-ROM.

All the tutorial files that you will use when working through the tutorials in this book are on the CD-ROM in the folder named "Tutorial Files." In this folder, you will find all the files referenced in the sessions.

Use the process described in the preceding section to copy the files to your hard drive. Windows users can access the Tutorial Files from the Start menu. Macintosh users can access the Tutorial Files from the Finder.

Applications

The following applications are on the CD-ROM:

» Macromedia Flash MX trial version for Windows 98, 2000, Me, NT, XP and Macintosh OS 9.1, OS 9.2, and OS X. Macromedia Flash MX is the program that you will use throughout this book to replicate the movies, create graphics, and do just about everything else in the course. Go to http://www.macromedia.com for more information and product updates.

» Trial versions for Windows and Macintosh of Macromedia's Dreamweaver MX and Fireworks MX. Go to http://www.macromedia.com for more information and product updates.

» Trial versions for Windows of Macromedia's Sitespring and Freehand. Go to http://www.macromedia.com for more information and product updates.

Shareware programs are fully functional, trial versions of copyrighted programs. If you like particular programs, register with their authors for a nominal fee and receive licenses, enhanced versions, and technical support. *Freeware programs* are copyrighted games, applications, and utilities that are free for personal use. Unlike shareware, these programs do not require a fee or provide technical support. *GNU software* is governed by its own license, which is included inside the folder of the GNU product. See the GNU license for more details.

Trial, demo, or evaluation versions are usually limited either by time or functionality, such as being unable to save projects. Some trial versions are very sensitive to system date changes. If you alter your computer's date, the programs will "time out" and will no longer be functional.

Troubleshooting

If you have difficulty installing or using any of the materials on the companion CD-ROM, try the following solutions:

» **Turn off any antivirus software that you may have running.** Installers sometimes mimic virus activity and can make your computer incorrectly believe that a virus is infecting it. Be sure to turn the antivirus software back on later.

» **Close all running programs.** The more programs you are running, the less memory is available to other programs. Installers also typically update files and programs; if you keep other programs running, the installation may not work properly.

» **Reference the ReadMe:** Please refer to the ReadMe file located at the root of the CD-ROM for the latest product information at the time of publication.

If you still have trouble with the CD-ROM, please call the Wiley Publishing Customer Care phone number: (800) 762-2974. Outside the United States, call 1 (317) 572-3994. You can also contact Wiley Publishing Customer Service by e-mail at techsupdum@wiley.com. Wiley Publishing will provide technical support only for installation and other general quality control items; for technical support on the applications themselves, consult the program's vendor or author.

Index

»N«

Named Anchor on Scene option, 67

navigation

creating glow bars, 289–290

creating masked animated buttons, 286–288

overview of, 281, 302

navigation ActionScript

for common submenus, 296–297

copying to other submenus, 298–299

in frames to other buttons, 296–297

function literals and, 296

to HTML pages, 292–293

for main menu buttons, 292–293

to other movies, 294–295

overview of, 281

page to page in single movies, 300–301

for shortcut to main menu, 291

for submenu buttons, 294–295

SWF files and, 292, 293

New Document templates, 269–273

No Color box, 104

Normal Mode scripting, 294, 306, 322–324

numbers in ActionScript, 310–311

»O«

objects. *See* **graphic objects**

operators, 313–315

Optimize (curves) option, 125

Oval tool, 4, 91

»P«

Paint Bucket tool, 99, 118

paintBrush.fla movie. *See also* **CD contents**

adjusting symbol alpha/brightness, 119

alpha fades in Motion tweens, 152–153

breaking apart/coloring text, 114–115

coloring objects, 113

creating keyframe changes, 138–139

navigation within movies, 300–301

Paint Brush tool, 84, 94–95

setting color palettes, 116

palettes. *See* **Color Swatches panel**

Panel Sets

customized, saving, 58

customizing, 57

defaults, changing, 56

saving Panel Layouts, 58

panels. *See also individual panels*

Accessibility, 36

Actions, 34, 36

adding to dock, 57

Align, 32, 202, 203

Answers, 32

Color Mixer, 32

Color Swatches, 32

Components, 34

Debugger, 36

disabling docking, 66

docking, 29, 31

Info, 33

Library, 35

Movie Explorer, 34

Output, 36

overview of, 31

Properties, 30–31

Reference, 36

Scene, 33, 59

Transform, 33

Pen tool, 68, 89, 91

Pencil tool, 84, 93

PICT settings, 69

Pin script options, 323

pivot points, moving, 130, 209–210

play ( ) **action, 320**

player programs, 263, 264, 265

playheads

defined, 25–26

moving, 158

in pseudo-timelines, 363–364

playing movies, 78

plug-ins, 21, 265

pointer tool. *See* **Arrow tool**

Polygon Mode options, 88

Portfolio button, 293

Portfolio page, 48

PortfolioPortal.fla movie, 294–295, 323–325

Preferences dialog box

ActionScript Editor tab, 71

Clipboard tab, 69

default preferences, 67

Editing tab, 68

General tab, 66–67

Warnings tab, 70

Preloader scene. *See also* **Flash Web design studio project**

ActionScript for, 326–327

adding, 59

adding frames, 72–73

adding objects, 74–76

defined, 47, 59, 326

document properties, 60–61

naming, 59

testing speed of, 261–262

previewing publication, 79, 263, 264

Printing options, 66

Projector options, 263, 264

properties. *See also* **Text Properties panel options**

bitmap properties, 110

layer properties, 65

object properties (ActionScript), 317

sound properties, 234, 236

converting text blocks to, 115

defined, 28–29, 112

drawings versus, 85, 112

editing all instances, 113, 118, 284–285

editing button symbols, 122–123, 284–285

editing color parameters, 119–120

editing colors, 113

editing, overview of, 85

editing single instances, 119–120, 122–123

instances, Motion tweens of, 144

nested, opening with Arrow tool, 85

overview of, 24

pivoting on offset center points, 130

removing colors, 113

types of, 112

Sync (sound/event) options, 246–250

Syntax Coloring option, 71

system requirements, 49, 383–384

»T«

Target (Web page) option, 167

templates. *See also* **movie clip publication**

for banner ads, 269–271

creating, 276

for mobile devices, 272–273

for publishing in HTML format, 267

testing movies

movie clip speed, 261–262

shortcut keys, 186

with Test Movie command, 14, 78, 364

text. *See also* **dynamic text fields; input text fields**

animating, 169–173

blinking cursors with, 177–179

changing proportionally, 167

from external sources, 355–360

overview of, 165, 192–193

selecting, 177

static text fields, 165, 166

text blocks. *See also* **graphic objects; shapes**

breaking apart, 114–115, 175

coloring fill and strokes, 115

converting to graphic symbols, 115

creating laser effects with, 180–183

creating masked layers from, 218–220

filling with bitmap graphics, 174–176

Motion tweens of, 144, 167, 218–220

Text menu, 42

Text options in Preferences dialog box, 68, 71

Text Properties panel options

align buttons, 167

Bold, 167

Character position, 167

Character spacing, 167

Color Well swatches, 166

defined, 166

Device Fonts, 168

Font menu, 166

Font size, 166

Format, 168

Height (H), 167

Horizontal (X) position, 167

HTML, 167

Italic, 167

Kerning, 166

opening, 77

Rotation, 167

Selectable, 167

Show borders, 167

Target (Web page), 167

Text Direction, 167

Text Panel icon, 166

Text type, 166

URL Link, 167

Vertical (Y) position, 167

Width (W), 167

Text ("A") tool, 77, 90

3-D objects, animating, 365–368

timelines

creating pseudo-timelines, 363–364

defined, 26–27

in movie clips, 199

using pseudo-timelines, 377–379

tint, 120, 161. *See also* **color**

Tint slider, 120

To Stage button, 203

Toolbox. *See also* **drawing tools**

defined, 29–30

Fill color well, 30, 117

Free Transform tool, 130

overview of, 83–84

Snap to Objects button, 149

Stroke color well, 30

Text tool, 77, 90

Trace Bitmap settings, 111

Transform panel. *See also* **Fill Transform tool; Free Transform tool**

changing object scale, 144, 158

with Constrain option, 167

Distort option, 128

Envelope option, 128

Flip Horizontal/Vertical options, 128

overview of, 128

Rotate option, 201

transparency. *See* **alpha levels**

trial programs, 386

troubleshooting book's CD, 386–387

turning on/off. *See also* **hiding**

dock visibility, 65

fill, 4

stroke lines, 4

(P-35) - Comma libs → useful buttons, etc.

(P-36) - File → New From Template

42 - Movie can be stepped 1 frame forward/backward using control menu.

43 - window → reference — for Ac & reference.

About Seybold Seminars and Publications

Seybold Seminars and Publications is your complete guide
to the publishing industry. For more than 30 years it
has been the most trusted source for technology events,
news, and insider intelligence.

Workflow
Media Te
Creation [
Manageme
Digital As
Fonts an
Digital M
Content N
Managem
Workflow
Media Te
Creation [
Manageme
Digital As
Fonts an
Digital M
Content N
Manageme
Workflow
Media Te
Creation [
Manageme

Produced by

PUBLICATIONS

Today, Seybold Publications and Consulting continues to guide publishing professionals around the world in their purchasing decisions and business strategies through newsletters, online resources, consulting, and custom corporate services.

○ *The Seybold Report: Analyzing Publishing Technologies*
The Seybold Report analyzes the cross-media tools, technologies, and trends shaping professional publishing today. Each in-depth newsletter delves into the topics changing the marketplace. *The Seybold Report* covers critical analyses of the business issues and market conditions that determine the success of new products, technologies, and companies. Read about the latest developments in mission-critical topic areas, including content and asset management, color management and proofing, industry standards, and cross-media workflows. A subscription to *The Seybold Report* (24 issues per year) includes our weekly email news service, *The Bulletin,* and full access to the seyboldreports.com archives.

○ *The Bulletin: Seybold News & Views on Electronic Publishing*
The Bulletin: Seybold News & Views on Electronic Publishing is Seybold Publications' weekly email news service covering all aspects of electronic publishing. Every week *The Bulletin* brings you all the important news in a concise, easy-to-read format.

For more information on **NEWSLETTER SUBSCRIPTIONS,**
please visit **seyboldreports.com**.

CUSTOM SERVICES

In addition to newsletters and online information resources, Seybold
Publications and Consulting offers a variety of custom corporate services
designed to meet your organization's specific needs.

○ **Strategic Technology Advisory Research Service (STARS)**
The STARS program includes a group license to *The Seybold Report* and
The Bulletin, phone access to our analysts, access to online archives at
seyboldreports.com, an on-site visit by one of our analysts, and much more.

○ **Personalized Seminars**
Our team of skilled consultants and subject experts work with you to create a
custom presentation that gets your employees up to speed on topics spanning
the full spectrum of prepress and publishing technologies covered in our publications. Full-day and half-day seminars are available.

○ **Site Licenses**
Our electronic licensing program keeps everyone in your organization, sales
force, or marketing department up to date at a fraction of the cost of buying
individual subscriptions. One hard copy of *The Seybold Report* is included with
each electronic license.

For more information on **CUSTOM CORPORATE SERVICES,**
please visit **seyboldreports.com**.

EVENTS

Seybold Seminars facilitates exchange and discussion within the high-tech publishing community several times a year. A hard-hitting lineup of conferences, an opportunity to meet leading media technology vendors, and special events bring innovators and leaders together to share ideas and experiences.

Conferences

Our diverse educational programs are designed to tackle the full range of the latest developments in publishing technology. Topics include:

- Print publishing
- Web publishing
- Design
- Creative tools and standards
- Best practices

- Multimedia
- Content management
- Technology standards
- Security
- Digital rights management

In addition to the conferences, you'll have the opportunity to meet representatives from companies that bring you the newest products and technologies in the publishing marketplace. Test tools, evaluate products, and take free classes from the experts.

For more information on **SEYBOLD SEMINARS EVENTS**, please visit **seyboldseminars.com**.

Wiley Publishing, Inc.
End-User License Agreement

READ THIS. You should carefully read these terms and conditions before opening the software packet(s) included with this book "Book". This is a license agreement "Agreement" between you and Wiley Publishing, Inc."WPI". By opening the accompanying software packet(s), you acknowledge that you have read and accept the following terms and conditions. If you do not agree and do not want to be bound by such terms and conditions, promptly return the Book and the unopened software packet(s) to the place you obtained them for a full refund.

1. **License Grant.** WPI grants to you (either an individual or entity) a nonexclusive license to use one copy of the enclosed software program(s) (collectively, the "Software") solely for your own personal or business purposes on a single computer (whether a standard computer or a workstation component of a multi-user network). The Software is in use on a computer when it is loaded into temporary memory (RAM) or installed into permanent memory (hard disk, CD-ROM, or other storage device). WPI reserves all rights not expressly granted herein.

2. **Ownership.** WPI is the owner of all right, title, and interest, including copyright, in and to the compilation of the Software recorded on the disk(s) or CD-ROM "Software Media". Copyright to the individual programs recorded on the Software Media is owned by the author or other authorized copyright owner of each program. Ownership of the Software and all proprietary rights relating thereto remain with WPI and its licensers.

3. **Restrictions On Use and Transfer.**

   (a) You may only (i) make one copy of the Software for backup or archival purposes, or (ii) transfer the Software to a single hard disk, provided that you keep the original for backup or archival purposes. You may not (i) rent or lease the Software, (ii) copy or reproduce the Software through a LAN or other network system or through any computer subscriber system or bulletin-board system, or (iii) modify, adapt, or create derivative works based on the Software.

   (b) You may not reverse engineer, decompile, or disassemble the Software. You may transfer the Software and user documentation on a permanent basis, provided that the transferee agrees to accept the terms and conditions of this Agreement and you retain no copies. If the Software is an update or has been updated, any transfer must include the most recent update and all prior versions.

4. **Restrictions on Use of Individual Programs.** You must follow the individual requirements and restrictions detailed for each individual program in the What's on the CD-ROM appendix of this Book. These limitations are also contained in the individual license agreements recorded on the Software Media. These limitations may include a requirement that after using the program for a specified period of time, the user must pay a registration fee or discontinue use. By opening the Software packet(s), you will be agreeing to abide by the licenses and restrictions for these individual programs that are detailed in the What's on the CD-ROM appendix and on the Software Media. None of the material on this Software Media or listed in this Book may ever be redistributed, in original or modified form, for commercial purposes.

5. **Limited Warranty.**

   (a) WPI warrants that the Software and Software Media are free from defects in materials and workmanship under normal use for a period of sixty (60) days from the date of purchase of this Book. If WPI receives notification within the warranty period of defects in materials or workmanship, WPI will replace the defective Software Media.

(b) WPI AND THE AUTHOR OF THE BOOK DISCLAIM ALL OTHER WARRANTIES, EXPRESS OR IMPLIED, INCLUDING WITHOUT LIMITATION IMPLIED WARRANTIES OF MERCHANTABILITY AND FITNESS FOR A PARTICULAR PURPOSE, WITH RESPECT TO THE SOFTWARE, THE PROGRAMS, THE SOURCE CODE CONTAINED THEREIN, AND/OR THE TECHNIQUES DESCRIBED IN THIS BOOK. WPI DOES NOT WARRANT THAT THE FUNCTIONS CONTAINED IN THE SOFTWARE WILL MEET YOUR REQUIREMENTS OR THAT THE OPERATION OF THE SOFTWARE WILL BE ERROR FREE.

(c) This limited warranty gives you specific legal rights, and you may have other rights that vary from jurisdiction to jurisdiction.

6. Remedies.

(a) WPI's entire liability and your exclusive remedy for defects in materials and workmanship shall be limited to replacement of the Software Media, which may be returned to WPI with a copy of your receipt at the following address: Software Media Fulfillment Department, Attn.: *Flash MX Complete Course*, Wiley Publishing, Inc., 10475 Crosspoint Blvd., Indianapolis, IN 46256, or call 1-800-762-2974. Please allow four to six weeks for delivery. This Limited Warranty is void if failure of the Software Media has resulted from accident, abuse, or misapplication. Any replacement Software Media will be warranted for the remainder of the original warranty period or thirty (30) days, whichever is longer.

(b) In no event shall WPI or the author be liable for any damages whatsoever (including without limitation damages for loss of business profits, business interruption, loss of business information, or any other pecuniary loss) arising from the use of or inability to use the Book or the Software, even if WPI has been advised of the possibility of such damages.

(c) Because some jurisdictions do not allow the exclusion or limitation of liability for consequential or incidental damages, the above limitation or exclusion may not apply to you.

7. U.S. Government Restricted Rights.
Use, duplication, or disclosure of the Software for or on behalf of the United States of America, its agencies and/or instrumentalities "U.S. Government" is subject to restrictions as stated in paragraph (c)(1)(ii) of the Rights in Technical Data and Computer Software clause of DFARS 252.227-7013, or subparagraphs (c) (1) and (2) of the Commercial Computer Software - Restricted Rights clause at FAR 52.227-19, and in similar clauses in the NASA FAR supplement, as applicable.

8. General.
This Agreement constitutes the entire understanding of the parties and revokes and supersedes all prior agreements, oral or written, between them and may not be modified or amended except in a writing signed by both parties hereto that specifically refers to this Agreement. This Agreement shall take precedence over any other documents that may be in conflict herewith. If any one or more provisions contained in this Agreement are held by any court or tribunal to be invalid, illegal, or otherwise unenforceable, each and every other provision shall remain in full force and effect.